ENGLISH
GOVERNMENT FINANCE
1485-1558

VOLUME ONE

English

Government Finance

1485-1558

Frederick C. Dietz

Professor of History, Emeritus, University of Illinois

FRANK CASS & CO. LTD.

1964

First published in 1921 by the
University of Illinois, under the auspices
of the Graduate School, Urbana, Illinois.

This edition published by
Frank Cass and Co. Ltd., 10, Woburn Walk,
London, W.C.1.

First Edition 1921

Second Edition 1964

Printed in Great Britain by
Thomas Nelson (Printers) Ltd.,
London and Edinburgh.

PREFACE

The following pages are a reprint, with textual corrections, of three separate studies relating to Tudor and early Stuart public finance. The Introduction to Volume I is an essay contributed to the volume of essays edited by Professor N. S. Gras brought out by the Harvard University Press in honour of Professor Edwin F. Gay. In this paper there are some general observations covering the entire field under survey. The remainder of the first volume was originally published in 1921 as Volume 9 No. 3 of the University of Illinois Studies in the Social Sciences under the title of English Government Finance, 1485–1558. This book was a reworking of a Ph.D. thesis submitted to Harvard University in 1916 together with three additional chapters covering the reigns Edward VI and Mary. Volume II is a study made with the help of a grant from the John Simon Guggenhein Foundation, published in 1932 by the American Historical Association.

All these studies were printed in limited additions and have not been available for purchase for many years. It is rewarding to think that there is enough of value contained in them to warrant reprinting. A thorough study of the subject would have involved at least a year's work in the Record Office and the British Museum. My plea in avoidance is that I had neither the time nor the resources to add another year to the three already spent in these great archives. It is hoped that these studies may be of some value to scholars in the field of sixteenth and seventeenth century history.

FREDERICK C. DIETZ

Urbana, Illinois
February 9, 1963

BIBLIOGRAPHICAL NOTE

The limited secondary material available when these studies were made has been considerably enlarged by the work of such scholars as Richardson, Tawney, Judges, and Ashton. Their books should be consulted for the amplification of many sections of this essay.

The chief reliance in the preparation of these volumes was necessarily upon documentary sources, especially those preserved in the British Museum and in the Public Record Office. The British Museum material takes the form of letters and notes of lord treasurers and other officials, accounts and summaries of accounts—some of them parts of series missing from the Record Office—and papers drawn up by exchequer officers describing exchequer practice and procedure. There are also manuscript pamphlets detailing ways in which the kings of England have raised money, written chiefly for the delectation of James I and Charles I; documents relating to the various customs farms : letters of the council ; papers dealing with the subsidies, ship money, and almost every other matter of fiscal nature. Special mention may be made of the letters and memoranda of Lord Treasurer Winchester and of Lord Burghley in the Lansdowne Manuscripts and to the voluminous papers of Sir Julius Caesar scattered among the Additional Manuscripts and other collections. The Harleian Manuscripts, the Cottonian Manuscripts, the Hargrave Manuscripts, the Royal Manuscripts, the Stowe Manuscripts and the Egerton Manuscripts, are the other collections yielding the most valuable finds.

Of first interest in the Public Record Office material are the accounts of the exchequer and other revenue courts. The classification of these documents will be kept in mind more easily if certain exchequer practices are understood. The accounting system of the exchequer represented stratum upon stratum of different forms of bookkeeping superimposed upon each other. When older methods were discovered to be inefficient or when new categories of revenue were added to those received in the court, new methods of audit were introduced, but at the same time the old were retained.

The oldest of the exchequer rolls, the pipe rolls and their companion rolls, concerned only with the now unimportant conventional revenues collected by sheriffs, bailiffs, and escheators, proved of little service in this study. Of great value, however, were those forms of exchequer accounts known as *compoti*. These were engrossed on parchment in Latin by collectors of revenues and by disbursing officers and were presented for acceptance to the barons of the exchequer. When approved, the *compotus* was signed at the top by the barons and their clerk (auditor) and sent to be enrolled on the customs rolls, the subsidy rolls, the household rolls, or the roll of foreign accounts of the lord treasurer's remembrancer's office. The *compotus* was used for the customs to the end of Elizabeth's reign, for the parliamentary subsidies and fifteenths and tenths, and for the accounts of the cofferer of the household through the reign of Charles I.

Another extremely valuable group of documents based on the older exchequer practice are the Memoranda rolls of the king's remembrancer, together with the related Repertories of states and views of public accounts in the office of the lord treasurer's remembrancer, in that of the king's remembrancer, and in the Repertory rolls or indexes to the Memoranda rolls of the king's remembrancer. There is also a set of Memoranda rolls of the lord treasurer's remembrancer, which proved less valuable than those of his colleague.

In general these rolls and repertories contain notices of the appearance of all accountants before the exchequer to make their accounts, brief summaries of the accounts, notices of appointments of new officials by letters patent, memoranda of important debts adjudged due to the crown, and above all, the enrolments of the leases of many of the farms of the customs. For a history of the customs these rolls proved invaluable, and the wonder is that they have never been really used before. Occasional references have indeed been made to isolated rolls, but no systematic investigation has been attempted previously.

Henry VII degraded the exchequer by setting up new revenue courts to take care of the new revenues which he brought into being. In these courts, which were extended and perfected during the reign of Henry VIII, entirely new practices were developed. Among other things the receiver general or treasurer of each court was obliged to render directly to the king at stated intervals a formal account of all receipts and expenditures. Similar accounts were exacted from the exchequer of receipt and from the Duchy of Lancaster.

As the result of bitter rivalry between two officers, the auditor of the receipt and the clerk of the pells, the report of the exchequer of receipt developed into two series of reports, which, after 1597, duplicate each other. These are found in various forms, together with the original books of exchequer receipts and issues, in E. 401, E. 403, E. 405. Some miscellaneous accounts relating to exchequer of receipt business, such as the collections of forced loans, the fines of knighthood in 1630–1632, and summaries of crown debts, are found in E. 407. The reports of the Duchy of Lancaster are found in Duchy of Lancaster accounts, and those of the receiver general of the Court of Wards in Court of Wards, Miscellaneous Books.

The Augmentations Court and the Court of First-Fruits and Tenths were merged with the exchequer in the reign of Mary, but they kept their identity as departments in the exchequer. Headed by the remembrancer of first-fruits and tenths and by the seven auditors and the seven receivers general of land revenues, these departments carried on their peculiar systems of audit independently of the older exchequer practice, although exchequer officials made constant efforts to reduce them to conformity. No formal reports of the remembrancer of first-fruits and clerical tenths have been found, but particular accounts of tenths collected by the bishops are preserved by the thousands in E. 351 and A. O. 3. Occasional general reports of the auditors and receivers of the land revenues, much like the earlier formal accounts of the treasurer of the Court of Augmentations, are found in the British Museum and among the State Papers in the Record Office. The accounts of local bailiffs and ministers, and the annual accounts of each of the seven receivers general for single counties and groups of counties are found in Land Revenue accounts. Details of the terms of new leases and surveys of the value of the king's lands are preserved in Rentals and Surveys, and in Land Revenue accounts.

Henry VII made a further innovation in his insistence that certain spending officials must account directly to him for money received by them "in prest" or as an advance against future disbursements. Such officials drew up their accounts in the form of a "declaration of account," on paper, in English. The declaration was audited by one of the king's trusted advisers, and, on approval by the king himself, the accountant was free against the king without submitting to the cumbersome exchequer procedure. Later in the sixteenth century there developed the practice of appointing special commissions to "take" or examine and approve declarations of account, subject to the advice of the king's auditors or auditors of the prests. In the reorganized exchequer of Mary's time the older officials, such as the lord treasurer's remembrancer,,seem to have endeavoured to suppress the declaration of account, since it carried no fees for themselves. All through the reigns of Elizabeth and James I they sporadically renewed their campaign.

The declaration of account was made in duplicate, the original on paper, and the duplicate on parchment. After it had been certified by the auditors of the prests, the commission appointed for the purpose approved it by signing it at the bottom. Probably the finest collection of signatures of the great statesmen of Elizabethan and StuartEngland is that made up of the subscriptions to the declarations of accounts in the Record Office. The parchment copy of the declaration was returned to the accountant as his acquittance or receipt ; the paper original was kept by the auditors of the prests. In many instances a third copy, on parchment, was made, and found its way into the pipe office. The declarations of account include, among others, the accounts of the clerk of the hanaper, the keeper of the wardrobe, the treasurer of the navy, the treasurer of Ireland, the treasurer of Berwick, the treasurers of all military forces, the treasurer of the chamber, and the chief butler. They also include the accounts of many of the customs farmers, particularly of the great and petty customs, and the accounts of all collectors of new impositions, praetermitted customs, and all other customs dues imposed after 1608.

Among the Record Office materials must be listed also the hundreds of volumes of the State Papers for the reigns of Elizabeth, James I, and Charles I. The domestic papers for Elizabeth and James I were studied in manuscript, but for the reign of Charles I the printed calendars were used. There are in the printed calendars of the domestic State Papers of Elizabeth and James I certain documents not bound with the volumes of the domestic State Papers in the Record Office. These are referred to under the designation of *Cal. State Papers, Elizabeth,* and *Cal. State Papers, James I,* and the references are to pages.

In the printed calendars of the domestic State Papers of Charles I, the references are to numbers of documents when the citations are *State Papers, Charles I,* and to pages when the citations are *Cal. State Papers, Charles I.*

Of the other calendars, those of the State Papers, Venetian, the State Papers, Elizabeth, Foreign, and State Papers, Scottish have been most useful. These are cited as *Venetian Cal.*, *Cal. State Papers, Elizabeth, Foreign,* etc., and the references are to numbers of documents.

Other printed documents of great service in this essay were : the Cecil papers, in the *Calendar of the MSS. of the Marquis of Salisbury preserved at Hatfield House* (Historical MSS. Commission Reports), referred to as *Hatfield MSS.;* the letters in the appendix to Bishop G. Goodman's *The Court of James I ;* the collection of letters known as *The Court and Times of James I*, edited by Thomas Birch ; and Francis Peck's *Desiderata Curiosa.* Occasional reference is made in the text to numerous other collections.

Finally, among the materials used in this work, mention must be made of the Sackville Manuscripts, the property of Lord Sackville-West, now deposited with the Historical Manuscripts Commission. Through the courtesy of Lord Sackville-West and the kindness of the officials of the Historical Manuscripts Commission, it was possible to examine these documents, which comprise some nine thousand numbers of the papers of Lionel Cranfield, Earl of Middlesex, before they appeared in the printed calendar of the Historical Manuscripts Commission.

CONTENTS

Royal revenues derived from feudal dues, lands and
customs in the Middle Ages — Their decline in the
Fifteenth Century — More frequent use of direct
taxation by the Lancastrians — The fifteenth and
tenth — Unsuccessful experiments with other direct
taxes — Direct taxes not favored either by the crown
or the people — ''The King must live of his own'' is
the view of the gentry class which was most affected by
direct taxation.

The king in alliance with the lesser gentry and the
professional classes — The crown needs adequate revenues under its own control — The middle classes desire
relief from taxation — Increase of the customs, and
especially of the landed estates of the crown as a
result — Made practicable by the increased economic
unification of England.

Trade fostered to increase revenues by new trade treaties and by royal credit to merchants — Lands increased
by resumptions of alienated portions of the crown domains, by confiscation and forfeitures of attainder — Renewed insistence upon feudal rights of the king makes
possible great escheats to the crown — Wardship and
Marriage — The purpose of the *Inqpisitiones post Mortem* — Insistence upon suit of livery of lands by
heirs — Temporalities of clergy held by king during
vacations.

Increase of payments into the royal treasury ''by
obligation'' and ''by recognizance''— Their nature —
Closely connected with the activity of Empson and Dudley — The growth of the Empson and Dudley legend —
Examination of Dudley's own account book — Fines
and pardons for infringement of penal laws comparatively few, except in cases of invasions of the king's
feudal rights — Empson and Dudley not mere extortioners — Royal business agents — The importance of
their work in building up the crown estates — Their
unscrupulousness and unpopularity — Machiavellianism of
Henry VIII.

CONTENTS

CONTENTS

INTRODUCTION

An illustration of The Reinterpretation of certain larger problems in the early modern period made possible through the use of data provided by the study of Fiscal History.

While the extension of the scope of business over larger territorial areas which called the national state into being has already been discussed in some detail, the technique of the establishment of centralized governments in place of feudal monarchies has been somewhat neglected. Fiscal history affords one avenue of approach to this problem. A study of public finance not only indicates the administrative measures actually adopted to enlarge the royal authority, but gives certain clues to the reasons for the resulting character of the new state organisms and for their failure to satisfy the sociological aims which certain of their ideological proponents had in mind.

1. In that development of public administration in England which historians call the foundation of the national state, one of the characteristic qualities was the addition to the comparatively simple machinery of government of a more effective set of bureaus designed to secure real control at a distance from the capital. This development is particularly manifest in the realm of fiscal affairs, where the extension of royal authority through the centralized supervision of the crown lands and the customs is most striking.

The most significant of the new departures was the appointment, in connection with newly acquired lands, of the general surveyors and the auditors of the land revenues, who rode around from estate to estate collecting the king's rents, examining the condition of the property, and issuing the requisite royal directions. It may be that these officials, whose introduction seems to have been planned by Richard III, provided the model for the still more important committee of high officials who, in Henry VII's reign, rode about the country in search of all those who were guilty of breaches of the peace, illegal entry, livery and maintenance, riots, abduction of wards, and other offences which tended to disturb the country or to interfere with the fiscal rights of the crown.

In connection with the customs the existence of an embryonic nonfeudal bureaucracy dating from the period before the advent of Henry VII intercepted the early introduction of a new system of general surveyors and auditors along the lines of the Tudor land offices. The centralization of authority in the customs was expressed by the enforced use of semi-national, and then national, valuations as a basis for the collection of rates of duties, by the Elizabethan integration of all ports outside London under the general surveyors of custom causes, and by the unified farms of the customs on a national basis under the Stuarts.

It is noteworthy that the ultimate audit control over the new royal officers was exercised by the king in person in Henry VII's time, and by committees with delegated royal powers under his successors. This development involved a purposeful neglect of the exchequer, where traditions and practices favoured the sheriffs, bailiffs, and customers, with all their disintegrating localism. The exchequer system of elaborate parchment rolls, for instance, was not competent to provide that oversight from a distance which was a prerequisite of the new fiscal system. It was only after the king's money came into the collectors' hands that the exchequer checks were satisfactory. In the new scheme of things the minutiae of estate business behind the rents actually paid to the king were to be carefully watched. The introduction of easily handled paper account books in place of the parchment rolls, the use of Italian forms of bookkeeping, and the proper functioning of the itinerant inspectors would be easier in an entirely new organization. The Tudor fiscal committees were consequently developed into a series of revenue courts with separate treasuries attached, independent of the ancient course of the exchequer.

Royal commissions were used also to control many of the more important expenditures and disbursements, and such commissions continued to be used without formal institutionalization until after 1641. To assist the *ad hoc* commissioners, an office of the auditors of the prests[1] and foreign accounts appeared at a comparatively early period. When the new revenue courts, together with the office of the auditors of the prests, were finally amalgamated with the exchequer,

---

[1] Prests were advances of money to officials entrusted with its expenditure.

their forms of procedure were retained within the resulting organization. Late in Elizabeth's reign the newer methods of audit were applied even to the customs, which had hitherto remained subject to the more ancient exchequer practice. As a result of such mergers and shifts, the exchequer itself became in most respects merely a Tudor commission functioning in behalf of the royal interest at the king's will.

2. Even more suggestive than the study of typical Tudor administrative departments as revealing the processes attending the establishment of the national state is an investigation of the innovations in the functions of government. This process is somewhat obscured by the fact that medieval traditions and institutions were, through changes of connotation and nuance, virtually transformed under the outward semblance of continued integrity. Much that was really new passed for what was in form old. Thus, from Sir John Fortescue, chancellor to Edward IV, to the Earl of Middlesex, lord treasurer to James I, the practice of public, or rather royal, finance was conditioned by the traditional phrase that the king ordinarily must 'live of his own.' Every word in the phrase changed its meaning in the century and a half after the death of Edward IV. There were, of course, serious possibilities in the failure to recognize the new under cover of the old, and in critical times the medieval survivals might, and did, seriously hamper the crown.

Of considerable significance in the persistance of remnants of medieval views, which was by no means confined to England, was the circumstance that the revolution of 1485 was only imperfectly realized. It is a truism that Henry VII founded the national monarchy in England as did Louis XI in France, and Ferdinand and Isabella in Spain. Yet it is equally important for the future that the first Tudor was unconscious of the cataclysmic quality of the movement which he initiated. Unaware of the high destiny of his house as the English builders of a new type of state, Henry VII stressed his role as the legitimate vehicle of the feudal kingship by the allegation of his headship of the house of Lancaster and of the analogous place of his queen in the house of York. Consequently he took over a good deal of the nomemclature of the feudal world and made it possible to carry over into the new order many precedents and traditions of the dead Plantagenet monarchy.

Antecedent to the actual development of the new national monarchy there were certain social and economic needs and desires which paved the way for its successful advent. Medieval rulers no longer adequately met the expanding requirements of English life. Sir John Fortescue, writing before 1485, envisaged a centralized monarchy, which should be powerful enough to put down the local tyrants, with their disorderly brawls and forced perversion of justice through the practice of livery and maintenance, administer justice equitably, and enforce peace and order everywhere throughout the land.

In the early sixteenth century publicists, such as Starkey, Forrest, Fish, and Brinklow, the demand for amplification of the government's functions is more highly elaborated. Old evils, already known in the fifteenth century, had become national in extent. The wrongs of enclosures and the low standards of social morality were apparent to these critics. Wealth was ill used, and the rich ate up the poor. Merchants exported necessities and imported only luxuries. The great enclosing lords made it impossible for the poor to live. The enhancing of rents and the increase of fines of leases caused the decay of the realm. The relations of the sexes left everything to be desired, and the conduct of priests, monks, and friars did not better current sexual evils.

The church, having stressed regard for externals for too many centuries, had no real message for such troublous times. Her authority was so much decayed that she probably could not have enforced a new morality even if her leaders had seen the need for it. The only hope of salvation on a nationally extended scale lay in the king. The end of government was declared to be the promotion of the public good, and it was held that the functions of the state must be increased to set wrongs right.

> "For chiefly your crown to this intent you wear
> Wrong to reform that equity may rule bear."

The king was to "perceive the commonwealth's noyance, and for the same to take ordynaunce." To this end all individuals and all institutions, including the church itself, might be subordinated to the royal authority.

The climax of such views was reached in the notion of the organic state in which the king as head directed the activities, moral, religious, and economic, of all the members, who served him and owed all that they had to his protection and care. Such exalted views, frequently found even in the early seventeenth century, were of course little more than pious sighs for an ideal which had failed of realization.

The restoration of the golden age, which was merely the legalistically minded sixteenth century's way of demanding positive social benefits at the hands of the king, was not unconsidered by the Tudors. Henry VII's legislative and administrative acts to suppress disorder, to expand industry and trade with royal aid, and to improve economic conditions are well known. His son's assumption of supreme control over the English church was stimulated in part by the same purpose, and the step was welcomed by comtemporaries as a necessary preliminary to the preaching of a new social gospel. There was nothing, so far as the Tudor attitude went, which prevented the introduction of a modern type of all-controlling paternalistic state during the sixteenth century.

Nevertheless the national state founded by the Tudors and carried on by the Stuarts was not of this variety. In the actual work of the government as it affected the individual subject during the sixteenth century much attention was paid to treasons, riots, and breaches of the peace, to forgery, libel, and perjury, to "lewd and naughty words," to family quarrels, matrimonial disputes, and suits over land, to the control of the church, the maintenance of uniformity, and the suppression of dissent, to enclosures, the relief of the poor, the avoidance of idleness, and the training of the young. While all these matters have social implications, the attitude of the crown as the sixteenth century went on, seems to have been determinded more and more by considerations of the preservation of internal peace through the elimination of the causes of disturbance and the enforcement of outward unity in the interests of its own safety.

The failure of the well-ordered state of the Tudor-Stuart commonwealth to measure up to the most advanced thought of the day can be explained in considerable measure on fiscal grounds. From the very outset it was well understood that the new desired type of government would be very expensive. More than one writer went into an elaborate discussion of the necessity of the prince's being rich. He must have revenues adequate to meet all demands made upon him, and he must have sufficient income over and above his expenses to gather "some store for sudden events, either wars or dearth."

At the same time that more was expected of the king, skepticism about the value of state efforts persisted. Taxes, imprests, and imposts were generally believed to impoverish the realm "after the manner of France." There was no widespread faith that heavy payments by the people of the nation to the king would be anything else than wasted. Perhaps a better way of putting the situation would be to say that national feeling was still rather restricted and made headway only in the face of strong localisms. The county populations saw little advantage to themselves from the central government. They were willing to assume the costs of county affairs ; let the king carry the burdens of his own business. Some writers were willing to grant the state a free hand in increasing its revenues, even to the point of conceding that the crown might lawfully and with a safe conscience take taxes of its subjects. Yet this was not generally the case, and for practical purposes the whole period from 1485 to 1641 was a struggle over money between the king and his subjects.

The realization of the high hopes of those who had hailed the national state as the dawn of a new day was thwarted less by inability to raise money than by the circumstance that money was required for other objectives. On the assumption that the heart is where the treasure is disposed it seems that the real interest of the new national states was elsewhere than in domestic social policy. On the continent the national monarchies were already engaged in the game of seizing each other's territory. After an initial episode in France, Henry VII consciously prevented England during his own reign from following other national states in conforming to the pattern of a power entity, intent upon enforcing its views upon its neighbors and consequently under the heaviest obligations of providing for its own defence.

Given the circumstances of European life and England's position it is hard to see how she could have continued permanently to avoid being induced to follow continental fashions. Henry VIII had, however, no desire to follow his father's policy, although the most solemn abjurations to do so were addressed to him. Thus in the Tree of Commonwealth, written by Edmund Dudley while in prison during the first days of the young king's reign, Henry VIII was urged to avoid wars since "the commodities of this noble realm be so noble and with that so plenteous that they cannot be spended or all employed within the same, but necessarily there must be intercourse between this realm and the outward parts for the utterance thereof and specially for the wool and cloth, tin and lead, fell and hide." This plea for an international outlook as a necessity for foreign trade was backed up by the observation that "war is a marvellous consumer of treasure and riches : for I suppose aright great treasure is soon spent in a sharp war." Yet within a few years, Henry VIII as the ally of Ferdnand plunged his country into war with France and definitely obligated himself to assume the heaviest commitments for defense and offense. Choice and necessity led his successors to continue in his course.

A simple comparison between the normal peace time armed service budgets at various times between 1485 and 1641 is quite illuminating. In the latter part of his reign, Henry VII expended annually £1,200 for the wages of his private bodyguard of the yeoman of the guard. The sum of £88 a year was paid to the surveyor of the ordnance and his clerks. The keeping of Berwick and the east and middle marches against Scotland cost £2,500 a year. The wages of the garrison at Calais were about £10,000 annually, and certain small payments were made for the navy and for the English forces in Ireland[2]. A hundred years later the yeoman of the guard received £4,000 a year for wages and £1,222 for liveries. The more recently instituted gentlemen pensioners received £4,500 a year. The ordnance office had a budget of at least £10,000 annually. Calais fortunately had been lost. Berwick, where expenditures had just been reduced by James I, still needed £5,000 a year for some time to come. To other border stations and forts and garrisons, such as those at Land's End, St. Mary's, and Portsmouth, £5,000 a year was allotted, and this was soon to be increased. There were English forces in the Low Countries, maintained at a charge of £25,000 a year to guarantee the repayment by the Dutch of £40,000 a year, and the costs of the English occupation of Ireland, where during the recent wars Elizabeth spent as much as £336,000 in a single year, averaged £70,000 a year for the first decade of James I's reign. The navy, which as late as the early years of Elizabeth's reign had occasionally kept within a peace time appropriation of £6,000, now regularly required £40,000 annually for normal maintenance.

These figures, except those for Ireland, represent the peace time military appropriations. In the event of war the expenditures of the

[2] During the three years 1485, 1486, and 1487 the King's ships cost £1,841, or £600 a year. In the first year and a half of Henry VIII's reign the repair and building of ships and the purchase of bow staves amounted to £3,138. In the war periods 1492-1493 and 1495-1496 Navy payments were more considerable ; in other years, smaller. Irish revenues were said to be unable to meet the costs of the Irish garrison ; but except in the years 1494-1496 little money seems to have been sent to Ireland from England.

new power state skyrocketed remarkably. Figures here must be largely tentative, since it is impossible to determine all the extra disbursements which were due to war purposes. Definitely known expenditures in certain decades may, however, have certain relative values. In the decade between 1491 and 1500 Henry VII engaged in two wars, with France and with Scotland, besides crushing several rebellions. His military operations cost something over £107,600 in addition to certain incidental charges for aid to the Duchess of Brittany of which the accounts are not available. Between 1541 and 1550 Henry VIII and Edward VI again fought France and Scotland. From the beginning of the first alarums in 1539 to Henry VIII's death the crown spent £2,134,000 for the building of fortifications in England and at Calais and Guisnes, for the charges of the navy and the siege, capture, and keeping of Boulogne, and for the war against Scotland. To this sum Edward VI's government added £1,386,000 between 1547 and 1550. Again, in the decade from 1591 to 1600 Elizabeth spent approximately £4,000,000 in Ireland, France, and the Low Countries and for the navy with such little success that the drain had to continue through the last years of her own regime and into that of James I. As time went on wars became even costlier. In the single campaign of 1640 Charles I spent £570,000 in his failure to teach the Scots proper respect for his majesty.

There were two other factors by which the policies of any sixteenth century king, however much concerned he might have been with a social program, would have been restricted. The first of these was the sixteenth century price revolution, which worked so insidiously that even modern scholars tend to overlook its constant presence. There were also rising standards of taste and luxury, growing out of the increasing wealth of Europe, which the English court, following continental fashions, inevitably adopted. Conspicuous consumption was a real political factor. Few Englishmen would have been willing to forego it, lest the national honor, the king's dignity, and their own pride be injured. In the royal household alone, to use merely one of the great spending departments of the court for illustration, these two forces of rising prices and higher living standards drove up the cofferer's normal disbursements from a mere £13,000 in 1505–1506 to £25,000 in 1538, £45,000 in 1545, between £50,000 and £60,000 in the latter years of Elizabeth (in spite of Burghley's thrift and care), and £70,000 during the latter part of James I's reign. The same processes were at work to increase the pensions and annuities paid to courtiers and officials from £1,354 in 1506 to £102,000 in 1638.

Nor would a more detailed exposition of royal expenditure lead to a different conclusion than the one here indicated. The closest study of crown disbursements from 1485 to 1641 reveals constantly growing outlays for military preparations and actual warfare, larger advances for exchanges of diplomatic agents, pyramiding appropriations for the royal court in connection with the household, wardrobe, chamber, buildings, and royal parks, and larger payments of pensions and annuities. Virtually nothing was spent by the state directly toward the realization of the social ends envisaged by the contemporary publicists. What was done along these lines was done by the local authorities or by the reorganized church. The English government in the sixteenth and early seventeenth centuries devoted practically all its resources toward its own maintenance or toward the military ends of the system of *Der Staat als Macht*. The irony of the business was that the support of the court and the upkeep of a skeleton fleet and insignificant military departments used up most of the crown's resources. There was only a little left for the war chest, the accumulation of which was considered an important part of military activity. In the event of war, even second class efforts completely disorganized the revenue system, compelled the alienation of capital resources, and heaped up debts.

It is only a partial explanation of the neglect of social aims in the Tudor-Stuart state to say that since the money available was sufficient only for the support of the court and military affairs, only these were served and other matters were overlooked. A truer evaluation of the situation reveals an interesting mechanistic connection between the choice of purposes actually made by the crown and the compulsion to that course provided by the traditions of fiscal policy, that the king must live of his own except for aid from the nation in time of war.

Certain considerations of practical politics affecting Henry VII's fiscal program at the beginning of his regime colored the issue throughout the entire period. Owing to the rapid development of the spoils system during the fifteenth century, Henry VII received with the crown only the smallest endowments. He also enjoyed the customs dues of the capital, the wool customs collected at Calais over and above the wages of the garrison and the mortgage payments due to the Staplers, and such sums collected in the ports outside London as the local officials were willing to disgorge.

There were theoretically three possible courses open to King Henry. These were the continuation of experiments with direct taxes, which so far had had no positive results, the extension of the policy of developing large landed estates, and the increase of the customs revenues. Henry VII tried all three devices. His greatest success was achieved in connection with the crown lands, which, it may be noted, were widely recognized as the best endowment of the crown. In his own person Henry VII was a congeries of local feudal lordships, as indeed his immediate predecessors were to only a more limited exent. As the actual holder of the Lancastrian estates, the lands of York—the properties of Warwick and Spenser, and many another feudal holding, Henry VII was able to use his local feudal position to make a beginning of making land the fiscal basis of the Tudor state. The general inclination to sanction such revenue devices as might satisfy class prejudices, such as the detestation of Henry's middle class followers for the feudal baronage, gave great freedom to the king's activities. He was able to resume alienated royal domains, confiscate the lands of the "traitors" who had fought against him at Bosworth Field and of those who took part in the early rebellions of the reign, to revive fiscal feudal rights, such as marriage and wardship, and to insist upon the greatest extension of tenure *in capite* in the hope of eventual escheat to the crown.

Public opinion regarding the monasteries, the bishops, and the church in the sixteenth century made it possible for Henry VII's successors to continue his land policy by increasing the royal "livelihood" at the expense of the church. After Elizabeth's last exchanges of less valuable parcels for the bishops' best properties and her last great attainders of the northern feudal nobles, the increase of crown estates was still sought through such irritable devices as the search for assarts (parcels once part of the king's forests of which record had been lost) and the resurvey of the royal forests.

At the beginning of the Tudor regime the customs seemed less auspicious than the landed estates. The Calais revenues had for the most part perhaps permanently escaped royal control. More could be expected from London, where in 1507 the more adequate payment of customs dues was enforced by the substitution of an official scale of valuations in a book of rates in place of the merchants' declarations. Various trade treaties did something to stimulate the passage of goods through the customhouses, and royal loans to merchants were designed to accomplish the same end. The increase of revenue from the customs by about twenty-eight per cent between 1485 and 1509 was no mean achievement, but the real importance of the customs in the English fiscal system did not begin until the lands began to show the operation of a kind of law of diminishing returns in Mary's, Elizabeth's, and James I's reigns.

Although the more important categories of customs duties were granted by Parliament, the customs at least since Henry VII's reign were considered as a virtual part of the king's own inheritance. This view was stengthened by the principle, reported by Dyer, adduced in connection with the suit of London merchants against impositions in 1559, that customs commenced with the king's control of the ports and his right to close them against the payment for a royal license to import and export goods. There were other possibilities in the discovery that the customs could be used to serve domestic business interests. Although some writers insisted that duties on exports were in reality paid by English artisans through the lowering of the prices of their products, it was generally believed that the customs outward were paid by the foreigners. Such dues were less harmful than the customs on imports paid by English merchants, which increased the cost of goods to the consuming public. Levies on necessities were bitterly resented to such an extent that in 1610 Lord Salisbury removed the new impositions of 1608 as far as they were laid upon the necessities of life. Duties on luxuries, however, especially those which might be produced at home, were positively popular. Gerard Malines, the merchant economist, argued for a tariff to protect home industries on the ground that the highest function of the state was the maintenance of traffic. By this he meant the increase of national and individual wealth with the active help of the state, and the bait he held out to secure this boon was that such assistance would make the subjects the more willing to pay for the support of the crown. Finally, in the book of rates of 1610 industrial protection was openly avowed as a government policy as a kind of sugar coating to sweeten the pill of impositions.

Of greater immediate importance were the schedules to "equalize traffic," that is retaliatory duties or special levies on foreigners in the interest of the English merchant. Even Sir Edward Coke held that the king might lawfully levy countervailing duties to make equality in case of duties levied in foreign parts, since such duties were for the advancement of traffic, which was the life of every island, *pro bono publico*. When Lionel Cranfield somewhat later discovered that alien merchants were quasi-lawfully liable for an additional imposition of threepence in the pound beyond that paid by native merchants, he almost popularized the original exaction of 1608.

Under the cover of assertions of royal rights and the manipulation of customs duties to protect the native merchants and industrialists opposition to new duties was disarmed, and a vast extension of royal customs duties under the name of impositions was carried into effect without parliamentary sanction from Mary's time onward.

The political opponents of impositions feared that the income from the new customs dues would render the crown financially independent and thus end the possibility of a financial readjustment which would involve the parliamentary control of the state. There never was much possibility of such productivity on the part of the impositions or other customs dues. For though the crown income from the various types of customs went up remarkably, the increasing yield even when taken together with the lands and other revenues was never quite enough to provide for the needs of the court, the requirements of the services, and the rapacity of the courtiers.

It was more or less clearly recognized at least as early as Thomas Cromwell's time that even for such as were considered normal peace time expenditures direct taxation afforded the only adequate basis for royal finance. On the other hand direct taxes were cordially disliked. In their older form of purveyance they aroused continual protests, which ended only with the abolition of purveyance by the Long Parliament. In their more recent guise of fifteenths and tenths and subsidies they were always unpopular. Fortescue raised his voice against them, granting their permissibility only in the event of war or some other extraordinary occasion. Under the constitution such direct taxes had the added difficulty of requiring parliamentary appropriation. Unfortunately for his system, in the formative years of the Tudor state Henry VII did not grapple with the problem of direct taxes. His very success in dealing with his lands and customs is perhaps a partial explanation of his neglect. Moreover, the opposition of his middle class supporters to this method of raising revenue, as revealed in Fortescue's works and by several revolts directly attributable to efforts to collect taxes on Henry's own part, made the king loath to undertake radical innovations here. After a few cautious experiments, Henry VII left the matter of direct taxation pretty much where it had been under the Lancastrians. The nation was no more accustomed to meeting the expenses of its government by direct payment than it had been when Henry IV took the crown. Half a century after Henry VII's death John Hales, referring to Henry VII's experience, pointed out that "that way of gathering treasure is not always most safe for the Prince's surety ; for we see many times the profit of such subsidies spent in appeasing the people that are moved to sedition partly by occasion of the same."

Little progress was made in the use of the fifteenth and tenth and the subsidy by Wolsey, whose gravest difficulties with Parliament grew out of his attempts to secure grants in 1514, 1515, and 1523. In the disturbed third of a century after Wolsey's fall and again in the last fifteen years of Elizabeth's reign direct taxes were voted and collected often enough to inure the people to them. More than that, while the value of a single subsidy or a single fifteenth and tenth could not be raised and in fact depreciated, the number of grants in a single appropriation and the value of the sums annually taken from the people mounted steadily. It would seem as if by 1603 the payment of direct taxes should have been an habitual matter, and these taxes should have formed a regular portion of state revenues without regard for the necessity of a war before they could be obtained.

On at least two occasions the crown has tried to get the Parliament to make some acknowledgement of the inadequacy of the old notion of direct taxes as extraordinary war supplies. In 1566 Lord Chancellor Bacon made the suggestion that taxes should be voted for the payment of the Queen's debts. This novelty was so little liked by the Commons that the grant of this year was the smallest of Elizabeth's reign. Again in 1610, after the refusal of the nation to continue the heavy Elizabethan votes on the ground that the government no longer had the Spaniards, but only the Irish, left to deal with, James I tried to get Parliament to vote a large subsidy to pay past debts and to provide an annual "support" for the future. "Support and Supply" as used by James I in 1610 was another way of asking that the king be granted subsidies in peace as well as in war. This attempt, too, failed, and when the next grant but one was made, in 1624, a special commission was created with it, to see that it was spent for war purposes exclusively.

Even if fifteenths and tenths and subsidies could have been reduced to the status of regularly recurring taxes, they were in themselves unfitted to be made the foundation for a national fiscal system. The fifteenth and tenth was hopelessly stereotyped long before the Tudor era began. In 1334 it had assumed the form of a fixed tax on certain parcels of land, and since that time it was subject to no changes except diminution in yield to allow for "decays". The subsidy represented a Tudor attempt to levy on income from land or fixed capital (personalty). In actual practice the subsidy tended to become little more than a land tax. It was difficult to add the names of new men to the subsidy books so as to bring new wealth within the scope of the tax. The subsidy thus became a fixed tax also, capable only of declining in yield as "subsidy men" decayed.

Ship money, the later nonparliamentary direct tax, represented an effort to escape from the limited incidence and fixed yield of the subsidy as well as from parliamentary reluctance to vote appropriations and the desire of its leaders to use grants to increase their political power. The crown determined in advance the sum demanded, and required new assessments, independent of the subsidy rates, to be made. Yet even in connection with ship money no effort was made to escape the military connotation of direct levies. Ship money was said to be collected for the maintenance of the fleet, and every penny actually was used for naval purposes. The fact that a large part of the potential revenues were justifiable and leviable only for military purposes perhaps helped to make military efforts one of the chief forms of state activity in the first period of the national system from 1485 to 1641.

It was asserted by Hakewell in 1610 during a parliamentary attack upon James I's increase of his customs through the levy of impositions that each royal liability was covered by a corresponding source of revenue, and that the king might come to Parliament for funds if his own were not sufficient. It should be noted that not only was this view directly contrary to established ideas, but it was disproved by events. For James made appeals for taxes on just such grounds and came face to face with the old disinclination of the nation to appropriate funds to cover his deficiencies.

3. Henry VII's regard for tradition and political expediency prevented the adoption at the beginning of the Tudor regime of a revenue system adequate for more than the briefest time. The main reliance was placed on lands and customs, and public taxation remained a war revenue measure. Rising costs of maintaining the court

and the growing demands of the armed services in face of the European diplomatic situation left no funds for the adoption by the government of functions for which the times were crying out. The crown's failure to make the state mean very much to the average individual made him loath at a later date to permit the abandonment of the medieval tradition that the king was entitled to ask for aid from his people only in the event of war.

At the same time certain aggressive political leaders saw the possibility of capitalizing the fiscal difficulties of the crown and the ever present reluctance of the nation to pay taxes even for war by precipitating a conflict between the king and Parliament. Parliament under such inspirtion made the novel departure in the early years of Charles I's reign for refusing to respond to royal requests even for military appropriations in the face of a great war. The King's only possible recourse short of turning the government over to a group whose every action branded them as incompetent to act as the administrators of the state was to govern as an absolute ruler. Thus fiscal traditions, policies, and practices played an important part not only in determining the character of the first phase of the English national state but in terminating it in the bloody struggles of the Civil Wars.

CHAPTER I

THE FIFTEENTH CENTURY BACKGROUND

In the middle ages, the revenues of the English kings were derived from the *firma comitatus,* or farm of the ancient domains of the crown and of the king's share of the fines in the popular courts; the fee-farms of incorporated boroughs and cities; the fines and amercements in the king's courts; the farm of the ulnage and the profits of escheat and other feudal incidents. To these Edward I had added the great and small customs, the *magna* and the *parva custuma,* and Edward III the customs subsidies of tonnage and poundage, and of wool, wool fells and leather. The customs subsidies of tonnage and poundage and of wool, wool fells and leather were of parliamentary origin, and in the fifteenth century either were granted for periods of two or three years and renewed, or were voted for life. Though they were given theoretically for the safeguarding of the seas, and the defense of the realm, and though parliament endeavored to control their use, in actual fact, once they were granted by Parliament, the king used them as he pleased, and for all practical purposes they formed part of the annual regularly recurring revenues of the crown.[1] Besides the feudal

[1] Henry V received the grant of these subsidies for life after the battle of Agincourt (*Rot. Parl.,* IV, 641); Henry VI in 1453 (*Rot. Parl.,* V, 229); Edward IV in 1472 after Hexham (*Rot. Parl.,* VI, 154); and Richard III in 1485 (*Rot. Parl.,* VI, 238). A grant for life was never to be a precedent, (*Rot. Parl.,* IV, 64a). In 1404 the Commons in their grant declared that the sums received from these subsidies should be spent ''in especial expense in defence of the realm, according to the form and intent of the grant . . and for no other purpose.'' Anyone who received any sums out of the said grants ''for wars or for any debt due by King Henry before the day of this present Parliament except only for the defence of the realm to be made in time to come'' was declared guilty of treason. The disbursement was placed in charge of treasurers of war, to

11

dues and the customs, the king enjoyed the income from estates which had come more recently into the hands of the crown, especially in the course of the fifteenth century, either by inheritence like the lands of the Duchy of Lancaster, or by forfeiture like the estates of the Duke of Clarence.

The crown revenues from feudal sources and from customs diminished greatly in value in the course of the fifteenth century. In the reign of Henry VI the *firma comitatus*, and the fee farms of the chartered towns, and other feudal dues had yielded £17,000 yearly to the crown.[2] In the reign of Edward IV they returned only £2,500.[3] The customs revenues of all kinds had averaged £47,000 a year in Henry IV's reign. In the middle of the century they fell to £32,000 a year, and in the first half of Edward IV's reign to £25,000 a year. They rose to an average of £35,000 a year in the latter half of this reign, only to decline to £20,800 a year for the three years of the reigns of Edward V and Richard III.[4] The more recently acquired crown lands were in a similar case. During the fifteenth century the land which came to the crown by forfeiture was very great in extent. Fortescue estimated that during the reign of Edward IV alone, the king held possession of one fifth of the land of England, at one time and another.[5] Because faithful followers demanded rewards, and perhaps because a system of centralized control of crown lands had as yet not been sufficiently developed, the land passed out

report at the next Parliament (*Rot. Parl.*, III, 546b). Even as late as 1473-1476 Sir John Fortescue, in his *De Dominio Regali et Politico*, declared that the subsidy of the tonnage and poundage ought to be applied only to the keeping of the sea, and was not to be considered part of the king's ordinary revenues (Fortescue, *Works*, I, 456). But as early as 1406 Henry IV was permitted to use £6,000 of the revenues from customs subsidies as he pleased (*Rot. Parl.*, III, 568b); in Henry VI's reign it was made possible to use some of their returns to meet household expenses (*Rot. Parl.*, V, 246-247), and in Edward IV's reign assignments for the household were definitely made upon these subsidies (*Rot. Parl.*, VI, 198-199).

2 Ramsay, *Lancaster and York*, I, 145-146.

3 *Ibid.*, I, 458.

4 *Ibid.*, I, 151, 313; II, 254-257; 461-462; 559. These tables are based on the *Lord Treasurer's Remembrancer's Enrolled Customs Accounts*.

5 Fortescue, *Works*, I, 463.

of the king's possession almost immediately.[6] The hereditary estates of the crown, the Duchy of Cornwall, the Earldom of Chester, the Principality of Wales, and the Duchy of Lancaster were alienated only in part; but they were so burdened with charges that during the reign of Edward IV that they returned to the crown only five-eighths of their rental.[7] From all the more recently acquired crown lands Edward IV received per year on the average, during the last years of his reign,[8] £6,471 and during the reign of Richard III, the sums seem to have been less.[9]

The growing deficiency of the ordinary revenues gives a clue to the rising importance of direct taxes of parliamentary origin in the fifteenth century. The difficulties of the Lancastrian kings were not due to extravagance and mismanagement. Their shrinking revenues scarcely sufficed for their ordinary expenses, and their constant wars compelled them to find further resources in frequent parliamentary grants.

The usual parliamentary tax was the fifteenth and tenth. The fifteenth and tenth was a grant of the fifteenth part of the value of movable property belonging to persons outside the royal demesne; and the tenth part of such value in case of persons living on the royal demesne and in cities and boroughs. Though this tax was originally assessed anew at every grant, it was fixed in 1334 on the basis of a composition between the royal commissioners and the men who paid it.[10] The sum agreed upon was "entered on the rolls as the assessment of the particular township. And the tax-payers in the townships were required to assess and collect the amount upon and from the various contributors."[11] The fifteenth and tenth thus passed out of the control of the royal assessors and commissioners, since the tax-payers in each township assessed and collected the required sum, and it became a fossilized tax yielding at

6 Ramsay, *Lancaster and York,* I, 147; II, 459.

7 *Ibid.,* II, 459-461.

8 *Exch. of Receipt, Receipt Rolls,* nos. 941, 942, 943, 946, 947, 949; Michaelmas 1480-Michaelmas 1483.

9 *Exch. of Receipt, Receipt Rolls,* nos. 950, 951; Easter, 1484-Easter, 1485.

10 Stephen Dowell, *History of Taxation and Taxes in England,* I, 87.

11 *Ibid.,* I, 86.

first between £38,000 and £39,000.[12] But since no new groups could be added to those which paid the tax, nor the amount paid by any existing group increased because of the fixing of the assessment in 1334, as the old groups became unable to pay their full quotas, the value of the tax to the crown decreased. Allowances were made from time to time for decayed towns. In 1443 the specific sum of £4000 was allowed,[13] and this was increased in 1449 to £6000, when, in addition, the city of Lincoln and the town of Great Yarmouth were completely exempted from payment. From that time forward these allowances and exemptions were always made. The yield of the tax was thus reduced to between £32,000 and £33,000, and continued to fall. It is to be noted also that the fifteenth and tenth, originally a tax on movable goods became after 1334 a fixed tax on land. It did not however touch the demesne lands of peers, and it passed over the landless population entirely.[14]

For these reasons, the Lancastrian and Yorkist kings, and even their predecessors made every effort to replace the fifteenth and tenth by more productive taxes with a broader incidence, collected under royal control. In 1404 Henry IV declaring to Parliament that the grant of 1402 was insufficient, received a new tax, a grant of five per cent of the yearly value of lands and rents in England, or of one shilling for every £20 of personal property in the case of men without land. With this were combined two fifteenths and tenths.[15] During the next reigns various experiments were tried; a tax on householders combined with a tax on knights' fees,[16] a tax on land,[17] a graduated tax on land,[18] and in 1440 a graduated income tax combined with an act for the resumption of all grants from the royal demesne since the accession of Henry VI.[19] The remark-

[12] *Ibid.*, I, 87.

[13] *Rot. Parl.*, IV, 425a.

[14] *Nottingham Records*, II, 286; Vickers, *England in the Later Middle Ages*, 335.

[15] *Rot. Parl.*, III, 546-547.

[16] *Ibid.*, IV, 318b; anno 1427.

[17] *Ibid.*, IV, 370; anno 1431.

[18] *Ibid.*, IV, 486b; anno 1435.

[19] *Ibid.*, V, 172-174. A description of these taxes is given in Dowell, I, 104-126.

able thing is, that of all these experiments made during the first half of the fifteenth century, not one was successful enough to be repeated. The new taxes were perhaps sometimes too elaborate to be successfully managed with the existing governmental machinery; but the proviso added to nearly all the new taxes that they were not to be taken as precedents, lends some support to Dowell's statements that the fifteenth and tenth "came to be regarded by the people almost as of constitutional right" and that all the attempts to introduce other forms of taxation ended in failure for that reason.[20] Even in conjunction with some of the new taxes the fifteenth and tenth was used, as in 1404, 1431 and 1435; and it was always returned to in the intervals between experiments.

Edward IV made two great efforts to change the character of the parliamentary grants, in 1463 and 1472. In 1463 the £6,000 allowed in the fifteenth and tenth for decayed towns was to be levied upon the shires proportionately to the sum allowed for the decayed towns within each shire. This sum so apportioned to the shire, was to be levied upon the inhabitants having twenty shillings in yearly value of lands or ten marks in goods, by royal commissioners, and the money was to be collected by royal collectors. This plan was an attempt to recoup the crown in the collection of fifteenths and tenths to the amount of the allowances made to the shires for decayed towns; to alter the incidence of taxation by a new limit of exemption and the inclusion of the landless classes; to introduce the principle of a progressive charge; and to replace local by royal assessment and collection;—in short, "to revise the settlement of 1334."[21] The king was compelled to abandon the attempt. He remitted the £6,000 and agreed to collect the fifteenth and tenth under the old forms.[22]

In 1472 Edward IV made another attempt to change the old order. To pay for the support of 13,000 archers against France for one year, estimated to cost £118,625, he received from Parliament the grant of ten per cent of all issues and profits of lands and tenements, rents, fees, annuities, offices and

[20] Dowell, I, 88.
[21] *Ibid.*, I, 121.
[22] *Rot. Parl.*, V, 498.

other income from the Commons and Lords in Parliament.[23] The first collection of the tax yielded £31,140. To provide the balance, Parliament before its prorogation granted a fifteenth and tenth, and saddled £5,383 arbitrarily upon those counties whose certificates of assessment had not been returned in time for the first collection. There was still lacking £51,147, however, after this second grant had been collected. This sum was now assessed upon the shires in specific amounts, and royal commissioners were sent to subdivide the sum assesed on a county, among the inhabitants, levying on the value of goods and chattels, which were to be taxed before any land or landed possessions. The new tax was not successful. The House of Commons stating that "the most easy, ready and prone payment of any charge to be borne within this realm by the commons of the same, is by grants of fifteenths and tenths, the levy whereof amongst your people is so usual although it be to them full chargeable, that none other form of levy resembleth thereunto," prayed the king to remit the said £51,147. and take in its place one entire fifteenth and tenth and "three parts" of a fifteenth and tenth.[24] The next grant of taxes in 1482 was a fifteenth and tenth in the old form.[25]

The fifteenth century experiment of using direct parliamentary taxation to increase the governmental income was not regarded as successful by either the king or his people. For the crown it was accompanied by an unwelcome surrender of power to Parliament, which made opportunities of the king's necessities to endeavor to increase its own control of the state, and to interfere with the policies of the king. The "constitutionalism" of the century follows directly upon the financial difficulties of the Lancastrian sovereigns. Among the "people" taxation as a method of government finance was unpopular. As the "people" expressed themselves in Parliament and through the writers on political theory, like Sir John Fortescue, they show themselves to have an ingrained notion that the king should live of his own. Henry IV was petitioned by his Parliament of 1404 that he should live of his own,[26] Sir John Fortescue

[23] *Ibid.*, VI, 4.
[24] *Ibid.*, VI, 151.
[25] *Ibid.*, VI, 197.
[26] Oman, *The Political History of England, 1377-1485,* 191.

held that in general the king should live of his own "livelood" which was his in right of his crown,[27] and Edward IV, bidding for the support of the nation at large, announced in 1467 that he intended to "lyve upon my nowne, and not to charge my subjgettes but in grete and urgent causes."[28] Only when there fell "a case overmuch exorbitant," for the suppression of rebellion, the defence of the realm to repel invasion and the safeguarding of the seas, was it thought right and necessary that the people should be taxed.[29] The formulated reason for this attitude was that taxes, regularly levied for the support of the ordinary charges of the government impoverished the people. France where the aides and tailles together with the gabelle and certain excises were the important revenues of the king, was the horrible example. "There the same commons be so impoverished and destroyd that they may unneth (scarcely) lyve. Thay drynke Water. Thay eate Apples, with Bred right brown made of Rye. They eaten no flesche. . . Their Wifs and Children gone bare fote. . . Thay gone crokyd and ar feble not able to fyght nor to defend the Realme nor they have wepon nor monye to buy them wepon withal."[30] In England with the commons poverty-stricken by taxation, the archers would decrease, and the nation's military power be weakened. The people, being men of greater courage than the French might rise against the king. In time of special need they would not be able to help his necessities as they now did with subsidies and fifteenths and tenths.[31]

Behind such arguments, Lord Acton would have us seek the baser motives, the special self-interest. The articulate classes, who ever arrogate to themselves the designation of the people, who voiced these protests against taxation in the persons of such writers as Sir John Fortescue, or through the House of Commons, were the richer freeholders and gentry of the country; and the burgesses of the towns. The persons who paid the fifteenths and tenths and subsidies were precisely these same ones. Had they been given to deeper introspection, they would

27 Fortescue, *Works*, I, 458-459.
28 Vickers, *England in the Later Middle Ages*, 467.
29 Fortescue, *Works*, I, 457.
30 *Ibid.*, I, 451-452.
31 *Ibid.*, I, 464-466.

probably have acknowledged that their real objection to taxation as a method of financing the state was that it took their property and the property of their peculiar classes alone, for the support of the state and government. The continuance of the earlier developments of the country might have reconciled them to taxational finance; for in return they had acquired in their institution, Parliament, especially in Henry IV's reign, a large degree of control in the state. This control seems to have been asserted rather to limit expenditure and to keep down taxes, rather than for any desire to shape high policy. For the proper use of this control, in their own interests however, the gentry and burgesses had neither experience nor aptitude. When in the middle of the century they found Parliament and its power the tool of ambitious restless nobles like the Beauforts, York, Warwick, and later, Gloucester, for the disturbance of the peace of the land, they must have felt that government should be chiefly the concern of the king. Rather than power in the state, which they did not yet know how to use, they preferred for themselves relief from the necessity of supporting the state. Thus the ancient idea that the king should live of his own was reinforced, and became anew a vital article of their creed.

CHAPTER II

THE ESTABLISHMENT OF THE TUDOR DYNASTY

Henry Tudor's chief advisers and supporters in 1485 fall into two classes; on the one hand the Earl of Oxford and the Courtenays of Devon, and on the other, John Morton, Richard Fox, Reginald Bray, Richard Guildford, Edward Poynings, Richard Edgecombe, and Thomas Lovell.[1] Oxford and the Courtenays are representatives of the remnants of the old Lancastrian nobility. They had been exiled for their loyalty to the cause of Lancaster, and their property and wealth confiscated. To them the triumph of Henry Tudor meant the victory of the true Lancastrian claimant over the usurper of York, together with their own personal rehabilitation in title, estates and position.

Morton, Fox, Bray, Guilford, Poynings, Lovell and Edgecombe were all of them sons of yeomen or lesser gentry; men with university or legal training, or skilled in accounting — in a word — the professional men of the middle classes. The best trained and most experienced men of their classes, they may be taken as the best representatives of the attitude and interests of their classes, and their support of Henry Tudor was more than mere personal service. To them Henry Tudor was not a Lancastrian as opposed to the Yorkist Richard III, but the strong prince, the legitimate king, the enemy of the feudal nobility who for the last thirty years had made sport of the king and the crown. The revolution of 1485 was a revolution of the middle class in alliance with Henry Tudor, with such help as they could get from the Lancastrian cause against the old nobility. The Tudor commonwealth which followed was an alliance of the same middle class with the crown for mutual self interest.[2]

[1] There were of course also those Yorkists who resented Richard III's usurpation, like the Woodvilles.

[2] *Cf.* J. W. Burgess, *Political Science and Comparative Constitutional*

One of the chief interests of the crown was to secure a sufficient revenue, at least, large enough to make impossible a repetition of the humiliation and chaos of the fifteenth century. It might be increased so much even as to enable the crown to be freer in its choice of policies, or as it termed, to become more absolute. The middle class desire among other things was to shift from itself the burden of financing the state, or of contributing to its support, to be as free as possible from taxation.

The trend of the working of the alliance of the king and the middle class is clearly indicated in the first Parliament of Henry VII's reign. The question of an adequate revenue was taken up early in the session. The first grant made to the king was that of the subsidies of tonnage and poundage and of wool, wool fells and leather for life, for the defence of the realm and the safe-guard and keeping of the sea.[3] With a view to increasing the yield of these and other customs revenues, or at any rate to stop the decrease caused by merchants alien becoming denizens — since denizens paid at a lower rate than aliens — all merchants alien who became denizens were required to continue to pay at the higher rate.[4]

Further, since the present revenues did not suffice "to kepe and sustayne" the king's honorable household, and his other ordinary charges "which must be kept and borne worshipfully

Law, I, 93. "By the middle of the fifteenth century the actual power of the state had passed from the aristocracy to the people. It remained now for the people to organize themselves and seize the sovereignty. Nominally they were organized in the House of Commons, but really they were not. The House of Commons was then but a kind of overflow-meeting of the House of Lords. The people were not yet far enough advanced in the development of their political consciousness to create an entirely independent organization. An existing institution must furnish them the nucleus. They were deeply conscious of their hostility to the aristocracy. There remained, then, only the King. He, too, was hostile to the aristocracy. Through their common enemy, the King and the people were referred to each other. In the organization which followed, called in political history the absolute monarchy of the Tudors, the people were in reality, the sovereign, the state, but apparently, the King was the state. England under the Tudors was a democratic political society under monarchic government."

[3] Rot. Parl., VI, 268.

[4] Statutes of the Realm, 1 Henry VII, c.2.

and Honorably as it accordeth to the Honor of your Estate
and your said Realme by the which your adversaries and enemyes
shall fall into the drede wherein heretofore they have byne,''
the crown estates were increased by the resumptions of the alienated portions.[5]   The Duchy of Cornwall, the Earldom of Rich-
mond and other lands were assured to the crown.[6]   Finally,
acts of attainder were passed against Richard, Duke of Gloucester, John, Duke of Norfolk, the Earl of Surrey, Francis
Lovell, Walter Devereux, Lord Ferrers, John Lord Zouche, Richard Ratcliffe, William Catesby and others, and their lands were
confiscated.[7]   Even though important and numerous exceptions
were made to the resumptions, and lands were restored to persons
attainted under Richard III,[8] the crown estates were greatly
increased by these acts.   Whereas the income from lands had
been £6,471 a year during the last year of Edward IV's reign,
it was £13,633 during the first year of Henry VII.[9]

These revenue acts, and especially the statutes of resumption,
confiscation and forfeiture satisfied the desires and interests
of both the king and the commons.   They were the beginnings
of a revenue system which would become adequate for the
needs of the state and relieve the middle class, at the expense
first, of the merchants, especially foreigners, in whose control
most of the foreign trade lay; and secondly, of the common enemy, the feudal nobility.   The customs revenues and rents of

   [5] The first resumption comprehended all the lands of the Duchy of
Lancaster in the possession of Edward IV on March 4, in the first year
of his reign or at any time thereafter, or in the hands of Richard III at
any time in his reign, with the revocation of all their grants and alienations from the Duchy (*Rot. Parl.*, VI, 271-272).   Later in the same session
the great resumption of all such castles, lordships, honors, manors as
Henry VI had on October 21, 1455, as parcel and in right and title of
the crown of England and of the Duchies of Lancaster and Cornwall, the
Principality of Wales, and the Earldom of Chester was made.   All gifts,
grants and leases made by Richard III, and the gifts and grants of offices
made by Edward IV before August 21, 1485, were annulled (*Ibid.*, VI,
272, 336).
   [6] *Ibid.*, VI, 272.
   [7] *Ibid.*, VI, 276.
   [8] *Ibid.*, VI, 339-385.
   [9] *Exch. of Receipt, Receipt Rolls,* nos. 955, 958.   This figure does not
include the *firma comitatus,* or the fee farms of the cities.

landed estates in the possession or control of the crown were the bases of the new Tudor revenue system. In the later Tudor period the customs became more important, though they were never neglected from the beginning. During the earlier time the chief reliance was upon the crown lands and the special concern was to increase their extent and value.

The use of landed estates as a chief basis of the new revenue system, which political exegencies demanded, was made possible by the advancing economic development of the country. In the last analysis governmental revenue systems are efforts to turn the chief forms of wealth of the country most efficiently to the support of the state with due regard for the prevailing political idea or theory. Their nature varies with, and corresponds, sometimes tardily to the changing economic development and organization of the country. In the Middle Ages, when communication was poor, the country economically disunited and the state in general weak, feudal aids and incidents, the profits of jurisdictions and the farms of the demesne lands of the king by the sheriffs were the most effective means of diverting the wealth of the country, in its form of land to the support of the government. But towards the close of the fifteenth century, communication improved, money economy had developed rapidly, book keeping of a more modern form made possible exact supervision from a distance, England became more conomically unified, and London became the economic as well as the political capital of most of England. The extension of the domestic system in the fifteenth century, and its national regulation by the truck act of 1465, the regulation of the corn trade by the government, the parliamentary recognition of craft guilds, the protection of native artisans, and the complete adoption by the Tudors of the mercantilist policy foreshadowed in the legislation of Richard II, are special phases of the expansion of the economic unit and the more perfect nationalization of the economic life of the country.

This more perfect unification made practicable a more effective means of turning land, at the outset of the Tudor period still the chief form of wealth, to the support of the state. It was now possible for the crown to manage directly from London and to receive in money payments the rents and issues of vast estates owned or controlled by the crown in the several counties. On these lands and manors the demesnes were let on leases for money rents, and the peasant holdings were under the direction of royal bailiffs and stewards, the whole overseen by crown surveyors controlled directly from London by the expert accountants in the government service.

The beginnings of this use of lands as one basis for a revenue reach back into the early fifteenth century. The Duchies of Lancaster and Cornwall foreshadowed the new system; the confiscations of Edward IV were a groping toward it. Richard III drew up a plan of central administration and control of large landed estates.[10] Henry VII favored by the coincidence of economic practicability and the political desire of the most forceful group of his subjects brought to realization the tendencies and plans of the past decades.

[10] See below, chapter VI.

CHAPTER III

The Development of the New Revenue System
Customs and Crown Lands

"Being a king that loved wealth and treasure," says Bacon of Henry VII, "he could not endure to have trade sick." He fostered commerce by opening new markets for English trade and by bettering old facilities. Treaties with Denmark in 1489 and 1490 opened Iceland, renewed privileges to English merchants in Norway, especially at Bergen, and taken with the unratified treaty with Riga in 1499 were attempts to break the Hanseatic League's monopoly of the Baltic. Trading relations with the Netherlands were reestablished by the Intercursus Magnus of 1496 with a removal of restrictions imposed during the past fifty years. The treaty of 1486 with France provided for free intercourse and the removal of all special burdens imposed during the past twenty-one years. Nine years later, as a price of his neutrality in the Italian war, Henry compelled Charles VIII to restore other ancient trade privileges. The English penetration of the Mediterranean was furthered by the treaty of Medino del Campo with Spain, and the pact with Florence in 1490.

In the later years of the reign, Henry VII stimulated foreign trade by advancing capital to English and Italian merchants, to the extent of at least £87,000 between 1505 and 1509. The king accepted no interest, as indeed it was illegal for him to do; but he required that the borrower bind himself to import into England enough goods each year, as long as the loan stood, to pay certain amounts in customs dues.[1]

In this fashion, by providing easy conditions of trade and credit, Henry VII developed his customs revenues. He did

[1] *Exch., Treasury of Receipt, Misc. Books*, 214.

not make any but unimportant increases in the existing duties
of the tonnage and poundage and the old and new customs.
He satisfied himself with the increased revenues resulting from
an increase in the bulk of transactions. He tried further to
abolish the exemptions and special privileges of foreign merchants in England and to secure more faithful fulfillment
of their duties by custom house officials. A better valuation
of the goods upon which duty was paid was probably secured
by the substitution in 1507 of an official Book of Rates for the
port of London, for the declaration by the merchant on his
oath.[2] During the first ten years of the reign, the customs
revenues averaged £32,951 a year; during the remainder of
the reign they were increased to £40,132 a year.[3]

For many years the customs yielded a revenue larger than
the crown rents and other income based on land. Yet it was
in the increase of the landed revenues that the most rapid and
remarkable progress was made. The resumptions and confiscations made in the Parliament of 1486 more than doubled
the value of the royal estates proper. Since however £7,723
of the rents was at once assigned to the maintenance of the
household and wardrobe each year,[4] there were only a few
thousand pounds available for the king's other purposes. During
the next ten years, large additions were made to the crown
estates by the attainder and the forfeiture of the estates of
Sir Simon Montford, Sir Robert Ratcliffe, William Daubeney,
Humphrey Stafford and others, and especially of Sir William
Stanley "the richest subject for value in the kingdom." From
his castle of Holt, the Treasurer of the Chamber received £9,062
in ready money beside the small sum realized from the sale
of his goods;[5] and his lands yielded the king over £1,000 a
year clear.[6] The lands of Cecilie, Duchess of York, valued at

[2] Gras, *Tudor Books of Rates, Quarterly Journal of Economics*, XXVI,
766ff.

[3] The whole subject of the customs and the commercial policy of Henry
VII, and of Henry VIII is admirably and exhaustively treated by Georg
Schanz, *Englische Handelspolitik gegen Ende des Mittelalters.*

[4] *Rot. Parl.*, VI, 299f.

[5] *Accounts, Exch., Queen's Remembrancer*, 413/2, f. 85.

[6] *Exch., Treasury of Receipt, Misc. Books*, 212.

£1,200 a year came into the king's hands by escheat,[7] and Parliament made the further resumptions of the alienated portions of the manor of Woodstock and of all the York lands.[8] Other great additions to the crown lands were made later, by the acquisition of the queen's land, on the death of Queen Elizabeth, and of the lands of Jasper, Duke of Bedford, of Sir Francis Cheyne, of Edward de la Pole, of Lord Ferrers and of Lord Audeley, leader of the Cornish rebels.[9]

Henry VII was not content merely to increase the extent of the crown estates; he sought to make their revenues as productive as possible. In February of 1486, Sir Reginald Bray, Chancellor of the Duchy of Lancaster was ordered to carry out a "reformation" of officials in charge of the royal lands as far as was thought necessary "for our most profit and avail,"[10] and in the following year an act of Parliament not only annulled all grants of office of receiver, auditor, customer, collector of customs and subsidies, controller, searcher, surveyor, "aunager," but revoked all leases on manors and lordships of the king, in order to enable the king "providently" to make new leases "for his most profit and approvement of his revenues."[11] Again, in 1495 all leases in the Principality of Wales were declared void by Parliament, because "much less rent reserved unto the king and the prince than the said lordships manors lands and tenements might reasonably be set for."[12] The success of this policy of maximum productivity can be illustrated very well in the case of the Duchy of Lancaster. It was the practice after the first years of the reign, to pay the clear surplus of the revenues of the Duchy, after all allowances had been made, fees and annuities paid, and the assignments in favor of the household and wardrobe discharged, into the Treasury of the Chamber. In 1488 the Treasurer of the Chamber received £666 13s. 4d. from the Chancellor of the Duchy; in 1490 £2,800;

[7] *Exch., Treasury of Receipt, Misc. Books,* 212.

[8] *Rot. Parl.,* VI, 459-462.

[9] These acquisitions from time to time can be traced in the memoranda in the back of the account books of the Treasurer of the Chamber, especially *Exch., Treasury of Receipt,* 214.

[10] Campbell, *Materials for a History of the Reign of Henry VII,* I, 324.

[11] *Rot. Parl.,* VI, 403.

[12] *Ibid.,* VI, 465.

in 1495 £3,600; in 1499 £4,400; in 1504 £5,368 and in 1508 £6,566.[13]

The increase of the revenues from the crown estates proper as a whole, as the result of Henry VII's various measures was remarkable. The clear annual yield from the crown lands in the first years of the reign was about £10,000;[14] of which £7,723 was assigned by act of Parliament as has been noted, for the payment of the costs of the household and wardrobe, leaving about £2,500 available for other purposes. This clear excess, after all expenses of collection and administration and all assignments for household and wardrobe (which in practice ranged from £7,500 to £4,650 a year) had been paid, increased very rapidly. In 1491 it was £3,764 18s. 7d.; in 1494 £7,789 17s. 7d.; in 1497 £12,746 17s 2d.; in 1503 £20,689 8s. 11d. and in 1504 £24,145 4s. 10d.[15]

Much attention has been attracted to Henry VII's revival of feudal relations and his refurbishing of the royal feudal rights. Cities and gilds paid handsomely for the confirmation of their liberties.[16] Every year after 1494 men were fined for not appearing to be made Knights of the Bath.[17] In 1504 the king requested Parliament for the two feudal aids to which he was entitled "on the knighting of his son Arthur, now dead," and on the marriage of his eldest daughter to the King of Scotland.[18] In 1486, 1500 and 1503 proclamations were issued, ordering all men with £40 a year in lands to take up knighthood.[19] Henry's object in compelling men to take up knighthood

---

[13] *Accounts Exch., Queen's Remembrancer*, 413/2, I; 414/6; *Add. Mss.* 21480.

[14] *Duchy of Lancaster, Accounts Various* 6/1, 6/7.

[15] *Accounts, Exch., Queen's Remembrancer*, 413/2, I, II; 414/6; 414/16; *Add. Mss.* 21480.

[16] The men of Cheshire paid £2,000 for the confirmation of their liberties, with a pardon for their intrusions and alienations (*Accounts, Exch., Queen's Remembrancer*, 413/2, III; *Lansd. Mss.*, 127, f. 37). The merchant tailors paid £100 to have their liberties enrolled. (*Lansd. Mss.*, 127, f. 16) The citizens of London paid 5000 marks for the confirmation of their liberties. (*Fabyan's Chronicle*, 688).

[17] In one year fines of £1125 13s. 4d. were collected on this account. *Accounts, Exch., Queen's Remembrancer*, 413/12, II, III.

[18] *Rot. Parl.*, VI, 532.

[19] Campbell, *Materials*, II, 76; Rymer *Foedera* O. XII, 770; Gairdner, *Letters and Papers, Richard III and Henry VII*, II, 379.

D

was not to levy fines for neglect to do, but to bring as great as possible a portion of the land of England into feudal relations with the crown as a matter of recent record. The two feudal aids requested in 1504, would have given an opportunity and legal occasion to search out all titles and tenures, and make a new record of those lands which were held directly of the crown, *in capite*.[20]

Land holden of knight service *in capite* was subject to the incidents of wardship and marriage upon the death of the holder, if his heir was a minor or a woman; and to escheat into the king's hands, upon the holder's death without heirs.   The further extension of the crown domains temporarily by wardships and marriages, permanently by escheat was the real purpose of what has hitherto been regarded as petty insistence on outgrown and forgotten feudal obligations.

The protection of the king's rights in lands held *in capite,* and the transference of all marriages, wardships and escheats, legally due, to the king's hands, was assured by the rather notorious *Inquisitiones post mortem* of the reign. On the death of a man who held land of the king or was suspected of doing so, it was usual for the Court of Chancery to issue a writ to the escheator of the district to conduct an inquiry to ascertain the extent of the possessions; and the tenures by which they were held, the heirs and their age, and whatever else might be needful that the king receive the profits justly due him. The royal policy is explained by a letter of 1495, which though written to Irish officials, is applicable to England, and explains the policy there followed. ''Item to have a remembrance to see that all escheators may duly inquire upon the writs of *diem clausit extremum* and such other writs of *mandatum* after the death of the king's tenants, of their lands, and the age of their heirs and of their tenure, and that the true extents may be made thereof and so returned; and then both the ferme of the wardships where such happen and also the king's relief and

---

[20] The Commons recognized the king's purpose. Because of their great uneasiness on account of ''the search and non-knowledge of their several tenures, and of their lands chargeable to the same'' aids, the Commons prayed the king accept £40,000 in place of the aids. The king, defeated in his purpose, graciously covered his retreat by remitting £10,000 of the grant. *Rot. Parl.*, VI, 532; Roper, *Life of More*, 12.

such other profits shall be the more; and if ye think the escheat-
or to be favorable to the party or insufficient or indiscreet
whereby the profit of the king may be hurt by the finding of
any such inquisition as is daily in England to the king's great
hurt: howbeit his council think that some time if a fine be made
for the recompense of the profits thereof the king shall have no
loss nothing remembering the hurt of the crown which shall ensue for lack of a matter of record; but it were better for the
title of the king and of his heirs to lose such profit which
needeth not if true and sufficient officers be deputed, that the
king's title were found of record, and to cause such sufficient
persons to be commissioners to inquire after the decease of
all such tenants, so that the king's title might be found of record,
but that shall not be only for the profit of the king, but also
of his heirs.'' [21] The last sentence quoted is especially illuminating.   Even though a large fine to the king for the relin-
quishment of his rights would in some cases yield a larger immediate gain, it was of greater importance that the king's
rights be reasserted and found of record; since in that way
the profits of wardships and marriages in the future would come
to the king's hand, and the land itself might eventually come
into possession of the crown, by escheat, either during Henry
VII's own lifetime or later.

To keep a check upon the escheator, who was a local official
and perhaps too well disposed to the family of the deceased,
the Chancery clerks probably examined very carefully the records of previous inquisitions; and the Exchequer records too,
as was commanded in Ireland.[22] If, when compared with the
information from these sources, the inquisition was found to
be faulty, it was returned with a writ *ad melius inquirendum.*
In some cases the escheator was joined by a royal commissioner
or even superseded entirely, doubtless in order that the rights
of the crown might be ascertained most completely. In their

[21] Royal Mss. 18c. XIV, f. 231. The document is printed with the in-
sertion of words which destroy its meaning in Gairdner, *Letters and Papers,*
Richard III and Henry VII, II, 65-66.

[22] Gairdner, *Letters and Papers, Richard III and Henry VII*, II, 66.
Empson and Dudley searched in the Exchequer records for information
about tenures, and Heron, Treasurer of the Chamber, seems to have had
information from spies. See below p. 30, n. 45.

eagerness to profit the crown, these officials went so far as to cause untrue "offices" or verdicts to be found, sometimes returned into the courts of record offices and inquisitions that had never been found, and sometimes changed the matter of offices that were truly found "to the great hurt and disheryson of the king's true subjects, that like beforetime have not been seen in the realm," as was admitted in a law of Henry VIII's reign, designed to prevent a repetition of the injustice in the future.[23]

As part of the same policy Henry VII insisted that heirs of lands held of the crown must not enter upon them without suing out their livery from the king's hands. The fines for the livery of lands (except in cases of special livery) were very small, averaging £437 a year for the last four years of the reign.[24] The real purpose of the requirement was that the transfer to the new heir might be a matter of record, and might not be made prejudicial to the king's rights. If the heir entered without suing his livery, no record of the king's rights in the land against the new possessor would exist, or his rights might otherwise be injured, and it was to prevent this that intrusion upon lands by heirs, that is entry without the king's writ, was punished by a large fine, by confiscation of the rents from the death of the former holder until such time as suit for livery was made, or even by confiscation of the land itself.[25]

Though eventual escheat of lands held *"in capite"* was of first importance, the profits of wardship and marriage were not inconsiderable. In some cases the king's rights of wardship and marriage were sold;[26] but as a rule the king retained the lands

[23] *Statutes of the Realm,* 1, Henry VIII, c. 8.

[24] *Exch., Treasury of Receipt, Misc. Books,* 211, book of fines for writs of entry before the King's Bench, annis 21-24 Henry VII.

[25] Examples of fines of intrusion taken from *Lansd. Mss.* 127 are, Sir William Say, 2,500 marks; Sir Philip Calthrop, £500; Sir Edward Harward and Alice his wife, £533. John Heron, Treasurer of the Chamber, in his account books, especially in *Add. Mss.* 21,480 has noted the names of those who have had no livery of their lands, the rents of which belong to the king until the suit for livery is made. In *Exchequer of Receipt, Misc. Books,* 253, there is a list of lands in the king's hand, "ratione intrusionum" annis 21-22 Henry VII.

[26] In the first year of Henry VII, £1,803 was realized from the sale of the king's rights of wardship and marriage. *Exch. of Receipt, Receipt Rolls,* nos. 955-958. Such sales continued throughout the entire reign.

of wards in his own hands and administered them for his own profit through his ministers and receivers, just like the rest of the crown estates of which they were practically a part for the time. From a few hundred pounds in 1487, income from ward's lands increased to more than £6,000 in the year 1507.[27] This may perhaps be taken as a measure of the success of the king in reasserting his ancient feudal ownership and its obligations.

Closely analogous to the feudal incidents taken from lay subjects was the practice of the king's taking possession of the temporalities of abbots and bishops when they died. The estates were administered by the king during the vacancy of the office, and when the new bishop or abbot was elected he made a large fine to the king for the restoration of his possessions. As Bacon observed, it it was Henry VII's practice to advance bishops from one see to another "by steps, that he might not lose the profit of the first fruits." [28] The income from this source was of course subject to great fluctuations, depending upon the number of bishops and abbots who died in the course of a year. Thus in the summer of 1492 the Treasurer of the Chamber received £1,800 from the bishop of Bath's lands; in 1494 £1,200 from the temporalities of Bath and Durham, and in 1495 a larger sum from the temporalities of Lincoln. In the year 1503 the total payments of this nature to the Treasurer of the Chamber were £1,673 6s. 8d.; in 1504, £6,049 10s. 6d. and in 1505, £5,339 2s. 1d.[29]

[27] Income from ward's lands under Crown management:

1487	£ 353	6s.	8d.	*Accts. Exch. Q. R.* 413/2 I.
1491	343	6s.	8d.	*Accts. Exch. Q. R.* 413/2 II.
1494	1,588	0s.	0d.	*Ibid.*
1504	3,003	0s.	0d.	*Exch. T. R., Misc. Books,* 247, pp. 72-100 Mich. 1503-1504.
1505	5,422	8s.	10d.	*Ibid.,* Mich. 1504-1505.
1506	5,626	3s.	11d.	*Exch. T. R., Misc. Books,* 248, pp. 1-98 Mich. 1505-1506.
1507	6,163	15s.	5d.	*Ibid.,* pp. 99-222, Mich. 1506-1507.

[28] Bacon, *Henry VII*, 19.

[29] *Accounts, Exch., Queen's Remembrancer,* 413/2 II, III. The payments were probably even larger. In these books, with no reason given for the payment, are many sums from bishops, abbots and priors, who according to Le Neve's *Fasti* had just taken office. These were certainly payments for

Such, in a brief sketch, were the main lines of development of Henry VII's new revenue system. The fostering of trade and the increase of the customs receipts proceeded more quietly than the augmentation of the crown estates, and the extension of royal rights and claims over the land of the kingdom. In these matters, the organized disorder of the last thirty years was still an obstacle, and sometimes demanded the use of the strongest and the most unscrupulous measures by the king and his ministers.

restitution of temporalities, but because of possible doubt they have not been included.

CHAPTER IV

OBLIGATIONS AND RECOGNIZANCES:
THE WORK OF EMPSON AND DUDLEY

Among the entries of payments to the Treasurer of the Chamber certain miscellaneous payments "by obligation" begin to appear in 1493. Before the end of the reign, payments upon obligations, together with somewhat similar payments "by recognizance" became very important. In the year Michaelmas 1493 to Michaelmas 1494 less than £3,000 was received at the Treasury of the Chamber in this way; but in the year Michaelmas 1504 to Michaelmas 1505 £30,824 18s. 4d. were received by obligation and £4,175 by recognizance. Obligations and recognizances were bonds, providing either for the deferred paymnt of some debt due to the king, or for the forfeit or payment of some sum to the king contingent upon a future event. An obligation to pay the king a certain sum in installments for customs dues belongs to the first class; a recognizance for faithful performance in office with the forfeit of the bond in case of failure to do so belongs to the second class.

Unfortunately in nearly all cases the entries of payment upon obligations or recognizances in the receipt book of the Treasurer of the Chamber run very briefly, as "Received of the Abbott of Abbingdon by Recognizance £100," and do not specify the reason for which the money was due. In the back part however, of his books of payments, John Heron, Treasurer of the Chamber, kept careful lists of all the obligations and recognizances in his hands, upon which money was due to the king. These lists, which in some cases bear the marks of the king's examination, in notes in his own hand, give a fuller description of the bonds that is found in the books of receipt. They show that obligations and recognizances were made for the payment of money to the king, for many reasons — for the restitution of bishops' temporalities, for loans made by the king to Italian and English merchants, for the money remaining in the hands of the Mayor and Fellowship of the Calais Staple after they had paid the wages of the garrison there, for arrears of accounts in the hands of the king's receivers, for the purchase of wards, for licenses to export wool and to import wines, for deferred customs (often for very large amounts especially for customs at Southampton) and for the hire of the king's ships. Then there were recognizances for fines of various sorts, those assessed in court for offences, those made by culprits for release from prison or for pardon of their offences, fines laid upon sheriffs and especially upon bishops for the escape of prisoners from their prisons, and those assessed upon the rebels in Kent and in the southwest after the Cornishmen's rebellion. There were also bonds for faithful performance of duty in royal offices, for the keeping of the peace and for good conduct.

While all the bonds made in favor of the king appear in these lists, the reason for the bond is not always given even here, and from Heron's lists it is not possible to make any definite statement about the exact relative importance of the various classes of these obligations in relation to the crown revenue. One of the most important single classes of obligations however, was that of bonds taken by John Dawtry for the deferred payment of customs at the port of Southampton. These averaged about £7,000 a year, during the last years of the reign.[1] Obligations for loans, for the restitution of temporalities and for wardships were also very important. The returns from fines and pardons sold, excepting the fines levied on the Cornish rebels, were not very great; at least as late as Michaelmas 1505, when Heron's receipt books end.

Further light is thrown upon the subject by a study of the activity of Empson and Dudley; for it was in connection with these payments by recognizances and obligations that they worked, and it was on the basis of this work that the traditional story of their exactions grew up.

Edmond Dudley, commoner, was educated at Oxford; and trained in law at Gray's Inn, London, and so was one of the

---

[1] *Exch., Treasury of Receipt, Misc. Books*, 214, pp. 477, 509, 577.

great company of men versed in the new learning and in the law, who were making their sovereigns' fortunes and their own at the end of the fifteenth, and the beginning of the sixteenth centuries in all the courts of western Europe. He helped to negotiate the peace of Etaples in 1492; in 1497 he was undersheriff of London, and in 1504 he was Speaker of the House of Commons. In the autumn of the same year he entered the employment of Henry VII in the peculiar capacity of some sort of financial agent in which he was to win so much fame.

Richard Empson was also a lawyer; somewhat older and longer in Henry VII's service. Empson became attorney general of the Duchy of Lancaster in 1485; in 1491 he was speaker of the House of Commons; in 1493 he was receiver of certain of the king's manors and in charge of the wood-sales from the king's lands.[2] As late as 1505-1506 he was still receiver of the wood-sales,[3] but in the meantime he had risen to great offices in the state. In 1504 he was knighted, nominated High Steward of the University of Cambridge and in the same year he became Chancellor of the Duchy of Lancaster to succeed Sir Reginald Bray. As early as 1495 he was prominent enough to be named in Warbeck's proclamation as one of "the caitiffs and villains of simple birth" whose subtle inventions and pilling of the people "supported the misrule and mischief" then reigning in England.[4] Beyond these bald facts little has been known of Empson and Dudley or their work apart from the legend which has grown up about them.

To trace the growth of the legend is in itself rather instructive. Kingsford's Chronicles, which are practically contemporary diaries, make no mention of Empson and Dudley, though they do record the mulcting of the London mayors and aldermen, — Sir William Capel, and Thomas Kneysworth and his sheriffs, for offences in office.[5] The continuation of Fabyan's Chronicle from 1485 to 1509 which was written after 1509 does not mention Empson and Dudley; but the second continuation which appeared in 1542 speaks of their execution.[6] Arnold's Chron-

[2] *Accounts, Exch., Queen's Remembrancer,* 413/2 II, f. 41b.

[3] *Exch., Treasury of Receipt, Misc. Books,* 212.

[4] *Harl. Mss.,* 283, f. 123.

[5] Kingsford's *Chronicles,* 205, 261, 262.

[6] Fabyan, *Chronicle,* 695.

icle which was printed about 1521 tells the story of the "troubles" of the London mayors, and adds that this happened by the king's commandment "by means of Empson and Dudley."[7] Finally Polydore Vergil in the Historia Anglica which was finished in 1533 gives the story of Empson and Dudley at some length. About 1501 Henry VII began to hate civil war more than death; and "he resolved to take such measures that all material for disorder of this kind in the future might be destroyed; and this he thought he would achieve only if he took his subjects down a little, knowing very well that men were easily made proud by abundance of possessions and loved nothing more than wealth, since their choice of peace or war was generally influenced by the fear of loss or hope of gain. But that it might not be said that he acted unjustly toward men whom he attacked, he took thought of how he might act with a show of right. As he thought upon this it occurred to him that his people were in the habit of paying so little heed to the laws of the kingdom that if the question were raised, without doubt very many not only of the distinguished men, but also of the merchants, craftsmen, farmers and fishermen would be found guilty of violating them. This resolve taken, he began to search out the laws and impose small fines on those who did not observe them. Then he appointed two fiscal judges (fiscales judices), Richard Empson and Edmund Dudley men learned in the ancient law of the realm. That they might find the greater favor with the king, these men, armed with a horde of informers who reported the names of offenders, showed more zeal for collecting money than regard for justice, the danger to the state, and their proper functions, altho they were often admonished by the leading men in the nation to be less exacting. After great treasure had been heaped up however, the king, moved by the continual prayers of the people to God for an end to their misery, was stirred by thoughts of mercy and generosity, and resolved to have done with both Empson and Dudley, and to restore their money to those from whom it had been extorted."[8]

Hall translated the story from Vergil almost literally; and addd to it in another place in his text a description of how

---

[7] Arnold, *Chronicle*, p. XLIII.

[8] P. Vergil, *Historia*, 755ff.

Empson and Dudley would bring against a man an action of which he had no knowledge; and on his failure to appear to answer the charge he was outlawed and his goods confiscated. "These outlawries, old recognizances of the peace and good abearing, escapes, riots and innumerable statutes penal were put into execution and called upon by Empson and Dudley, so that every man, both spiritualtie and temporaltie having either land or substance was called to this pluckying bancket according to the Psalmist's saying, all declyned and fell together and no man although he were never so clere and guiltless in conclusion durst aventure a tryall, seynge the experience of them that had passed afore. For these two ravenynge wolves had suche a guard of false perjured persons appertaining to them which were by their commandment empanyeled on every quest that the king was sure to wynne, whosoever lost. Learned men in the laws when they were required of their advice would saye to agree is the best council I can give you. By this undewe means these covetous persons filled the king's coffers and enriched themselves. And at this unreasonable and extort doynge noble men grudged, meane men kicked, poor men lamented, preachers openly at Paules Cross and other places exclaimed rebuked and detested but yet they would never amend." [9]

Bacon next took the story, added to it some badly remembered details from "a book of accompt of Empson's that had the King's hand almost to every leaf" "seen long since," [10] transfused it with his own wonderful style and made Empson and Dudley famous forever as two of the greatest extortioners in history. The finishing touch is given by Sir Robert Cotton in his little tract, "A Discourse of Foreign War," where he wrote "but that whereby he (Henry VII) heaped up his mass of Treasure . . was by sale of Offices, redemption of Penalties, dispencing with laws and such like to a yearly value of £120,000." His authority is noted in the margin as "Ex Libr(o) Acquittance inter Regem et Dudley." [11]

The book to which Sir Robert Cotton referred is apparently Dudley's book of accounts, a copy of which is preserved among

[9] Hall, *Chronicle*, (Ed. of 1809), 502, 503.
[10] Bacon, *Henry VII*, 192, 193.
[11] Robert Cotton, *A Discourse of Foreign War*, 53.

the manuscripts of the British Museum.[12]   The book begins, ''Memorand. that hereafter followeth all such obligations and somes of money as I Sir Edmund Dudeley have received and had of any person for any fine or duty to be paid to and for the use of our most dread sovereign lord King Henry of that name the Seventh, since the first time that I the said Edmond entered the service of our said soveran lord, that is to say the 9 day of September the 20th year of his most noble reign.'' The account, covering 60 folios, runs from the 9th day of September 1504 to May 28, 1508.   The entries for each day are signed by the king on the middle of the page directly below them, and before the entries for the next day, in a way which shows that the account was examined by the king himself each day on which entries were made.   Each folio is added, and signed by Dudley.

   Obligations were made to the king's use by a number of men beside Empson and Dudley; generally in association with them, like Richard Fox Bishop of Winchester, Sir Giles Daubeney, Sir Charles Somerset, Lord Herbert, Sir Thomas Lovell and Sir Henry Wiot, as appers from those obligations which have been preserved.[13]   All obligations made by these men seem to have been taken in charge by Dudley and were delivered by him to John Heron, Treasurer of the Chamber, who collected the sums due on them.   The obligations made by John Dawtry for the deferred payments of the customs due at Southampton, the obligations for the re-payment of money loaned to merchants by the king, except in a few cases, and the obligations of the Calais Staple except in the year 1507-1508, do not appear in Dudley's accounts.   But apart from these very important classes Dudley entered into his book practically all the obligations and recognizances made to the use of the crown, as appears from a comparison of the totals of Dudley's accounts and of John Heron's lists.[14]   The figures do not agree with Sir Robert Cotton's.   The sum total of all obligations, recognizances and money (for Dudley generally took a small part payment in money) received by Dudley during the year Sep-

[12] *Lansd. Mss.*, 127.

[13] *Letters and Papers*, I, 342, 600, 642.

[14] The lists kept by Heron of all obligations and recognizances for the years 1505 to 1509 are in *Exch., Treasury of Receipt, Misc. Books*, 214.

tember 9, 1504-Michaelmas 1505 was £44,882 14s. 10d.; for the year 1505-1506, £60,655 16s. 6d.; for the year 1506-1507, £65,361 13s. 7d. and from Michaelmas 1507 to May 28, 1508, £48,416 2s. The money received by Dudley varied from £2,700 in the first year of his activity to £7,500 in the second year, and £10,000 in each of the two last years. After these sums are deducted from the totals received, the remainders represent only the face value of the bonds turned over to Heron by Dudley; and not the amount the king realized on them. As Heron's lists show, many bonds were cancelled by the king, and others were suspended during pleasure so that perhaps only three quarters or even less of the face value eventually came to the king.[15] In his entries except for a few at the beginning of the book, Dudley gave a full description of the consideration for which the obligation was made. It is therefore possible to make an analysis of these causes, which for the year 1504-1505 gives the following result:

Recognizances and obligations for the hire of the Royal ships Sovereign and Regent and for customs of goods carried in them	£ 6,600	0s.	0d.
For the confirmation of the liberties of London and North Wales	5,886	13s.	4d.
For the restitution of bishop's temporalities	4,260	0s.	0d.
For faithful performance of duties by the king's officers	4,400	0s.	0d.
(This item is not included in the total for the year by Dudley)			
For pardons of murder, felony, rape and false verdicts	3,846	13s.	4d.
For special livery of lands	2,024	15s.	3d.
For wards sold by the king	1,866	13s.	4d.
For fines for the escape of prisoners	1,680	0s.	0d.
For the proceeds of the sale of goods confiscated in the ports for contravention of customs regulations	1,488	3s.	4d.
For lands purchased from the king	1,324	0s.	0d.

[15] The loss of the Receipt books of the Treasurer of the Chamber after 1505 makes it impossible to compare the amounts received in money or bonds by the king with the face value of the bonds made during the years 1505 to 1508. In 1504-1505, when £42,645 in bonds were made £35,000 in money was received on bonds. But since payments of bonds taken in any one year were extended over many years, no relation can be worked out from these sums.

For re-payment for money borrowed from the king	1,000	0s.	0d.
For the payment of customs dues on wines.	928	0s.	0d.
For the purchase of offices	720	0s.	0d.
For licenses of widows to wed	586	13s.	4d.
For licenses to amortize lands	526	13s.	4d.
For fines for hunting and riots	393	6s.	8d.
For the discharge of offices found to the king's use in lands	200	0s.	0d.
For alum sold by the king	200	0s.	0d.
For treasure trove	40	0s.	0d.
For causes not stated	11,315	0s.	0d.

The other years covered by Dudley's account book show a similar variety of causes for which obligations were made and money collected by him.[16]

To the obligations and payments for the hire of the royal ships, for the sale of alum (which was very great during the year 1505-1506), for licences to export wheat and to import

[16]	1505-6	1506-7	1507-8
Calais		£3,944	
Hire of royal ships	£ 13	3,000	£ 200
Sale of alum	15,086		
Licenses to import and export wheat and wine	1,153	987	1,064
Ecclesiastical temporalities	1,333	7,166	5,566
Licence to amortize land	300	2,266	393
Sale of wards	2,177	1,110	2,686
Licences of widows to marry	1,273		1,106
Special livery of lands	1,205	1,584	1,535
Restitution of lands	6,025	3,038	
Discharge of the king's title to lands	2,833		150
For discharge of obligations	1,877	668	636
Old debts and arrears	4,370	907	1,374
Sale of charters	450	2,240	50
Bonds for good 'abearing'	2,100	500	
Bonds for good behavior in office		4,000	8,666
Fines for escape of prisoners	1,143	910	1,020
Sale of offices	2,006	2,856	936
Purchase of the king's favor	2,926	3,263	2,453
Fines and pardons	4,583	5,756	18,483
Pardons of offences in office	1,986	133	640
Fines and pardons of intrusion	4,012	7,600	
Fines for mills and Cedells on rivers	973		
Forfeit merchandise	16	220	25
Loans		3,143	5,500
Miscellaneous	5,635	2,122	655

wine and for those to pay the customs thereon in deferred payments, not the slightest objection could be made. Nor could any protest be raised against obligations for payment for the restitution of ecclesiastical temporalities and for licences for free election of abbots and priors, for licences to amortize lands, for the sale of wards, for licences to widows to marry and for special livery of lands. The king was certainly within his rights when he insisted upon the payment of old debts and arrears of subsidies as he did from 1505 onwards. The sale of charters and liberties to cities and corporations was not contrary to law, and bonds for good behavior in office are recognized and used today. That the ends of justice be served it was necessary that prisoners be safely kept and the danger to the state of their escape had to be checked by heavily fining keepers of jails for laxness in their duties. The sale of offices by the king does not come up to the standards of present day social morality but it probably did not shock the men of the fifteenth century overmuch.

The purchase of the king's favor, for which obligations are found in 1505 and later, is much more questionable. In some cases it was quite innocent; as when the Merchant Adventurers paid £200 for the king's most gracious favor to them to be showed concerning their going into the parties of Flanders,[17] and £50 at another time to have their free liberty in choosing their governor.[18] In other cases the king's favor was sought by candidates for appointment to offices where the king could use his influence, as when 1000 marks were paid for the king's favor in the Deanery of York; or it was desired that the king use his influence in other ways, as when Sir Richard Haddon paid 1000 marks for the king's favor to have Wyndont's daughter wed his son.[19] But when Lord Stafford paid £400 for the king's favor in the matter at variance between him and the Duke of Buckingham,[20] or money was accepted by the king to write letters to the justices of the peace, apparently insttructing them to favor one side in a suit, or when £1,000 was paid for the

17 *Lansd. Mss.*, 127, f. 44.
18 *Ibid.*, f. 49.
19 *Ibid.*, f. 17.
20 *Ibid.*, f. 49.

king's gracious favor to have the course of his laws against one Metcalf,[21] the matter became reprehensible.

The attention of the chroniclers and of Bacon however has been turned more largely to fines and pardons for offences alleged to be against the old penal laws, than to the obligations of the various classes just noted. Obligations for fines and pardons form only a fraction of the yearly total of all obligations made by Dudley and his co-workers, and this fraction is not large, except in the year 1507-1508 when the value of obligations for fines and pardons was greatly increased by two obligations for the payment of £5,000 each — made to the king's use by the Earl of Northumberland and Lord Burgevenny.[22] Few fines imposed by the king's courts were collected by Empson and Dudley. In nearly all cases they went directly to the law-breakers and compounded with them for payment for the king's pardon. Such payments or promises of payment for the king's pardon were in essence fines levied by an irregular procedure. Some of these fines or payments for pardon seem eminently just, as when Giles Lord Daubeney paid £2,000 for his pardon for the receipt of money at Calais by reason of his office which belonged to the king's grace, in other words for embezzlement.[23] Others, especially pardons for murderers, which were frequent, cannot be defended. Even here there was once shown a curious kind of practical justice, when one Orrel was pardoned "for the murthering and robbing of certeyn straungers upon the see" for £100, but was required to pay another £100 "in recompense to the friends of the same straungers."[24]

There is no evidence of a general resuscitation of the old penal laws, as Vergil and Hall allege, in these obligations for fines and pardons. Hunting and the reversal of outlawry are insignificant factors in Dudley's accounts.[25] On the other hand,

[21] *Ibid.*, f. 23.
[22] *Ibid.*, ff. 51, 54.
[23] *Ibid.*, f. 34.
[24] *Ibid.*, f. 47.
[25] In 1508, however, fines for outlawry became important enough to be placed with licenses for widows to marry in charge of Edward Belknap, "surveyor of fines for outlawries and marriages of the king's wards" (that is, widows). Such fines for outlawries were apparently assessed by

the fines for maintenance of retainers, for ravishing of the king's wards and for intrusion are very large; as were the payments for restitution to lands. These last were a kind of backhanded fine for intrusions paid to the king for the restoration of lands seized for that reason into the king's hands. Large fines of these kinds, from a comparatively few persons make up a very large part of all obligations for fines and pardons. Thus Lord Dacre made an obligation of £200 for intrusion of certain lands; Lord Fitzwater agreed to pay £6,000 for his restitution to his lands; Sir William Say bound himself in 2,500 marks to be freed from the charge of intrusion of certain lands of the inheritence of one Hill; for the discharge of the king's title to certain lands recovered by him, worth £120 a year Lord Dudley had to pay £1,000; the Earl of Derby agreed to a recognizance of £6,000 for his pardon; Thomas Kneysworth, Shore and Grove, aldermen of London compounded for their offences in office by a fine of £933 6s. 8d.; the Lady Percivale gave £1,000 for her pardon; the Earl of Northumberland was pardoned for the ravishing of Elizabeth Hastings, one of the king's wards, for £10,000, of which £5,000 was to be paid and the balance to hang at the king's pleasure; Lord Conyers agreed to pay £1,000 for a riot committed against Lord Darcy by him; Thomas Tyrrel paid £1,728 for restitution to his lands; Nicholas Vaux and Thomas Parre gave obligations for 9,000 marks for the marriages of the two daughters and heirs of Sir Thomas Grene and for the discharge of their lands of intrusions and other condemnations; and Lord Burgevenny who confessed to "forfaictors of his retainors" before the "lord Chiff Juge and also the Chief Justice of the commyn place" to the amount of £69,000[26] made a fine of £5,000 to the king for his offences and gave other bonds for sure payment of the sum, and for his good behavior in the future.

From these instances it appears that many noblemen were very badly mulcted. Henry VII had in this the ulterior purpose of drying up the springs of political opposition by reducing

the king himself. From July 1, 1508, to March 10, 1509, £2,910 15s. 5d. was received from goods, chattels and fines of outlawed felons. *Accts. Exch. Q. R.* 517/14, and 517/15, Belknap's account books.

[26] *Exch., Treasury of Receipt, Misc. Books*, 214, p. 534.

the great nobles if not to poverty, at least to a wholesome fear. But two other facts stand out in the cases cited. Breaking the peace, keeping retainers, creating disorder by the ravishing of women, especially those who were the king's wards, and other breaches of the law were severely dealt with; and in the second place intrusion of lands was especially harshly punished. After the disorders of the wars of the Roses, it was of primary importance that the turbulent nobles should be kept in check and made to fear the law. The royal courts were too slow-moving, and perhaps too weak to do this. Much earlier in the reign, after the rebellion of the Cornishmen, Henry VII had not relied upon the courts to assess fines upon the rebels, but had sent Paulet and Sherborne as royal commissioners to make the king's power felt and to fine all who had taken part in the revolt. Just as they had asserted the royal authority in the Southwest, so Empson and Dudley vindicated it against the nobles, more directly, more quickly and more quietly than any court, even the Star Chamber could have done. Moreover the fines they assessed came entirely to the royal treasury and were not subject to deductions as were the fines assessed by judges before they reached the treasury. Besides the establishment of respect for the law, the fines for intrusion had a second object, to force heirs to properly sue out the livery of their lands, the importance of which in the light of the Tudor policy to base the revenue system on landed estates has already been pointed out.

In judging Empson and Dudley's work and activities, it should not be forgotten that fines and sales of pardon occupied only part of their attention, and that there were many other important classes of payments made to them. Moreover the king was thoroughly cognizant of all their activities, as is shown by his daily examination of Dudley's book. They were not mere irresponsible extortioners. They were the king's business and collection agents, who went up and down the country taking care that no money due to the crown went unpaid and no royal right violated. They were the king's long arms with which he reached out from one end of England to the other and took what was his. When the accounts of the Staple at Calais were cast, Dudley was present and probably drew up the recognizances by which the Merchants of the Staple bound themselves to payment;[27] when the recognizances forfeited in the king's bench for the first twenty years of the reign were examined, Dudley took charge "to make out process" for all that be unpaid;[28] When it was reported to the king that Sir E. had taken no livery of his lands, Empson searched the records;[29] when obligations in Heron's hands were not promptly paid they were delivered to Dudley to be put in suit,[30] and when the king's greatest mercantile transaction was made, the sale of £15,166 13s. 4d. worth of alum to Lewis de la Fava, Dudley was Henry VII's agent and received de la Fava's bond.[31]

Their activity against the great nobles did not make Empson and Dudley popular, and their unpopularity was greatly increased by the chicanery to which they stooped to accomplish their ends. They doubtless spent a great deal of time in searching the records, and apart from the fines levied for intrusion there is some evidence to indicate that when a defective title was found (going back even a long time) process to dispossess the present holder was begun for the king's benefit, and their own, since they received grants out of such lands recovered.[32] In the Plumpton Correspondence there is the account of how Empson tried to dispossess Sir Robert Plumpton of his lands for the benefit of the heirs general of Sir William Plumpton his father, to one of whom Empson was planning to marry his daughter. "Accompanied by Edward Stanhopp, Gervis Clifton, Robert Dimmoke and William Perpoynt knights and other gentlemen and yeomen to the number of 200 persons and more, and divers of the garde of our Sovereigne Lord the King arrayed in the most honorable livery of his said garde (he) came to Yorke to maintaine the foresaid Robert and Richard (that is the representa-

[27] *Add. Mss.*, 21480, f. 159.
[28] *Accounts, Exch., Queen's Remembrancer*, 516/17.
[29] *Add. Mss.*, 21480, f. 191.
[30] *Lansd. Mss.*, 127, f. 35.
[31] *Ibid.*, f. 29.
[32] *Letters and Papers*, I, 1965, 3284. Lands recovered by Empson, Dudley Wiot, Andrew Windsore, Sir James Hobart, Thomas Lucas, William Mordaunt, William Gascoigne, Richard Fox Bishop of Winchester and others, some of which were granted to Empsom and Dudley and their co-workers.

tives of the heirs general) in the said assise, and theare abode with the said companie at their costs and charges to the time that the said assize passed against the foresaid Sir Robert.''[33] Judge Vavosour who appeared with Empson and Dudley more than once in cases of dissesein,[34] ''then shewed in open courte a fine exemplified under the greate seale of England, saing that therin wear comprised the foresaid manors taled to the heires generall of Sir William Plompton and the Counsell of the foresaid Sir Robert desired hearing thereof and might not have it by any meanes.''[35] Before the trial Sir Robert was warned ''to labor as well the Schereffes as all your frynds,'' since Empson would avail himself of the favor it was possible for him to show as one of the king's council sitting to assess fines upon such as had not taken up knighthood, and would have persons thus made friendly put upon the jury. ''Thus he under myneth.''[36] The Plumpton case is only one instance in which these men reaped dislike by taking care of themselves. A second such case came to notice in 1527 when John Maryng petitioned the Lord Chancellor that twenty-eight years ago Edmund Dudley craftily attempted to disinherit him of certain lands by inducing a man named Fowler to lend him £10 on mortgage to be repaid within a year. Shortly after the loan he was imprisoned in the Tower; and Dudley redeemed the lands although he had the redemption money ready himself. Dudley obtained the deeds during his imprisonment and forged a conveyance in his name.[37] The sale of justice outright, cases of which have been quoted in connection with the sale of the king's favor, as in the case where £1,000 was paid ''for the king's favor toward John Layton, to have the course of the king's common law in assise against one Metcalf'' probably served to increase still more popular displeasure. Dudley himself repented of this, and in the Tree of Commonwealth, a little book written by him in the Tower before his execution, he advised Henry VIII to give judges ''a great charge to minister justice

---

[33] *Plumpton Correspondence*, p. CVII.

[34] *Letters and Papers*, I, 1965.

[35] *Plumpton Correspondence*, p. CVII.

[36] *Ibid.*, 151, letter cxlx.

[37] *Letters and Papers*, IV, 3727. If this incident took place 28 years before 1527, that is in 1499, Dudley was not then in the king's service.

truly and indifferently under pain of his high and great displeasure,'' and to take care that ''they let not for fears nor displeasure of any of his own servants or counsellors to do true Justice nor for fear of any great person in the realm.''[38] Finally Dudley was not even above forging obligations, as is shown by annotations made by Brian Tuke, Treasurer of the Chamber on the margins of certain old obligations in 1530, ''Not subscribed and the seale of Mr. S. saithe it was on of them that was counterfaict by Dudley,'' and ''discharged by matter of recorde in the common place as counterfaict By Dudley,''[39] At times Henry VII seems to have been troubled by some of his methods of getting money. On August 19, 1504, which was before Dudley came to his service, a proclamation was issued that all who had claims against the king for any loan or prest, or injury done to them might deliver their complaints during the term before Michaelmas two years hence to certain commissioners.[40] In his will Henry VII made provision for a similar proclamation.[41] But that he did not intend to have such money as was collected by Empson and Dudley very much questioned and disputed, seems clear from the appointment of Empson and Dudley as executors of the will, and as commissioners to examine any complaints.[42]

Practically all that is known of the next events comes from Vergil again. ''When the proclamation was read, all who had been in any way mulcted, rightly or wrongly (jure vel injuria) rushed to court and set forth each for himself the injury done him, asserting with wails of complaint, that his own case merited restitution. The Council heard the cases and ordered restitution, where manifest wrong had been done. When this was known, great Cæsar! the way the others, even those who had been justly punished stormed about and pressed their claims! To recover their losses they added all sorts of flourishes to their

[38] Edmund Dudley, *Tree of Commonwealth*, 11-12.

[39] *Letters and Papers*, IV, 6798. The original document is in the Record office, *State Papers, Henry VIII*, IV, §59, pp. 22-27, and the annotations there, which do not appear in the calendars were called to my attention by Professor E. F. Gay.

[40] Gairdner, *Letters and Papers, Richard III and Henry VII*, II, 379.

[41] Thomas Astle, *Will of Henry VII*, 11-12.

[42] *Ibid.*, 11-12.

stories. They distributed money freely (largitiones faciunt), used the influence of their friends and finally stopped at nothing. Their excessive zeal and greed worked destruction to Empson and Dudley and loss to themselves. The Council giving up the hope of being able to moderate the popular outcry and satisfy the demands of those who sought restitution, decided to hear no more cases but to arrest Empson and Dudley with their informers and agents to placate the excitement and desire of the people, who called for their punishment more than anything else.'' [43]

Some clue is given to the nature of ''the people'' (plebs populus) by the sentence, ''they distributed money freely and used the influence of the friends.'' ''The people'' were those classes against whom Empson and Dudley had been most active in asserting the rights of the king. Lord Dacre was probably typical of those who cried out against Empson and Dudley. In a letter to the council he prayed for the discharge of various obligations and recognizances, some of them surety bonds which he alleged had been retained although the purpose for which they had been made had ceased to exist, or had been turned into debts by Empson and Dudley ''against all right.'' Another was a bond for 1,000 marks in which he was bound with George Lord Fitzhugh for his mother, Dame Mabel Dacre accused of having ravished Richard Huddlestone, one of the king's wards. He had paid 600 marks of the bond and requested to be discharged of the remainder since Huddlestone was never a king's ward. [44] It was with men of Dacre's class that the execution of Empson and Dudley, which was ordered not on the charge of extortion for which there could have been no real evidence which did not compromise the late king and his whole policy, but on a trumped-up charge of constructive treason was best liked.

By his repudiation of Empson and Dudley, Henry VIII at once won a reputation for liberality. The Venetian Ambassador in England reported the new king's great liberality, [45] and William Lord Mountjoy wrote to Erasmus just after the ar-

[43] P. Vergil, *Historia Anglica*, p. 2 of the second part.
[44] *Letters and Papers*, I, 380.
[45] *Venetian Calendar*, I, 942, 945.

rest of Empson and Dudley, "All England is in ecstacies. Extortion is put down — liberality is the order of the day." [46] The stern justice of Henry VII's day was no longer needed to insure respect for the laws; and, like the true Machiavellian that he and all the Tudors were, Henry VIII broke the tools by whom in large part the supremacy of the law had been established. Some of the land won by Empson and Dudley for the crown was returned, notably to Lord Darcy and his wife;[47] some of the unpaid portions of large fines for intrusion were remitted; for example to Vaux and Parre for the intrusions of their wives;[48] the Earl of Northumberland's fine of £10,000 for ravishing Elizabeth Hastings was pardoned,[49] and nine of the smaller recognizances were cancelled since, because of their manifold injustice they "may not be levied without the evident peril of our said late father's soul which we (Henry VIII) would for no earthly riches see nor suffer."[50] Many other bonds were put in respite, but not discharged,[51] while others perhaps the greater part were levied and put in suit if not paid promptly.[52] They probably represented debts justly owing to the crown, for after all the great bulk of Empson and Dudley's work, and certainly the great bulk of all obligations made to the king's use in Henry VII's reign were for just and legitimate causes.

Order had been reëstablished and the crown lands vastly extended. The terrorism of great fines was no longer necessary and was repudiated. But the practice of collecting the king's debts and dues in installments by means of obligations continued, and the Treasurer of the Chamber long kept lists of obliga-

[46] *Letters and Papers*, I, 5736.

[47] *Ibid.*, I, 367, 721.

[48] *Ibid.*, I, 600, 612, 1026.

[48] *Ibid.*, I, 945, 961.

[50] *Ibid.*, I, 1004, 1372. See also *ibid.*, I, 5522. Other recognizances were cancelled in the course of the first four years of the reign to which this note was not attached. These were in some cases expired surety bonds, and in other cases, apparently just debts; in other cases it is impossible to tell their nature.

[51] *Ibid.*, I, 777, Book of such obligations as were respited but not discharged.

[52] *Ibid.*, I, 3497. Echoes of bonds put in suit reached as fan down as 1530, — see *ibid.*, IV, 6798.

tions and recognizances in the back of his account books, just as he had done in Henry VII's time — for the repayment of loans made by the king, the sale of wards, the livery of lands and deferred payment of customs.[53]

In Mary's reign, after long disuse in the later years of Henry VIII's reign, obligations and recognizances reappear as the "stalled debts" which figure largely in government finance through the second half of the sixteenth century.

[53] *Ibid.*, II, pp. 1481-1490; III. pp. 1545-1546.

CHAPTER V

TAXES, LOANS AND BENEVOLENCES, THE FRENCH PENSION

The new financial system for which the foundations were laid in 1485, and the work of Empson and Dudley did much to build up, took some years before it yielded an adequate revenue. Until it did, Henry VII was not able to abandon older devices to eke out his resources. At the beginning of the reign, the Marquis of Dorset and Sir John Bourchier were in Paris as pledges for money borrowed,[1] and to the Duke of Brittany Henry owed sums exceeding 10,000 crowns of gold on promises "as a prince to repay . . as soon as he had obtained the kingdom."[2] The coronation was planned on a scale that would show an "estate royal" and befit a king. The royal jewels had been pledged by Richard III, and had to be redeemed,[3] and some of Richard III's debts were ordered paid. The king was obliged to resort to short time loans, as Edward IV and Richard III had often found it necessary to do. The Archbishop of Canterbury for example lent the king £100;[4] the Bishop of Winchester 100 marks, and Italian merchants in London, sums ranging from £100 to 500 marks.[6] The merchants of the Staple at Calais advanced above £1,000 for wages and fees of the Calais garrison,[7] while the mayor and aldermen of the city of London lent £2,000,[8] in addition to the gift of 1,000 marks voted by the

[1] Bacon, *Henry VII*, 18.

[2] J. Gairdner, *Life of Henry VII*, 19.

[3] *Exch. of Receipt, Receipt Rolls*, no. 949; entry of receipt of loan on pledge of jewels by Richard III.
Hist. Mss. Commission, *Mss. of Lord Edmond Talbot*, 296.

[4] *Exch. of Receipt, Receipt Rolls*, no. 955.

[5] *Ibid.*

[6] *Ibid.*

[7] Campbell, *Materials*, I, 233, 266, 273.

[8] *Exch. of Receipt, Receipt Rolls*, no. 955; Kingsford's *Chronicles*, 193.

common council of the city before Henry's entry.[9] Reginald
Bray, Allen Cornburgh Clerk of the treasurer, Lord Dynham
the lord treasurer, the cofferer of the household and other financial officials lent large sums. All these loans, amounting to
£10,121 17s. 4d. during the first year of the reign, were for short
periods, a few weeks in some cases, and all were repaid.[10]

In 1486 and 1487 the king had to meet the expense of his
marriage to Elizabeth of York, his progress to the north, and
the suppression of the insurrection of Lambert Simnel and of
the disorders in Ireland. Toward the end of 1486, commissioners,
with letters under the king's signet were sent into various parts
of England to raise money for the king by "agreements."
Though the amount raised was small, this loan is important as
being the first of the forced loans which figure so prominently
in the Tudor period.[11] In the early part of 1489 commissioners
again visited the various shrines to collect loans.[12] Much greater
in amount than the loans from the people during these years,
were the advances made to the king by Reginald Bray, Lord
Dynham, the great ecclesiastics, and the city of London.[13] The
city of London lent the king £4,000 in 1487,[14] £2,000 in July
1488,[15] £4,700 in February and March 1489,[16] £1,000 in August
1489,[17] and £2,000 in 1490.[18]

[9] Campbell, *Materials*, I, 6, *Journ. Civit. London*, IX, 84, August 31,
1485.

[10] *Exch. of Receipt, Receipt Rolls*, nos. 955, 958, Michaelmas 1485 to
Michaelmas 1486. All the loans are noted with the date of their repayment.

[11] The amount borrowed from individuals was small, the average being
20 shillings; though in London, it was about £5. The costs of collection
were very large, being £29 5s. 10d. to collect £264 in Bedfordshire and
Buckinghamshire and £18 6s. 8d. to collecet £203 in Lincolnshire. Of the
money raised from this loan £3,250 were paid to the Treasurer of the
Chamber and £2,031 at the Receipt of the Exchequer. See Campbell,
Materials, II, 91, 92, 95, 96, 97, 105, 106; *Accounts, Exch., Queen's Remembrancer*, 413/2 I, Receipt book of the Treasurer of the Chamber; *Exch.,
Treasury Receipt, Misc. Books*, 125, payments at the Exchequer.

[12] *Exch. of Receipt, Receipt Rolls*, no. 964.

[13] *Ibid.; Exch., Queen's Remembrancer*, 413/2, I.

[14] Kingsford's *Chronicles*, 194.

[15] *Ibid.*, Fabyan, *Chronicle*, 683.

[16] *Exch. of Receipt, Receipt Rolls*, no. 964.

[17] *Exch. of Receipt, Receipt Rolls*, no. 966.

[18] *Exch., Treasury of Receipt, Misc. Books*, 124, p. 19.

More important in the early years of the reign, is the ingenious use of foreign complications by the king for his own pecuniary advantage. As Bacon phrases it, Henry VII used wars and rumors of wars to exact grants from Parliament for the defense of the realm, while peace, succeeding, "coffered up" the sums so received.[19] Henry VII's success in this respect was so well known in his own day that Sanuto commented in one place in his diaries, "under the pretence of this war (against Scotland) he amassed much money."[20] The Milanese Ambassador in England, Raimondo de Soncino, speaking of a rumor of war between England and Flanders in 1498 is sure that nothing will come of it, except that under the "name of war, possibly by way of fifteenths a certain sum of money may find its way to the king's purse; but the sovereigns are certain to come to terms and the losers (the taxed subjects) will have to bear their loss."[21] Perkin Warbeck made it one of the charges against Henry VII, in his proclamation of 1495, that the king "hath trodden under foot the honor of this nation, selling our best confederates for money, and making merchandise of the blood, estates and fortunes of our peers and subjects, by feigned wars and dishonorable peaces, only to enrich his coffers."[22] Taxes were legitimate, and justifiable war measures, and it was as war measures that Henry VII obtained them. Careful of the susceptibilities of his tax-voting and tax-paying subjects, Henry stimulated his people's patriotism against France and Scotland before asking for grants. The Parliamentary votes were then made almost automatically. Little did his subjects know how disingenuous were the purposes of the king until after the event. Besides taxes wars were made to yield further profits to the king in the way of a benevolence and of indemnities of no mean value.

The first parliamentary tax was voted in November, 1487, after the battle of Stoke, in which Lambert Simnel had been

[19] Bacon, *Henry VII*, 51.

[20] *Venetian Calendar*, I, 743.

[21] *Ibid.*, I, 776.

[22] Bacon, *Henry VII*, 141-142. Bacon asserts that he had seen a copy of the proclamation. The extract quoted does not however appear in the transcript of the proclamation preserved in the British Museum, *Harl. Mss.*, 283, f. 123 b.

defeated. Two whole fifteenths and tenths, and a poll tax on aliens, such as had been used by Henry VI, were granted "for the hasty and necessary defence of this your realm."[23] In December 1486 and February 1487 the convocations of the clergy of Canterbury and York had met at the king's summons, and each voted one entire tenth of the value of their benefices.[24]

The very success with which the king obtained these taxes, and the improvement in the financial situation which appears very noticeably after they were collected, may have made him the more willing to obtain new levies when he was enabled to do so easily by reason of the situation in Brittany. When the question of the annexation of Brittany to France became acute, early in his reign, Henry VII offered his mediation. He did not desire to see Brittany annexed to France any more than did other Englishmen. Mediation was a politic way of maintain his truce towards both sides, France and Brittany, to each of which he was under obligations; and at the same time, it kept his hand in the game of European politics, while it might put off the absorption of the Duchy of France.[25] But the cause of Brittany was very popular with Henry's subjects; they demanded intervention, rather than mediation; and the Commons even desired that he should command the troops in person.[26] Ambassadors were sent to Spain to seek an alliance there, though not exclusively on account of the Breton question; and commissioners were dispatched to Brittany and to Maximilian, Henry's natural ally. When Parliament assembled on January 13, 1489, its chief business was to make provision for the war; especially to provide funds for its prosecution. A grant of £100,000 was asked for. It was a very large amount of money, more than three fifteenths and tenths. All agreed to vote the sum, even extending it for two years additional, if the army were maintained that long.[27] There was a long dispute between the laity and the clergy about the proportion to be assessed on each; each wishing to escape as much as possible of the heavy burden of

23 *Rot. Parl.*, VI, 401.

24 Wilkins, *Concilia*, III, 618, 621.

25 Ant. Depuy, *Historie de la Reunion de La Bretagne a la France*, II, 165-166.

26 *Ibid.*, II, 163, 164.

27 *Rot. Parl.*, VI, 421ff.

the war for which they were clamoring.[28] It was finally agreed that the laity should pay three-fourths of the grant, and the clergy one-fourth. On February 8, 1489 the treaty of Redon was signed. By its terms a defensive league was made by Henry VII with the Duchess of Brittany, and in return for numerous concessions that the Duchess would not marry without Henry's consent, and that she would aid him if he should ever seek to recover his lost French possessions, Henry agreed to send her 6,000 men to serve until All Soul's Day next, at her own expense. As security for the payment of the cost of these troops, two strong places in Brittany were to be handed over to Henry VII, to be held and garrisoned by him.[29] A treaty with Maximilian was signed February 14,[30] and with Spain, March 27, 1489.[31] When the treaty of Redon, and the meanness of the operations of the English forces which aided Maximilian in Flanders are compared with the parliamentary grant, the conclusion is suggested that Henry VII had no heart for the war and was already chiefly thinking of his own enrichment.

Maximilian deserted Henry at the peace of Frankfort, July 22, 1489. After this the war, hitherto actuated by more than financial motives, became a purely business proposition. "Weighing one thing with another, he (Henry VII) gave Britain up for lost; but resolved to make his profit out of this business of Britain."[32] To the French ambassadors who came to London in August, 1489, to urge the English king to accept the peace of Frankfort, Morton insisted upon the renewal of the tribute once paid by Louis XI to Edward IV in recognition of the king's title to France as a *sine qua non*.[33] When no agreement could be reached, Parliament, assembled in October 1489, voted supplies for the continuance of the war. The tax of £100,000 had been an innovation. It was now admitted to be a failure, for only £27,000 had been collected of the £75,000 to be paid by the laity. For the remission of the remaining £48,000 a grant of one

28 *Venetian Calendar*, I, 550. Papal Collector de Gilis to Innocent VIII.
29 Rymer, *Foedera*, O. XII, 362.
30 *Ibid.*, XII, 359, 361.
31 *Spanish Calendar*, I, 34.
32 Bacon, *Henry VII*, 84.
33 *Ibid.*, 36.

fifteenth and tenth was made by Parliament.[34]   The clergy
of Canterbury and of York each granted one tenth.[35]   Henry
VII however, was sure of his hand, knowing the eagerness of
Charles VIII of France to be free to undertake his Italian
expedition, which had been revealed to Henry by the French
embassy of 1489.   Henry therefore continued to aid Anne
of Brittany, taking good care to secure her bonds and promises
for repayment.[36]   When Charles VIII by capturing and mar-
rying the Duchess made it impossible for Henry to put pressure
on him from that quarter to renew the tribute, Henry VII
determined to invade France in person, and recover his kingdom of France.

In this patriotic cause, Henry could ask for benevolence without much fear of opposition despite the unpopularity of the
benevolence under Edward IV, and the condemnation of the
practice by Richard III's first Parliament.   In July 1491, commissions were issued "for obtaining contributions for a war
against France," setting forth "that Charles of France not only
unjustly occupies the king's kingdom of France, but threatens the
destruction of England."[37] In December other commissioners were
sent to Yorkshire.[38]   When Parliament assembled the king told
his just cause for waging war.   "The cause of this battle did
every man allow, and to setting forth the same promised all
they could make."[39]   A liberal grant of two fifteenths and
tenths was made, with the promise of a third if the army remained abroad more than eight months.[40]

The invasion of France by an English army in 1492 was a
gorgeous military show.   It soon accomplished its purpose.
Charles VIII sent early proposals of peace; he would pay certain
arrears of the pension due by Louis XI to Edward IV, and
assume the debts of Anne of Brittany.   By the treaty of Etaples
he acknowledged that he owed for the costs of the war, the

[34] *Rot. Parl.*, VI, 438.

[35] Wilkins, *Concilia*, III, 625, 630.

[36] Rymer,*Foedera*, O. XII, 435, 436, 438, 442, 443.

[37] *Ibid.*, XII, 446; Gairdner, *Letters and Papers, Richard III and
Henry VII*, II, 372, The commissions are dated July 7, 1491.

[38] Rymer, *Foedera* O. XII, 464.

[39] Hall, *Chronicle* (Ed. of 1809), 451.

[40] *Statutes of the Realm*, 7 Henry VII, c. 11.

debts of Anne, the expenses of ambassadors, 620,000 Ecus d'or; and for the obligations of Louis XI to Edward IV 125,000 Ecus d'or, or 745,000 Ecus d'or in all.[41] This sum was to be paid at the rate of 50,000 francs yearly, in semi-annual installments due May 1, and November 1.[42] This "pension" was regularly paid by Charles VIII, and on his death, Louis XI renewed the obligation.[43]

The peace was not popular in England. "Men stuck not to say 'That the king cared not to plume his nobility and people to feather himself.' And some made themselves merry with what the king had said in Parliament, 'That after the war was once begun, he doubted not but to make it pay itself,' saying he had kept promise."[44] And he had, even though his profits were not so large as Bacon believed them. On the one hand he had received generous grants from Parliament and from the clergy, collected a benevolence of £48,484,[45] and received the assurance of a pension of 50,000 francs a year for a long term of years. On the other hand, in the preliminary contest in Brittany something was spent, and the invasion of France in 1492 cost £48,802.[46] The difference was the king's profit.

[41] £159,000 sterling.

[42] Rymer, *Foedera*, O. XII, 506, The treaty of Etaples.

[43] *Ibid.*, 684.

[44] Bacon, *Henry VII*, 103.

[45] *Cott. Mss., Cleopatra* F. VI, f. 314 — "King Henry VII in the 16th year had Benevolences of the clergy, nobility and commons towards his wars in France amounting to the sum of 48,484 pounds, besides the fifteenths and tenths at the same time. The book of this appeareth in the treasury as Westminister with the chamberlains." There was however no benevolence in the 16th year, and no fifteenths and tenths, but both were taken for the French war in 1491-1492, in the sixth year of his reign. The book referred to is perhaps, *Exch. of Receipt, Misc. Books*, I, which records receipts from the benevolence. Some pages are missing; the total of that part of the book which is preserved is £41,930 18s. 1d., paid in money. Another record (*Accounts, Exch., Queen's Remembrancer*, 516/23) shows the receipt by the collectors of £6,396 9d. worth of plate. The two sums added approach closely the figure given in the quotation above.

[46] The account of the expenditures in Brittany is preserved in the Chapter House at Westminster, but access to it, or to other documents such as letters of Empson and Dudley, preserved there could not be arranged. The account for the expenditures for the invasion of France is in *Accounts, Exch., Queen's Remembrancer*, 516/23.

More successful financially was the Scotch war of 1496 and 1497. Upon the news of a raid by James IV across the English borders in 1496, Parliament granted two fifteenths and tenths, with the usual exceptions and deductions, and, in addition "an aid and subsidy of as great and large sums of money as the said two fifteenths and tenths" with the abatement and reduction of £12,000, but no other reductions. This meant that the exempted towns were to pay the tax, paying as much toward the subsidy, as their fifteenths and tenths would amount to.[47] At the same time, the clergy of Canterbury made a grant of £40,000, despite the grant of a tenth in the year before.[48] Taking the fifteenth and tenth at £29,000 the entire clerical and lay grant at this time was nearly £160,000. The book of payments of the Treasurer of the Chamber shows the dispatch of money for soldiers wages, a total of £41,300.[49] The "rigging forth" of the navy took £4,408,[50] and the revolt of the Cornishmen, who objected to being taxed for the defence of the Scotch frontier, and the defeat of Perkin Warbeck cost £13,155 more.[51]

It might be noted in passing that after the suppression of the Cornish rising, Henry VII characteristically turned it to his own pecuniary advantage by sending Amis Paulet and Robert Sherborne, the Dean of St. Paul's and other commissioners "to plague and scourge them according to the quality of their crime and offence with great fines and assessments."[52] The commissioners visited every hundred, and levied fines on very great numbers of people. One roll in which fines of £8,810 are assessed contains over 3,400 names.[53] In all the Cornishmen and Warbeck's adherents were fined £14,699, payment of which was extended over many years. The last payment was made in 1507; as is shown by a note in the king's own hand at the end of one of the rolls.[54]

[47] *Rot. Parl.*, VI, 514, 515.

[48] Wilkins, *Concilia*, III, 645.

[49] *Accounts, Exch., Queen's Remembrancer*, 414/6.

[50] *Accounts, Exch., Queen's Rmembrancer*, 414/6.

[51] *Exch., Treasurer of Receipt, Misc. Books*, 126, pp. 40, 74-78.

[52] Hall, *Chronicle* (Ed. of 1809), 486.

[53] *Rot. Reg.* 14 B. VII. This roll is calendared in Gairdner, *Letters and Papers, Richard III and Henry VII*, II, App. B, 337.

[54] There are four rolls of the fines; *Accounts, Exch., Queen's Remem-*

In the large, the use of foreign troubles for financial ends is merely an episode in the history of Henry VII's reign. The king was willing to profit by them when they came ready to his hand, but considerable risk attended their use. With the improvement in the situation, which became very marked even before the Scotch war of 1496-1497, Henry VII preferred to abandon them and the devices and dangers they involved.

brancer, 516/24, to which the king's note is appended, 516/27, 516/28, and *Rot. Reg.* 14 B. VII.

F

CHAPTER VI

THE NEW ORGANIZATION OF THE FINANCIAL SYSTEM

De Ayala, the Spanish ambassador once described King Henry VII as spending all his time, when not in public or in his council chamber, in writing the accounts of his expenses with his own hand. The description is scarcely overdrawn; for while Henry VII did not actually write his own accounts, he spent a very large part of his time in examining, annotating and marking with his sign manual the account books of his several revenue officials. While his earliest, and always his chief interest was given to the new revenues which he himself had developed, he gradually extended his attention to the older revenues and their expenditure. Before the end of his reign, consequently, he had worked fundamental changes in the organization of the financial system, as a result of which the king in person was his own chief treasury official. He personally knew all his receipts and expenditures; he personally gave acquittances or discharges to the special treasurers, and to him, as the final officer of audit the great treasuries and revenue courts themselves submitted their accounts. The independence of the Exchequer was broken down in all its essential parts, and it, together with the new revenue bodies, were brought under the unified control of the monarch himself.

When Henry VII became king the great financial institution of the government was the Court of the Exchequer. It consisted of two distinct divisions, the Exchequer of Account, and the Exchequer of Receipt. The leading officials of the Exchequer of Receipt were the Under Treasurer, the two Chamberlains, and their clerks, and four Tellers.[1]

[1] The Lord Treasurer, being a great official, busied in other affairs of state, had ceased to attend personally to his duties in the Exchequer of Receipt. His work was performed by his clerks, one of whom became the

60

When the sheriff, collector of customs or other accountant came to London on the summons of the court, with his account and the money due to the king, he went first to the Exchequer of Receipt, and paid his money to one of the Tellers. The Tellers entered the amount of money which they received into a small paper account book.[2] Here we have modern business methods; but in the figurative back room, known as the Court of the Receipt there was a complete set of medieval machinery which had to be put into motion before the accountant could have a receipt for his money. After the teller had made the entry into his paper book, he copied the entry upon a slip of parchment, giving briefly the particulars of the payment.[3] This slip or bill was either "cast into the court of Receipt by a trunck made for that purpose" or according to other document given to the accountant to be by him carried to the Court of Receipt and handed to the Treasurer's Clerk for writing the Tallies, the *Clericus ad Tallia Scribenda*. A second clerk of the Treasurer, the Clerk for Writing the Pells entered the bill, letter for letter into a record called the Pell, or Treasurer's Roll of Receipts, and two Clerks for Writing the Controllment of the Pells, each representing one of the Chamberlains entered it into two other records, the so-called Receipt Rolls. The Usher of the Receipt then cut notches representing the sum paid as stated in the bill and read aloud by the Clerk for writing the Tallies into the side of a square stick of hazel wood, or tally. When the tally was properly notched, the Clerk for Writing the Tallies copied the bill upon the two sides of it word for word. Finally the Clerks of the Chamberlains for Splitting the Tallies, the *Clerici ad Tallia Scindenda* compared the notches in the tally and the two inscriptions upon the sides of it with the bill, and the three entries in the three receipt rolls. If all agreed the Clerks for Splitting the Tallies split the tally down the center

Under Treasurer. The Under Treasurer is sometimes called Clerk of the Treasurer even in the early years of Henry VIII's reign. *Exch. of Receipt, Declarations of the State of the Treasury*, II, III, IV.

[2] Examples of these account books, many of which are preserved for the reigns of Henry VII and his successors are *Exch., Treasury of Receipt, Misc. Books,* 124, 125.

[3] Many files of these slips are preserved as "Tellers Bills," among the manuscripts of the Exchequer of Receipt in the Public Record Office.

of the notched side, so that each half carried a record of the payment. One half, called the stock was given to the account-ant, and the other, the foil, was deposited in the court, to be sent to the Exchequer of account, there to be compared with the stock by the Chamberlain's Clerks for Joining the Tallies when the accountant should present his account for audit.[4]

In earlier times, the money received at the Exchequer of Receipt was kept in the custody of the Lord Treasurer and the Chamberlains. But in Henry VII's reign or before, the Lord Treasurer and Chamberlains "were clearly discharged of their account of the king's money," and the money received by the Tellers remained in their own custody.[5] It was paid out by them on warrants of the king under the great and privy seals, formally directed however as in the past, to the Treasurer and Chamberlains. When the Tellers issued money, they simply entered the payment, giving the name of the person, the amount and other particulars into their paper account books, and had the man who had received the money either sign the book di-rectly below the entry, or sign a simple paper receipt.[6] In earlier times, when the Lord Treasurer and Chamberlains still had the custody of money, a very elaborate process was neces-sary before money could be disbursed at the Exchequer by the Tellers, and the record of the payment was entered into issue rolls in triplicate, very similar to the three receipt rolls.[7] But now that the Tellers had actual custody of the money and were rsponsible for it, the simpler system of keeping accounts of issues was possible.

[4] The practices of the Exchequer of Receipt are taken from a bundle of documents in the Record Office, *Exch. of Receipt, Miscellanea*, 396, relating to a dispute between two officials in the time of Elizabeth. In these it is stated on the evidence of men who had been in the court in Henry VII's reign, that practices were the same in the reigns of Henry VII and Henry VIII. Especially valuable are the papers numbered 2, 7, 17, 82.

[5] The earliest evidence that the Tellers actually retained custody of the money is in one of the Teller's account Books, *Exch., Treasury of Receipt, Misc. Books,* 124, pp. 76, 130, 188, anno 5-6 Henry VII.

[6] Examples of such receipts and signatures are found in *Exch., Treasury of Receipt, Misc. Books,* 126, 131.

[7] The triple issue rolls cease with Richard III's reign. When they were resumed in Elizabeth's reign they were at "first merely transcripts from the teller's entry books."

The amount of money actually received at the Exchequer of Receipt in Henry VII's, and in the early part of Henry VIII's reign was very small, except in years when a subsidy was collected, or a loan levied.[8] Most of the "receipts" of the Exchequer was never brought to London at all, but was assigned by tallies. Warrants for disbursements directed to the Treasurer and Chamberlains were sent either to the Tellers, who paid them in cash, or to the Court of Receipt. A warrant sent thither might call for the payment of £1,000 to the Duke of York for the custody of the East and Middle Marches against Sctoland. At the Court of Receipt direction would be given that the Duke of York should be paid the sum by the collectors of customs at London, Pole, Yarmouth, Lynn, Bridgewater, Hull, Exeter and Dartmouth, and Chichester. After the amount to be paid by each collector had been determined upon, for example, £100 by the collector at Hull, much the same performance ensued as though these amounts had actually been paid into the Exchequer. Tallies were cut, written, split and enrolled in the three Receipt Rolls for the amounts; but in the margin opposite the sums the words *"pro duce Ebor. per tall"* with the reason for the assignment were written, instead of the usual *sol.* (paid). The foils of the tallies were preserved in the court, but the stocks were given to the Duke of York. They were in the nature of checks or drafts. The Duke presented them to the various collectors named, who on sight of them paid the sums represented by them to him, instead of the Tellers of the Receipt, and received the tallies as their acquittance. Assignments by tallies were not without their inconveniences. They occasioned long delay, and in some cases could not be collected at all. Every year many "desperate tallies" were returned to the Exchequer for redemption.[9] In Henry VIII's reign the use of assignments by tallies was reduced, so that by 1541 the

---

[8] During the first year of Henry VII, £1,866 19s. 10d. in money was received at the Exchequer of Receipt; in the eighth year £3,860 17s. 3½d. and in the last year £4,717 1s. 7d. *Exch., Treasury of Receipt, Misc. Books,* 125; *Exch., Treasury of Receipt, Declarations of the State of the Treasury,* I.

[9] The history and method of assignment by tallies are more elaborately described by Hilary Jenkinson, *Archeologia,* LXII, part II, 369-371, *"Exchequer Tallies."*

greater part of the business of the Exchequer was done in cash, with as a consequence, an increase in the prestige of the Tellers, and a lessened importance of the medieval elements of the Exchequer of Receipt.

The examination and audit of the particulars and details of the accounts of revenue collectors was left to the Exchequer of account, or Upper Exchequer. Here a very elaborate system of checks which had grown up in past centuries, examination by Exchequer auditors, formal engrossing, and enrollment in the great parchment rolls of the Lord Treasurer's Remembrancer's office, insured considerable honesty, even though not efficiency and speed.[10] With this formal audit system of the Exchequer of Account, Henry VII never interfered, though he did withdraw from its purview certain important kinds of accounts, leaving there the only customs accounts and the account of the Calais Staple for the wool subsidy, the accounts of the feudal revenue of the sheriffs, bailiffs, escheators, the accounts of collectors of the subsidy, the accounts of certain crown lands, the mint accounts, the account of the Clerk of the Hanaper, and the accounts of the expenditures in the Household and Wardrobe.

The Exchequer of Receipt, where the revenues were actually received and paid, was gradually brought more directly under the royal control. Before Henry VII's reign the Receipt and Issue Rolls, drawn up from the Tellers' entry books and bills were the formal records of the Exchequer of Receipt. In them no classification of receipts and expenditures was made to show the revenue derived from the several sources, or the expenditures for various purposes. In no case was any addition made to show even the total of all revenues or all expenditures. Toward the close of Henry VII's reign however, the Under Treasurer began to draw up each year a Declaration of the State of the Treasury, showing the total revenue received or assigned in the Exchequer

[10] The original particulars and bills of the accountant were carefully examined by the auditors; from them a Compotus, written on parchment was drawn up, which when approved was signed at the top by the auditors and Exchequer barons and enrolled on the Pipe Roll, the Foreign Roll, the Customs Roll, the Subsidy Roll or the Wardrobe and Household Roll. When enrolled a line was drawn down the center of the compotus, and with the original particulars and bills in a little leathern bag, it was sent to the office of the King's Remembrancer to be preserved.

of Receipt, and the various purposes for which money was expended, with the total expenditure for each.[11] These Declarations for the first time made it possible for the king to know exactly the state of his receipts and expenditures in this office, and they symbolized also the king's more perfect supervision over the lower branch of the Exchequer Court.

By the nature of its development, with so many medieval methods part and parcel of its organization, the Exchequer was ill-fitted to be adapted to more modern requirements. Its officials were slow in levying the revenues due to the king; accountants were respited from year to year, and payments were deferred "by space of many years." It was moreover, the stronghold of noble privilege and reaction. It had been weakened by royal control over the Exchequer of Receipt, but even more desirable was the creation of new bodies entirely free from the old traditions and influences. Richard III had already recognized its deficiencies and purposed to institute changes in the revenue system and its organization. In the management of the newly acquired estates of the crown the Exchequer of Account, and all its methods were to be superseded, while a new treasury to take it place beside the Exchequer of Receipt was to be instituted. Following and improving upon the plan used for the lands of the Duchy of Lancaster,[12] Richard III proposed clearly to discharge and dismiss the court of the Exchequer from any meddling with any livelihood in taking of accounts, such as the principality of Wales, the Duchies of Cornwall, York and Norfolk, the earldoms of Chester, March, Warwick and Salisbury and all other lands in the king's hands by forfeiture.[13]

[11] The first declaration known is for the year Easter 1505 to Easter 1506. It is found in a Jacobean copy, in *Lansdowne Mss.*, 156, f. 124ff. The Declarations were made regularly by the Under Treasurer until 1551.

[12] In 1399 by a charter of Henry IV all the lands and possessions of the Duchy were declared to be a distinct inheritance separate from the lands and possessions of the crown. The management of the Duchy lands was placed under a separate establishment, the Chancellor and Council of the Duchy of Lancaster, and the distribution of the revenues by a distinct treasury was ordered. Although the Chancellor and Council audited the accounts of ministers and receivers of the lands of the Duchy, the clear revenues were paid into the Exchequer of Receipt, and no new treasury was established.

[13] The old feudal demesne lands of the crown, the *corpus comitatus,*

These lands were to be placed in charge or receivers to collect their revenues and rents and of "foreign" auditors to take their accounts, for the purpose of increasing their yield to the crown, and strengthening the control of the crown over them.   These new auditors and receivers should yearly ride, survey, receive and remember in every behalf that might be most for the king's profit, and thereof yearly to make report of the estate and condition of the same by which the king's grace should know all the lordships that pertained to his crown.   These officials were not to be unlettered knights and squires who took great fines and rewards of the king's tenants to their own use, but "learned men in the law," who would be most profitable to be stewards of the said livelihood for many causes concerning the king's profit and weal of his tenants.[14]   These officials were not to account before the Exchequer but should make yearly declaration of all such revenues as they had in charge before such persons as the king's grace would assign at London, between Candlemas and Palm-sunday.   Exchequer auditors were to make a similar declaration at the same time, so that the king might know every year the total of his revenues, and "what thereof is paid and what is owing."[15]

This was equivalent to the establishment of a new system for the land revenue, with an independent revenue court of farmed out by the sheriffs, were so unimportant through the alienations of *terrae datae* that no change in their management was contemplated by Richard III, and none was made in Henry VII's or his successor's reigns.

[14] Foreign auditors and receivers, riding around the country are found as early as the reign of Richard II in the Principality of Wales, and the Duchy of Cornwall, and in the reign of Edward IV in the lands of the Duke of Clarence. *Calendar of Patent Rolls, Richard II*, V, 24; *Ibid., Henry V*, I, 139-140; *Ibid., Edward IV, Edward V, Richard III*, III, 98, 220.   The Exchequer apparently had jurisdiction over such auditors and receivers, and perhaps Exchequer officials ever reexamined accounts passed by the foreign auditors.   Richard III once ordered the Exchequer to accept the account of the Receiver-General of Cornwall already examined by the foreign auditor, as final and give a discharge for it. *Exch., King's Remembrancer, Memoranda Rolls*, 260 Brevia Directa, Hilary term, membrane 4.

[15] Richard III's plan, entitled "A Remembraunce made for the more hasty levy of the Kinges revenues" is printed in Gairdner, *Letters and Papers, Richard III and Henry VII*, I, 81-85.

audit and account; but Richard III did not carry out his plans completely. At the beginning of Henry VII's reign the recivers were still rendering their accounts at the Exchequer of Account. But the beginning of the establishment of a new treasury for the receipt of revenue, along side of the Exchequer of Receipt had been made even as early as the reign of Edward IV. For during his reign, the benevolences do not appear on the Receipt Rolls as paid at the Exchequer; while on the other hand, large payments from the king's own coffers suggest that it was to the coffers directly that the benevolences were paid.[16] During the reign of Richard III, the amount of money paid into the Exchequer of Receipt from the crown lands was very small, and the money from the lands was in some cases at least, and may usually have been paid not at the Exchequer, but to the king's own hands, in his chamber.[17]

Henry VII carried out the plans of Richard III completely. For the royal lands he erected a new court of audit and account, and to receive his new revenues and some of the old ones, he transformed the King's chamber into a treasury which was of vastly greater importance than the Exchequer of Receipt during the next third of a century. The new court of audit was for a long time very informal, and even on Henry VII's death it was not completely developed. Its beginnings are shrouded in obscurity. There is however, certain circumstantial evidence about its origin. In the first years of Henry VII's reign the great Roll of Foreign Accounts of the Exchequer is quite full. It contains the enrollments of the accounts of the receiver-general of the Warwick and Spencer lands, and of the Duchy of Cornwall, the Chamberlain of Berwick, the Treasurer of Calais, the Mayor and Fellowship of the Staple, the Clerk of the Hanaper and the Treasurer of the Mint. Certain of these accounts disappeared from the Foreign Roll after the eighth year, — those of the Warwick and Spencer lands, of the Duchy of Cornwall, of the Chamberlain of Berwick and of the Treas-

[16] Ramsay, *Lancaster and York*, II, 465, 467, 557.

[17] A note is found in the *Memoranda Rolls* (*Exch., King's Remembrancer, Memoranda Rolls,* 260, Brevia baronibus Directa, Hilary term, membrane 12) that John Hayes, receiver of the Warwick lands has paid four hundred Marks ''to our (Richard III's) own hands in our chamber.''

urer of Calais. Moreover, no accounts of the lands newly acquired by Henry VII ever appeared in the Foreign Roll.[18] The evidence of the Foreign Roll in which all land revenue accounts audited at the Exchequer (except those of the ancient firma comitatus) would be enrolled, suggests that the lands newly acquired by Henry VII were never in the province of the Exchequer, while some of the most important of the older estates were removed from the Exchequer jurisdiction. The Repertoires to States and Views of Public Accounts, an index kept in the Lord Treasurer's Remembrancer's office, of all accountants who came to the Exchequer, shows that during the first eight years of the reign receivers and receivers-general of the king's lands came to the Exchequer in lessening numbers, and practically ceased to account there.[19] The Ministers' Accounts, preserved at the Public Records Office are also of service.[20] For the first three years of Henry VII's *compoti* are found for many crown lands, so marked as to show that they were audited and enrolled in the Exchequer.[21] The *compoti* of John Walsh, one of the receivers general of the Warwick, Spencer and Salisbury lands are signed and marked as audited and enrolled in the Exchequer for the first five years of the reign, to Michaelmas

[18] *Exch., Lord Treasurer's Remembrancer, Foreign Roll*, 119. The accounts of receivers of certain very small parcels of land continued to be "enrolled in" the Foreign Roll for a long time after this.

[19] *Repertoires to States and Views, Public Record Office Indexes*, 7025.

[20] Though there are several thousand Minister's Accounts in the time of Henry VII, very few are of value for this problem. As the royal land system was organized the individual manors were in charge of bailiffs and ministers who paid the money they collected from the tenants to a receiver who was in charge of a large district. If the particular estate was very large, there might be four or five receivers, who paid the revenues to a receiver-general. Many of the Ministers' Accounts are the accounts or bailiffs and receivers, from which the Receiver-General made up his account, and he submitted these with his account in London, as the original particulars and bills. These original particulars are of no value in determining where the account was audited, since no distinguishing mark of any kind was ever placed on them. Only the final account of the Receiver-General, the *compotus*, is of service.

[21] They are signed *at the top* by the Barons and auditors of the Exchequer and have a line drawn down through the center. Enrolments of all are found in the Foreign Roll. *Ministers' Accounts, Henry VII*, 1101, 1102, 1239, 1240, 1356, 1472.

1490. *Compoti* of this same account for the seventh and a later year are neither signed or marked as enrolled in the Exchequer. In the Foreign Roll, the last enrollment of Walsh's account was in the eighth year of the reign, for the revenues of the sixth year. The *Compoti* of John Hayes, the other receiver general of the Warwick, Spencer and Salisbury lands are marked as audited and enrolled in the Exchequer to the end of the sixth year. The last entry in the Foreign Roll of Hayes's accounts is for the sixth year. The only *Compoti* which are signed by the Barons and auditors of the Exchequer, and marked as enrolled later than the sixth year are the *Compoti* of the Constable of Windsor Castle from the ninth to the seventeenth years of Henry VII, and these duly appear on the foreign roll.[22] Many *Compoti* later than the sixth year are preserved which are not marked with any Exchequer mark. More than that, certain of them differ in form and phrasing from the old *Compotus* and the money for which they account is noted as paid to John Heron, or to the Kings Chamber.[23] It may be that at the end of the eighth year of the reign. that is after Michaelmas 1493, when the accounts of the sixth year were rendered, changes in the organization of the revenue system were made. Lands were taken out of the jurisdiction of the Exchequer, and their accounts no longer received there. Yet the accounts were drawn up and audited regularly without break. The new auditing body was the beginning of the new revenue court of audit.

Butlerage and Prisage were also withdrawn from Exchequer jurisdiction later in the reign. In this case there is preserved

[22] John Walsh's accounts are found in *Ministers' Accounts, Henry VII*, 1370-1374. John Hayes's accounts, *ibid.*, 1356-1361. The accounts of the Constable of Windsor, *ibid.*, 20.

[23] The *Compoti* of Sir William Stanley's lands in Chester for the eleventh and eighteenth years of the reign are examples. The membranes of the accounts of the bailiffs are attached to the membrane on which the *Compotus* is written and the payment of money is noted, "Et in denariis liberatis ad Receptam coffuri domini Regis tam de arragiis quam de parte Recepte sue supradicta ad manum Johannis Heron ad duas vices, una vice per billam suam apud Westmonasterium X. die Novembris . . sub signeto et signo manuali dicti Johannis Heron suprt compotum liberatis et penes praedictum Receptorem remanentes." *Ministers' Accounts, Henry VII*, 1562, 1564. Other examples ar found *ibid.*, 133, 134, 1047, 1373, 1374, 1391-1393.

an original indenture telling something of the new court and the names of its chief officials. "This indenture, twentieth February, anno XX. (1505) betwen Roger Bishop of Carlisle and Robert Southwell knight, on the one part, and William Hodre knight, Chief Baron of the King's Exchequer, Bartholomew Westby, William Bollyngay and John Allen, Barons of the Exchequer on the other part, witnesseth the names of such of the King's officers and accountants as have appeared and entered their account before the said Roger Bishop of Carlisle and the said Robert Southwell, having the King's authority to call them in that behalf. Against all which persons underwritten so being in account before the said Bishop and Robert Southwell, the said Bishop and Robert desire Remanentes processes hanging in the said Exchequer for causes underwritten to be put in suspense according to the King's letter in this behalf directed." [24] The Bishop of Carlisle and Robert Southwell are named again in the accounts of the receiver-general of the Duchy of Cornwall for the ninteenth year, where an item in the account is noted as respited "per mandate Rogeri Carl. episcopi et Robert Southwell consiliari domini Regis." [25] Finally, for the nineteenth, twentieth and twenty-first years of the reign there are the general declarations of the accounts of this new court, made to the king by Robert Southwell. These show that by that time the court, still dependent for its existence merely upon the king's authority, was highly organized, and took the accounts of practically all the crown lands, (except the Duchy of Lancaster), of wards' lands in the king's hands, and of Butlerage and Prisage.[26]

[24] *Accounts, Exch., Queen's Remembrancer,* 517/10.

[25] *Minister's Accounts, Henry VII,* 1084.

[26] *Exch., Treasury of Receipt, Misc. Books,* 213, 212. The preamble of the Declaration for the twenty-first year runs — "Liber declarationum de anno Regis Henry VII. XXI.mo tam de terris domini regis quam de terris wardorum domino regi accommodatis, de Butts et Prisage vinorum per Robertum Southwell." The account of each separate estate is set forth on a page by itself, and the gross revenue, the costs of repairs and of management, the money paid to Heron and the unpaid arrears are shown. Other account books of the court, dealing with the wards' lands alone are also found, *Exch., Treasury of Receipt, Misc. Books,* 247, 248. Each page of all these books is signed by the king himself with his sign-manual.

The new court early known as the Court of General Surveyors, was a court of audit like the Exchequer of Account. A
treasury, like the Treasury of Receipt, was a necessary adjunct.
This place was filled by the Treasurer of the Chamber, who
already in Richard III's reign, and possibly in the reign of
Edward IV, had received certain of the royal revenues. In
as much as he was in personal attendance upon the King,
treasure in his hands would be more directly under the control
and at the disposal of the King than in the Exchequer of
Receipt. Sir Thomas Lovell was appointed Treasurer of the
Chamber in the first year of Henry VII's reign, and as late
as 1506 he held the office. The actual work, however, certainly
from 1487 on, was done by his deputy, John Heron, who himself
became Treasurer of the Chamber before the end of the reign.
To him were paid the new revenues of all kinds from lands,
the proceeds of the benevolence and the forced loans, the French
pensions, the surplus of Calais and Berwick, some customs revenues and the later clerical and lay subsidies, and all the money
received by recognizance and by obligation. Some of these
items were paid to him by assignment of tallies from the Exchequer, and represent the unexpended surplus of the Exchequer,
paid to him by royal warrant. The accounts of such were
rendered in the Exchequer of Account. But the more important
of the items enumerated came to him as the regular treasurer
of the newly established court of audit. He was further appointed treasurer of the revenues of the Duchy of Lancaster,
such as were in excess of those appropriated by Parliament
for the purpose of the Household. The relations between the
Treasurer of the Chamber and the King were particularly personal and intimate. Until much later in Henry VII's reign,
it was unnecessary for the Treasurer of the Chamber to draw
up any formal declaration of his accounts, as was done by the
Exchequer of Receipt, the new land court of audit, and the
Duchy of Lancaster, since his account books of the receipts and
issues of his office were examined every day by the King himself.
Nearly every page of his books bears the royal sign manual,
with notes in the King's own hand.[27]

[27] With the development of the Treasury of the Chamber under Henry
VII compare the analogous developments of the Wardrobe and Chamber

The new court of audit and the enhanced position of the Treasurer of the Chamber, were displeasing to the Exchequer and its officials. Even while Henry VII was still king, the Exchequer officials instituted processes against accountants who had ceased to present their accounts in the Exchequer, and Henry VII found it necessary to instruct his attorney-general to take these processes into his own hands and command the Exchequer officers to "surcease of any further process making, touching this matter, until they shall know therein our further pleasure."[28] But directly that Henry VII had died, the Exchequer bgan to vex and trouble such receivers and receivers-general who paid their money to John Heron and accounted before the General Surveyors. The Exchequer refused to accept the bills and books signed by the King or by Heron, and compelled the accountants to come personally and appear in the Exchequer, render accounts anew, and make a second payment, into the Exchequer of Receipt "as if they had never accounted nor made payment, to their importable loss, trouble, hurt and damage against all right reason and good conscince." Since Henry VIII and his advisers had no intention of returning to the slow, cumbersome Exchequer system, an act was passed in Henry VIII's first Parliament commanding the Exchequer officials to honor all bills and acquittances signed by Heron.[29] Shortly afterward, on February 6, 1511, the King, intending to continue the same order of account before his General Surveyors, and " to be answered of his revenues in his Chamber," issued a special commission to Sir Robert Southwell (who had been one of the General Surveyors under Henry VII), and Bartholomew Westby, who took the place of the deceased Bishop of Carlisle, to survey and approve the royal lands, and to continue the new court of audit for land revenue originated under Henry VII.[30]

The first thought of Henry VIII's government seems to have been to make the General Surveyors a department of the Ex-

in the 13th and 14th centuries, studied by Professor T. F. Tont, in his brilliant *Chapters in the Administrative History of Medieval England.*

[28] *Accounts, Exch., Queen's Remembrancer,* 302/14.

[29] *Statutes,* 1 Henry VIII, c. 3. This act was to continue to the next Parliament.

[30] *Statutes,* 3 Henry VIII, c. 23, page 45. The commission, incorporated into this statute of the following year, is recited here in full.

chequer. For in addition to the commission of February 6, 1511, there were issued two Privy Seals, dated June 30, 1510, and October 31, 1511, according to which accountants could be summoned only by the Exchequer, and process made out against them for failure to account only in the Exchequer. Moreover, Southwell and Westby were not empowered to administer oaths. All accountants had to be sworn before the Exchequer Barons before being sent to Southwell and Westby. But because no summons could be issued from the Exchequer in vacation times, which were notoriously long, many delays ensued to the great loss of the King, and of accountants who came to London during vacation periods. To remedy these defects and "for a further and strenger authority" to be given to Southwell and Westby than could be given to the royal commission and the Privy seals, Parliament at its second session, in 1511-1512 passed an act appointing the General Surveyors and Approvers of all and singular of the King's lands and estates, with supervision, but not direct control over the Duchy of Lancaster. They were given full power to summon accountants and to give the acquittance upon bills signed by Henry VII, Henry VIII or John Heron. By the same act Heron was confirmed in the office of the Treasurer of the Chamber to receive the land revenues, and to be responsible only to the King.[31] This act was valid only for one year; it was renewed in 1512 and in 1514, and repealed and reënacted in more systematic

[31] *Statutes*, 3 Henry VIII, c. 23. The act further provided that the accounts approved by the General Surveyors should be engrossed on parchment, and sent, with all original account books and tallies to the Exchequer, to be preserved by the Clerk of the Pipe. Provisions similar to this are found in the later acts relating to the General Surveyors. The reason for this seems to be connected with the assignments or appropriations made by Parliament for the Household and Wardrobe. These assignments, which were under Exchequer supervision, were made in large part upon the land revenues. Tallies were issued to the cofferer of the Household and to the Clerk of the Wardrobe by the Exchequer, directed to the receivers of the land revenues for payment. Since the Cofferer and Clerk of the Wardrobe rendered their accounts of receipts and expenditures in the Exchequer, it was necessary that the Exchequer should know what they had received upon the tallies issued to them. This could be done accurately only if the accounts of the receivers of the land revenues were sent to the Exchequer to be checked with their accounts. In practice

form in 1515. The act of 1515 was renewed in 1522 and made "perpetual" in 1535.[32]

But all the revenues of King Henry VII were not received and expended under the jurisdiction of the General Surveyors, the Treasurer of the Chamber and the officials of the Exchequer. In the two most outlying parts of the kingdom, large sums were collected and spent by local officers for the charges of the garrisons and the administration of the King's government at Berwick and Calais. In 1487 £2068 6s. 8d. of the revenues of certain lands in the north of England and of the customs of Newcastle were set aside to be collected, administered and spent by the Chamberlain of Berwick for the wages of the garrison there. Later the assignment was increased to £2627 14s. 4d. on the crown lands, and on the customs of Newcastle and Hull.[33] During the two years from Michaelmas 1487 to Michaelmas 1489, the Chamberlain of Berwick received £4752 0s. 9d., and spent £4338 17s. 4d., and during the next two years he received £4822 8s. 13d., and spent £4343 13s. 1d.[34]

At Calais the customs subsidy on wool brought from England by the merchants of the Staple was collected by officers of the Staple. This arrangement had originated under Edward IV. He was in debt to the Society of the Staple, and at the same time the garrison of the town of Calais was disorderly, and threatened the property of the Staple, because their wages were not paid promptly by the King. In order to protect themselves against the garrison by securing prompt payment of their wages, and to recover the money which the King owed them, the Mayor and Fellowship of the Staple arranged to take over the collection of the wool subsidy at Calais, pay the garrison, make certain payments to the King's judges, sergeants at law, and his attorney, and to the customers and controllers of the

the auditors of the court of General Surveyors drew up two "Vewes" of of the accounts of receivers. Of these one was sent to the Exchequer, and one was preserved by the General Surveyors (*Augmentations Office, Misc. Books*, 313A 314, 318, 322.

[32] *Statutes*, 4 Henry VIII, c. 18; 6 Henry VIII, c. 24; 7 Henry VIII, c. 7; 14-15 Henry VIII, c. 15; 27 Henry VIII, c. 62.

[33] *Rot. Parl.*, VI, 394a, 496a.

[34] *Lord Treasurer's Remembrancer, Foreign Roll*, 119, anno 5, membrane E; anno 7, membrane C.

wool subsidy of the port of London, to provide for the convoy
of wools from England to Calais, to keep part of the revenues
each year to pay the King's debt to themselves, and to pay the
balance to the royal treasury. This arrangement was continued
under Henry VII, and during part of Henry VIII's reign.[35]
For the charges of the garrison, it was originally provided that
£10,022 4s. 8d. should be paid to the Treasurer of Calais
by the Staple each year. This sum was regularly paid until
1502, after which it was reduced to amounts which varied
between £5,011 and £7,753 for the remaining years of the
reign. To the king's attorney, sergeants at law and judges, and
to the London customs-house officers £675 4s. 4d. were paid each
year, and £316 13s. 4d. were paid annually for convoy. The
account for the whole sum collected for the customs by the
Staple was rendered at the Exchequer, and the surplus or balance, which averaged £4,000 a year after the reduction, in
1502, of the amount paid for the garrison, was entered among
the Exchequer receipts, and was paid by assignment from the
Exchequer to the Treasurer of the Chamber.

The costs of governing and holding Calais were not, however,
entirely defrayed by the money paid to the Treasurer of the town
by the Staple from the proceeds of the wool subsidy. In addition
to this he received rents from certain lands in the English pale
there, certain octroi dues and the profits made on the victuals
sold to the soldiers of the garrison by the government. These
items amounted to between £2,500 and £3,000 a year. The expenditures of the Treasurer of Calais were always well within
his receipts, so that he had an unexpended balance of from
£500 to £6,000 a year, which, like the surplus of the Chamberlain of Berwick was turned over, except in the early years of the
reign, directly to the Treasurer of the Chamber.[36]

With the details of the accounts of such revenues as the

[35] *Rot. Parl.*, VI, 55b, 268, 395a, 523b.

[36] The balance for the year August 22, 1493, to August 22, 1494, was
£524; for the year August 22, 1506, to August 22, 1507, £6382. The
accounts of the Treasurer of Calais are found in *Accounts, Exch., Queen's
Remembrancer*, bundles 200, 201, 202; and in *Duchy of Lancaster, Accounts
Various*, bundle 2. The accounts of the Mayor and Fellowship of the
Staple of Calais are enrolled in the *Foreign Roll*, 119, and some originals
are preserved in *Accounts, Exch., Queen's Remembrancer*, bundle 201.

G

customs and customs subsidies, and the old formal revenues collected by the sheriffs, and the expenditures of the Household and Wardrobe, which were audited by the Exchequer of Account, Henry VII did not concern himself. But the state of his revenues in the Exchequer of Receipt, the Treasury of the Chamber, the Court of General Surveyors and the Duchy of Lancaster he knew intimately from his personal examination of their account books, and from the Declarations which were submitted to him each year as supreme financial minister.[37] Under his personal view were brought also the accounts of the Chamberlain of Berwick, and of the Treasurer of Calais.[38] In connection with the accounts of these two officials, who accounted to the king personally in detail for certain revenues and expenditures, a new form and method of accounting developed, applied later especially to the accounts of expenditures. Here is the origin of the Declared Account, long most important in English government finance. The first Declared Account is the *Status sive Declaratio Compoti* of the Treasurer of Calais for the year 1493-1494. The Exchequer *Compotus* was written on parchment, the new declaration of account was written on paper; the *Compotus* was a summary of the account prepared by an Exchequer auditor from a schedule drawn up by the accountant himself, the new declaration was made up by new officials, the King's auditors, from the accountant's original books; the *Compotus* was presented to the Barons of the Exchequer to secure a *quietus* or discharge for the accountant, while the declaration was "declared" before the king, either in person or dele-

[37] In addition to the Declaration of the State of the Treasury made by the Exchequer of Receipt, the Declarations of the General Surveyors, and the account books of the Treasurer of the Chamber, there were Declarations of the Duchy of Lancaster. These begin in the year 1505-1506, the same year in which the first preserved Exchequer Declaration was made (*Duchy of Lancaster, Accounts Various*, 23/14, 15, 16, 17). Like so many other account books, those of the Receiver-General of the Duchy, on which the Declarations of the Duchy were based, were personally examined and signed by the King (*Duchy of Lancaster, Accounts Various*, 6/1).

[38] The Chamberlain of Berwick ceased to account in the Exchequer after 1491; the Treasurer of Calais after 1492, when the last entry in the Foreign Roll, and the last *Compotus* of his accounts in the Exchequer are found.

gate in order that the accountant might have his acquittance.[38]

By the new institutions and methods which were developed in the course of his reign, Henry VII completely broke away from the medieval financial system, and laid the foundations for the more modern English revenue system, which was to be more completely perfected by his immediate successors, who merely elaborated on his ideas.

[38] For the reign of Henry VII the evidence for the declarations of account, or declared accounts as they became known at a later period, is rather scanty, since most of the preserved declarations and original account books of the reign are without distinguishing marks. In one case, however, the account books of Hugh Conway, Treasurer of Calais, for the year 1506-1507, are endorsed as delivered to John Clerk and Robert Cliff, the "King's auditors." Neither Clerk nor Cliff were Exchequer auditors. The declaration made from these books is signed "examinata per me, Robertum Cliff." See *Accounts, Exch., Queen's Remembrancer*, 202/6, 7, 13, 14. Some of the preserved declarations are annotated in a hand which may be the King's, and one of them has the following note,— "*lc cu dno Reg, lc cu J. Heron*" (lecta cum domino Rege, lecta cum J. Heron). *Accounts, Exch., Queen's Remembrancer*, 201/20. The method of accounting indicated by these scraps of material is exactly the same as the one which was used all through Henry VIII's reign for these new accounts. The declaration of account became the normal way of accounting for all special funds and expenditures. The particulars were examined and the formal declaration drawn up in three copies by special auditors, the king's auditors or auditors of the prests and foreign accounts. At first without much organization, in 1560 they were constituted the audit office and annexed to the exchequer. The Declaration drawn up by the auditors was presented to the king in person or in commission for approval and acceptance. A signed and sealed copy was given to the accountant as his acquittance, and the two other copies were preserved by the auditors. The later distinction between Pipe office and Audit office copies was not made.

CHAPTER VII

THE VALUE OF HENRY VII'S REVENUES

The construction of the new financial system, with the increase of the revenues and the reorganization of the treasury department was a work which occupied practically the whole of Henry VII's reign. His first Parliament began the great resumptions and confiscations; the work of Empson and Dudley was still proceeding at his death. But as early as 1490 there were indications in the cessation of short-time loans by the government, that the crown income was meeting normal expenditures, while a balance of over £5,000 in the hands of the Treasurer of the Chamber on September 30, 1489,[1] as the surplus of his receipts over his disbursements for the last two years suggests an even greater improvement. For this there is ample evidence after the end of the French war in 1492. Income began to exceed necessary expenditure to such an extent that the king was able to spend large sums on plate and jewels, and new buildings and palaces.[2] He was even beginning to create a surplus, as is evidenced by his ability to send £14,000 to Ireland for wages of soldiers between December 1494 and October 1496, apparently without difficulty.

But it was only after the time of the Scotch war in 1496 that

[1] The exact sum was £5,739 17s. 2d. *Accounts, Exch., Queen's Remembrancer*, 413/2, I.

[2] In 1492 he spent £5,325 on jewels, of which £4,875 went for cloth of gold, jewels and pearls for a ''harness'' in preparation for his voyage to Calais; in 1493 he spent £1,813 and in 1495, £4,853 for jewels and plate. In 1494 he began building at Woodstock and at Shene. Between January 22, 1494 and Michaelmas 1496 he had spent £5,329 19s. 2d. at Shene and Woodstock and £666 13s. 4d. at St. George's Chapel and Windsor Castle. *Add. Mss.*, 7099, Craven Ord's transcript of the payments of the Treasurer of the Chamber. The original books for the years 1492 to 1495 are missing.

78

any very considerable surplus treasure seems to have been accumulated. The king was unable, for instance, to meet the large initial expenditures of both the French and Scotch wars; and was compelled to borrow large sums from his subjects for the purpose.[3] Moreover, not once before 1497 is any mention made in any ambassador's report of Henry VII's wealth. Such notices are found, however, after the successful ending of the Scotch war in 1497. In September, 1497, Raimondo de Soncino, the Milanese ambassador in London wrote that the kingdom was perfectly stable on account of the king's wisdom and "secondly on account of the king's wealth, for I am informed that he has upwards of six millions of gold and it is said that he puts by annually five hundred thousand ducats."[4] In the following month, he again referred to Henry VII's wealth as one of the things which made him secure against fortune.[5] In reading Soncino's rather exuberant figures, however, the prothonotary de Ayala's comment should be borne in mind, "that the King of England is less rich than is generally said. He likes to be thought rich, because such a belief is advantageous to him in many respects."[6] But a year later, even de Ayala was enthusiastic about Henry VII's wealth. "His riches augment every day. I think he has no equal in this respect."[7] The evidence of the ambassadors regarding Henry VII's increasing wealth

[3] To meet the costs of an expedition to France perhaps £13,907 was borrowed and repaid. An example of the letter requesting the loan will be found in the *Reports of the Historical Mss., Commission, Report XII, App. 4, Papers of the Duke of Rutland*, p. 13. Records of repayment are found in the Treasurer of the Chamber's accounts, *Add. Mss.*, 7099. In 1496 privy seals for loans to the amount of £40,000 were issued from the chancery. Many of these cancelled privy seals, which were both a request for the loan and a receipt for repayment are preservd in the Public Record Office, *Exchequer, Treasury of Receipt, Privy Seals for Loans*, Bundles 2, 3. Calendared and printed examples are found in the *Reports of the Historical Mss., Commission, Various Collections*, I, p. 224, no. 109; *ibid., Report III, App.*, p. 420; R. I. Woodhouse, *Life of John Morton*, Appendix.

[4] *Venetian Calendar*, I, 751.

[5] *Milanese Calendar*, I, 548.

[6] *Spanish Calendar*, I, 210, a letter of de Ayala, July 25, 1498.

[7] *Spanish Calendar*, I, 239. Other notices of Henry VII's wealth are found in *Milanese Calendar*, I, 618, May, 1499; *Spanish Calendar*, I, 204, July, 1498; *ibid.*, 511, April, 1507; *Venetian Calendar*, I, 942, May, 1509.

is borne out and their guesses regarding his accumulated treasure are corrected by a study of the absolute figures of the revenues themselves.

The total receipts of the Exchequer, apart from the extraordinary subsidies, benevolences and loans varied between £32,000 a year at the beginning of the reign, and £48,000 a year at the end of the reign. In the year Michaelmas 1505 to Michaelmas 1506, an average year at the close of the reign, the Exchequer receipts were made up :[8]   . . .

Customs dues and subsides of wool, wool-fels and leather -	£27,597
Land revenues and fee farms	6,918
Sheriffs' profers, and issues and remains of accounts of sheriffs, bailiffs and escheators	6,009
Hanaper of Chancery, fees for affixing the great and privy seals	1,511[9]
Fines in the king's courts and forfeited bonds	988
Goods and merchandise confiscated in the ports for breach of customs regulations	893
Unexpended balance, returned from the Wardrobe assignment or appropriation	514
Arrears of subsidies	344
Farm of the ulnage	323
Profits of the mint	142[10]
Vacation of Abbeys	120
Fines for license of concord	63
Miscellaneous	114

The disbursements of the Exchequer were distributed over a variety of items. About one-fourth of the Exchequer revenue was assigned or appropriated by act of Parliament for the expenses of the royal household. The other payments met the expenses of the royal wardrobe; the fees and annuities of the great officials of state; the wages of the yeomen of the guard,

[8] *Lansdowne, Mss.*, 156, f. 124, the Under-Treasurer's declaration of the State of the Treasury, 1505-1506.

[9] The profits of the Hanaper fluctuated greatly. They were as high as £1,564 in the first year of the reign and as low as £284 in the tenth year (*Accounts, Exchequer, Queen's Remembrancer*, 217/4; 218/2, 6, 7; 219/1; *Accounts, Exchequer, Lord Treasurer's Remembrancer, Foreign Roll*, 119).

[10] The profits from the mint were small, never more than £200 a year during the reign. The mint accounts are found in *Exchequer, Lord Treasurer's Remembrancer, Foreign Roll*, 119, and *Accounts, Exchequer, Queen's Remembrancer*, bundle 295.

yeomen of the crown, heralds and sergeants-at-arms; the rewards to the sheriffs and collectors of customs and other charges, in a word, the general expenses of the administration of the government. The unexpended balance, about one-third of the Exchequer revenue in the last years of the reign, was paid over to the Treasurer of the Chamber. During the year Michaelmas 1505 to Michaelmas 1506 the Exchequer disbursements were:[11]

Expenses of Household	£13,059
Expenses of Wardrobe	1,395
Annuities and fees of divers lords, knights and others, officials of the state	1,354
Wages of the yeomen of the guard	1,200
Wages of heralds and pursuivants	66
Obligations to ecclesiastical persons	86
Wages of the yeomen of the crown	131
Wages of the sergeants at arms	142
Wages of the surveyor of the Ordnance and his clerks	88
Rewards to sheriffs	1,555
Rewards to collectors of customs	2,762
Other rewards	740
Payment of messengers	1
Payments for special causes, by the king's warrant	693
Wages for the Master of Works and the expenses of his office	333
Restitution of desperate tallies	263
Fees of the officers of the Exchequer of Account	753
Fees of the officers of the Exchequer of Receipt	480
Fee of the Keeper of the Privy Seal	365
The Duke of York, for keeping the East and Middle Marches against Scotland	1,000
Wages and allowances of ambassadors	2,000
Paid by assignment of tallies to the Treasurer of the Chamber	15,438

Since the greater part of the new or increased revenues were paid, not at the Exchequer, but to the Treasurer of the Chamber, the increase in the business of his office is much greater than that of the Exchequer. While the Exchequer revenues increased by fifty per cent during the reign, his augmented perhaps ten fold between 1487 and 1505.

His total receipts were:[12]

July 4		1487	to September 1	1487	£ 10,491

[11] *Lansdowne Mss.*, 156, f. 124.

[12] *Accounts, Exchequer, Queen's Remembrancer*, 413/2, I, II, III; 414/6; *Add. Mss.*, 21480, account books of the Treasurer of the Chamber.

September 1	1487	to	September 26	1488	10,811
September 26	1488	to	Michaelmas	1498	15,288
Michaelmas	1489	to	Michaelmas	1490	12,942
Michaelmas	1490	to	Michaelmas	1491	8,164
Michaelmas	1491	to	August 25	1492	14,693
August 25	1492	to	October 10	1493	14,716
October 10	1493	to	Michaelmas	1494	31,270 [13]
Michaelmas	1494	to	Michaelmas	1495	38,320
Michaelmas	1495	to	Michaelmas	1497	107,973
Michaelmas	1502	to	Michaelmas	1503	96,498
Michaelmas	1503	to	Michaelmas	1504	86,973
Michaelmas	1504	to	Michaelmas	1505	131,141

Many of the individual items which made up the receipts of the Treasurer of the Chamber and contributed to the total increase, by their greater productivity, have already been studied. An analysis of the receipts of the Treasurer of the Chamber for a single year will bring out still more clearly the relative importance of each of these. Further, certain reduplications, where the revenues are entered among both the Exchequer receipts and the receipts of the Treasurer of the Chamber can be checked, so that an accurate total can be arrived at. The receipts of the year Michaelmas 1504 to Michaelmas 1505 were as follows:[14]

I. Landed Revenues, Revenues of crown estates and ward's lands in the king's hands £32,630
   Vacation of bishoprics and abbeys, for the restitution of temporalities and licenses of free election — 5,339
   Sale of wardships — 765
   Woodsale from the king's lands — 115
   Fines for livery of lands — 268
   Licenses for mortization of land — 100
   Assignment on the Duchy of Lancaster for the Prince of Wales' household — 666
II. Clerical and Lay Subsdies, Arrears of Subsidies — 305

[13] In this year, 40,938 crowns from the first three payments of the French pension were receivevd by the Treasurer of the Chamber. French crowns were received in many of the following years by the Treasurer, but were not entered into his account because they formed ''no perfect sum.''

[14] *Add. Mss.* No. 21480.

Clerical subsidy granted in Yorkshire	677
The aid granted by Parliament in 1504	25,311

III. Cerain payments for ambassadors, the king's works, and the keeping of the Scottish marches are noted among the Exchequer disbursements. In practice the Treasurer of the Chamber advanced the money for these purposes to the men entitled to receive it, and the under-Treasurer of the Exchequer made repayment to him, instead of paying directly. In this way the Treasurer of the Chamber received £3,353

The Treasurer of the Chamber also advanced ready money to the Cofferer of the Household, averaging about £1,000 per month. This, being repaid, was accounted as "receipts." For the year there was thus repaid, and included in the income of the year £12,728

IV.	The payments from the Exchequer	13,273 [15]
V.	Payments by obligations and recognizances for causes not stated	21,565
VI.	Miscellaneous receipts, fines for hunting, riots, negligence in office	1,514
	Fines "for not being made knights of the Bath"	1,125
	"Marriage money" from the king of Spain	1,000
	Repayment to the king of money borrowed from him	900
	Payment of debts owing to the king	862
	Surplus of Berwick	685
	Surplus of the Treasurer of Calais and arrears of revenue administered by him	622

[15] The treasurer of the chamber made no note of these large payments of the Exchequer balance to him as coming from the Exchequer. They were all made by assignment of tallies; that is the Exchequer issued the tallies to the Treasurer of the Chamber, and he collected the money from the accountants. With the aid of the Exchequer account books, it is found that they comprised and are noted in the books of the Treasurer of the Chamber as:-

The surplus of the Staple at Calais from the wool subsidy collected by them, after the garrison and other charges had been paid	£ 4,757
Custom dues, chiefly from Southhampton, Exeter and Dartmouth	6,716
The profits of the Hanaper of Chancery	1,211
The profits of the mint	153
The profits of the sale of victuals to the garrison at Calais	270
The farm of the exchange	166

Licenses for the export of tin and wheat
and the import of wine   597
Sale of offices   125
Pardon, and confirmation of liberties to cor-
porations   66
Other miscellaneous receipts   2,234

The disbursements of the Treasurer of the Chamber were most varied, consisting chiefly of such payments as more intimately concerned the king and his court, rather than the civil administration, as did the Exchequer payments. The Treasurer of the Chamber paid the wages of servants attached to the court itself, notably the yeomen of the chamber, the musicians and minstrels. He purchased rich cloths and stuffs, perhaps for purposes outside the domain of the wardrobe; he rewarded ambassadors, paid out the king's weekly alms and offerings in church and provided the exhibitions or scholarships of the king's scholars at Oxford. Payments for these items constituted the regular charges of the Treasurer of the Chamber, and at times when no great payments by the king's special command were made, these charges varied from £9 5s. 9d. to £280 3s. 0d. a week. For the sixth year of the reign the king's ordinary charges of this sort, including the payment of "Espies" were only £4,029 6s. 79.; but this increased as the reign went on.[16]

But the ordinary charges formed but a very small part of the total disbursements of the Treasurer of the Chamber, as will be apparent from a table showing these totals:[17]

Michaelmas	1495	to	Michaelmas	1496	£25,707
,,	1496	to	,,	1497	73,366 [18]
,,	1497	to	,,	1498	42,302
,,	1498	to	,,	1499	32,836
,,	1499	to	,,	1500	46,183
,,	1500	to	,,	1501	52,934
,,	1501	to	,,	1502	81,252

[16] As an example of the rate of increase of these ordinary charges, the wages of servants and musicians of the court can be taken. In the sixth year, just instanced, these wages were £1,296; but in the years after 1505, they had been increased to £1,884 a year.

[17] *Accounts, Exchequer, Queen's Remembrancer*, 414/6; 414/16; *Add. Mss.*, No. 21480.

[18] This is the year of the Scotch war, and the amount includes the war expenditures.

''	1502	to	''	1503	90,327
''	1503	to	''	1504	79,408
''	1504	to	''	1505	169,003 [19]
''	1505	to	''	1506	124,358
''	1506	to	''	1507	66,046
''	1507	to	''	1508	54,657
''	1508	to	''	1509	132,643

A part of these great sums represents money paid for the wages of soldiers in Ireland and against Scotland; for the upkeep of the navy and the erection of new palaces and buildings for the king's use. The remainder may be considered as invested in jewels and in loans. Henry VII purchased jewels and plate on a very lavish scale, in all probability as a form of saving, just as Indian princes of the present day do. Between December 24, 1491 and the end of the reign, at least £128,441 was spent for jewels; while the crowns received in payment of the French pension were sometimes at least used for a similar purpose.[20] Much money was also invested in loans. The Archduke Philip and his son Charles borrowed a total of at least £260,000.[21] A very great deal was lent to English merchants and to Italian merchants in England. Such loans were unimportant and small before 1505, not above £3,400 a year; but from Michaelmas 1505 to Michaelmas 1509 £87,600 were loaned in this way.[22] The loan was generally secured by English noblemen, and the bond provided that if the loan were not repaid promptly on two months' notice, a penalty should be paid. Though no interest was exacted, it was often provided that the loan which had been made in silver should be repaid in gold. But more generally the borrower bound himself to import into England enough goods to pay a certain amount in customs dues, each year as long as the loan stood.[23]

[19] In this year £138,000 were loaned to the "Prince of Spain."

[20] On one occasion the gold crowns were turned over to the king's goldsmith to be made into a gold chain; and on another they were "sent to Paris in France to buy plate for the king's household." (*Add. Mss.*, No. 21480 f. 180; *Accounts, Exchequer, Queen's Remembrancer*, 414/6, March 1497).

[21] Add. Mss., 21480; *Exchequer, Treasury of Receipt, Miscellaneous Books*, 214.

[22] *Accounts, Exchequer, Queen's Remembrancer*, 415/3, 414/16; *Exchequer, Treasury of Receipt, Miscellaneous Books*, 214.

[23] This practice was followed by Henry VIII in the early years of his reign, on an even larger scale.

In addition to the revenues received and expended by the Exchequer and the Treasurer of the Chamber, there were certain not unimportant sums collected and expended locally, in the most outlying parts of the kingdom, by the Chamberlain of Berwick and the Treasurer of Calais for the charges of the government and garrisons there. At Berwick these sums averaged something over £2,000 a year, collected from land rents and the customs dues of Newcastle and Hull. At Calais, the Treasurer of Calais received from the Society of the Staple for the wool subsidy and from the rents of certain lands in the town, the octroi dues and the profits made on the victuals sold to the garrison, an average of £13,200 a year. His expenditures were always well within his receipts, by sums ranging from £524 in 1492 to £6,382 in 1507.[24] The unexpended balance was turned over to the Treasurer of the Chamber and has already been included in the receipts of his office, but account must be taken of the sums expended at Berwick and Calais in totals of income and disbursements of the government.

During the first few years of the reign the total receipts of the crown from all regularly recurring sources, received at the Exchequer, Berwick and Calais were about £52,000 a year, and the expenditures were so much greater that it was necessary to resort to subsidies and loans. During the last five years of the reign, the receipts averaged £142,000 a year, receivd at the Exchequer, the Treasury of the Chamber, Berwick and Calais, all duplications eliminated. The entire expenditures, including the heavy investments in loans and jewels averaged £138,000 a year.

At Henry VII's death it was believed that as a result of his financial measures £1,800,000 in gold and silver was found in his coffers.[25] Falier, the Venetian ambassador reporting to the Venetian senate in 1531 spoke of the treasure of Henry VII

[24] The accounts of the Chamberlain of Berwick and of the Treasurer of Calais are enrolled in the *Foreign Roll* (*Exch., Lord Treasurer's Remembrancer, Foreign Roll,* 119) and are found in the original in accounts, *Exch., Queen's Remembrancer,* bunbles 200, 201, 202 and in *Duchy of Lancaster, Accounts Various,* bundle 2.

[25] Bacon, *Henry VII,* 210. Bacon, it is to be noted gives the statement cautiously, on the authority of "tradition."

as six millions of gold, that is, about £1,300,000.[26] Sanuto, commenting on Henry VII's death wrote in his diary that "he had accumulated so much gold that he is supposed to have more than well nigh all the other kings of Christendom."[27] That Henry VII had accumulated a surplus, which if not as great, was comparable to that credited to him by report, is shown by Henry VII's lavish expenditure of his father's savings in the first period of his reign. But that this surplus was in the form of gold stored up in great chests is contrary to all evidence. The new revenues, and the unexpended balances of the Exchequer, of the Treasurer of Calais, of the Society of the Staple and of the Chamberlain of Berwick, together with the French pensions and the later subsidies were turned over to the Treasurer of the Chamber. His disbursements were only slightly less than his receipts in all the years for which there is a record of both, and the same was probably true in other years. As late as 1505 he had on hand in money, as the excess of receipts over expenditures up to that time, only £22,729.[28] Among his disbursements are included no large sums of money turned over to the king to be stored up by him in his private coffers. On the other hand, a great proportion of the Treasurer of the Chamber's disbursements had been for jewels, plate and loans, while great sums were owing to the crown for many causes in the form of obligations and recognizances. It was these jewels, plate and bonds of various sorts which made up the bulk of the wealth left by Henry VII to his son.

---

[26] *Venetian Calendar*, IV, 694.

[27] *Venetian Calendar*, I, 942, Sanuto's note on the death of Henry VII.

[28] *Accounts, Exchequer, Queen's Remembrancer*, 413/2, III, f. 120. The note is made at the close of business for the year ending Michaelmas 1505.

CHAPTER VIII

WOLSEY AND NATIONAL FINANCE

With the customs, and the customs subsidies of tonnage and poundage and of wool, wool fells and leather granted to Henry VIII in his first Parliament for life, the vacations of bishoprics, marriages and wardships and the income from the crown lands, together with the wealth inherited from his father, Henry VIII was well fitted to meet financial demands made upon him.

The ordinary payments of the Treasurer of the Chamber continued to be much the same as they had been during the last years of Henry VII's reign. The extraordinary payments which Henry VII had ordered each year for buildings, loans and the purchase of jewels almost ceased; so that the disbursements of John Heron actually decreased to £156,000 for the first three years of the reign.[1] This sum included the expenses of the father's funeral, and the son's coronation, and even £37,000 paid to the old king's executors for carrying out his will. A close study of the Treasurer of the Chamber's payments for a greater number of years gives several indications that the frugality which marked Henry VII's court gradually gave way to slightly greater luxuriousness. This is seen for example in the increase in the number of servants attached to the court. At the very beginning of the new reign, the wages of the royal musicians, minstrels, yeomen of the chamber and falconers came to £2,500 a year. The employment of additional servants and the institution of the king's spears of honor, increased the wage charge to over £5,000 a year, early in 1510. Cloth of gold, purple velvet, russet and "tylsent" satin, rich sables and other furs, gold embroidery, spangles and beads were purchased from Italian merchants in much larger quantities than had ever been

[1] *Letters and Papers,* II, pp. 1441-1480, book of the Treasurer of the Chamber, April 22, 1509 to January 1, 1512.

the case in Henry VII's time. The wages and diets of ambassadors and the number of embassies sent abroad showed a considerable increase. Before 1509, the yearly costs of the household scarcely exceeded the £13,059 assigned for that purpose by Parliament.[2] Henry VIII's first Parliament increased the household assignment to £19,394.[3] For a few years this sum was more than sufficient to cover the household expenses, which comprised the costs of food for the tables of the king and court, and the wages of the cooks and other servants, and officials of the household. During the first five years of the reign, more than £3,000 of this assignment was returned each year to the Exchequer unspent; then for a few years, the expenditures about equalled the assignment. In the year 1520-1521 the assignment was no longer large enough, and the Treasurer of the Chamber began to contribute augmenting sums to make up the deficit.[4] This may have been due in part to the rise in prices; but it was chiefly due during the earlier part of the reign, to the increase in the number of servants and officials who lived at the court, and were fed in the household. The rise in prices did not begin seriously to affect the royal household until the end of the decade of the 1530's, when the expenditures rose from less than £25,000 a year in 1538-1539 and previous years, to £45,700 a year in 1545-1546.[5] Wardrobe expenditures also increased.

Concurrently with the increased expenditures for ordinary purposes there was a decrease in receipts. In the Exchequer, the customs revenues showed a slight diminution after 1516. In the office of the Treasurer of the Chamber, £2,535 a year was lost by the restoration of lands by act of Parliament, to their former owners, and £7,585 by grants of land by the king by letters patent to his favorites. These losses, together with the increased assignments for the household on the royal lands, and new fees, wages and annuities, rendered the clear yearly land revenues payable to the Treasurer of the Chamber £24,719 smaller in 1515 than they had been in 1508,[6] and reduced the income received by the Treasurer of the Chamber from the lands

2 *Exch. L. T. R., Wardrobe Enrolled Accounts*, roll 8, membranes 1-26.
3 *Statutes of the Realm*, 1 Henry VIII, c. 16.
4 *Exch. L. T. R., Wardrobe Enrolled Accounts*, roll 8, membrane 32 b. ff.
5 *Ibid.*, membranes 43-47 inc.
6 *Rentals and Surveys*, no. 837.

and revenues in the survey of the General Surveyors and the Duchy of Lancaster to £16,367 a year.[7]

The decreases in revenue through the decline in the customs, and the alienations of the crown lands, with the increase in expenditures, especially in the household, were important. On the other hand, Henry VII's revenues had far exceeded his real expenditures, and as the increases in expenditure made by Henry VIII were comparatively small, and in no way show undue luxury or extravagance on the part of the king or court, it seems that the crown resources, the yearly revenue and the surplus left by Henry VII would have been sufficient for many years to meet the needs of the government, had no extraordinary drains been made upon them.

In view of this fact a brief analysis of the expenditures of the Treasurer of the Chamber during the early years of the reign is enlightening.

	Total expenditures of the Treasurer of the Chamber	Paid for wages of soldiers and sailors, and for purchase of ships, victuals and ordnance	Paid as subventions and aid to foreign governments and princes
1509	£ 65,097	£ 1,231	
1510	26,725	1,775	
1511	64,157	1,509	
1512	269,564	181,468	
1513	699,714	632,322 + 10,040 crowns	£14,000 lent to the Emperor
1514	155,757	92,000	
1515	74,006	10,000	
1516	106,429	16,538	38,500 subsidy to the Emperor
1517	72,359	60	13,333 loaned to Charles V
1518	50,614	200	
1519	52,428		
1520	86,030		

[7] *Rot. Reg.* 14 B. XI. This is an account for the year ending Michaelmas 1515.

[8] *Letters and Papers*, II, pp. 1441-1480; *ibid.*, III, 2750; Add. Mss., 21481 and *Exch., Treasury Receipt, Misc. Books*, 215.

This table shows how insignificant were all the ordinary payments — not to speak of increases in those payments — of the most important financial official of the government compared with expenditures for war and foreign affairs. From the beginning of his reign, Henry VIII was eager to play an important part in the politics of Europe. Already in November 1511 he was at war with France as the paladin of the church, and the ally of Ferdinand of Aragon in causes in which England had no interest.[9] It was by his active foreign policy and his participation in two wars with France[10] which were not thrust upon him, but which he espoused with the enthusiasm of a reckless boy, that the financial situation was first made acute, and the revenue system as perfected by Henry VII rendered inadequate.

In the three and one-half years between the spring of 1511, when a small expeditionary force was sent to Guelderland and the fall of 1514 £892,000 had been paid for the wages and provisioning of the army, and navy and the purchase of ordnance and military stores.[11] Aids and subsidies to the Emperor took 32,000 golden florins in 1512, and at least £14,000 in 1513. After the accession of Francis I to the French throne, Wolsey continued these subsidies to the imperial cause, as an effective means of checking the pretensions of the French king, and of quieting

[9] Fisher, *Political History of England, 1485-1547*, 170-171, ''Henry had no direct interest either in Italy or in Navarre; and it was nothing to England that a papal legate should rule in Bologna, . . But from the first Henry had been jealous of the French victories. . . The young theologian was on his mettle.''

[10] The first war with France continued from 1511 to 1514, and the second war with France from 1522 to 1525.

[11] For the expedition of the Marquis of Dorset to Guienne, of 10,000 men assisted by 3,070 men in 18 ships under Lord Howard, £173,057 was appropriated; of which £34,394 was not expended (*Letters and Papers*, I, 3496, 3762). The expeditions of 1513 against France and Scotland required between November 1, 1512 and December 31, 1513, £607,000 for the army to France, £16,500 for the army against Scotland, £10,000 for ordnance and £28,500 for the purchase of ships (*Letters and Papers*, II, pp. 1441-1480 ; *Accounts, Exchequer, Queen's Remembrancer*, 56/26-27 ; *Letters and Papers*, I, 4533 ; II, 54, 254, 2123 ; IV, 5724 ; *Accounts, Exchequer, Treasury of Receipt Misc. Books*, 2 ; *State Papers, Henry VIII* §5, 114-120). The preparations for the year 1514 and the payment of the bills of the past year took another £92,000 (*Letters and papers*, pp. 1463-1466).

the war spirit at home.[12] In the form of payments to Swiss mercenaries, and of loans to Maximilian and his grandson, Charles, probably £80,000 was advanced in 1515 and 1516.[13] Fatuously enough, too, Henry VIII had insisted in the treaty of 1514 upon the retention of Tournai in France, conquered by himself in 1513; and Tournai absorbed £40,000 a year every year between 1514 and 1518, when Wolsey surrendered the town to Francis I.[14]

After the shameful failure of Dorset's expedition to Guienne in 1512, Wolsey took personal charge of the direction of the war, including its finances. The money appropriated to war purposes was turned over by the Treasurer of the Chamber to John Daunce, John Dawtry and other treasurers of war. They came to Wolsey for instructions how to act,[15] and paid out money on his warrants, which he issued for the payment of bills after he had personally examined them and found them correct.[16] While thus carefully watching expenditure, the problem of obtaining revenues received his careful attention, as memoranda in his hand show.[17] His activity drew from Bishop Fox, at the time of Fox's resignation from the council in 1516 the tribute "more diligence and labor for the king's rights, duties and profits . . be in you than ever I see in times past in any other."[18]

[12] Brown, *Dispatches*, I, 100, 105, 110, 154, 155; *Venetian Calendar*, II, 706.

[13] *Letters and Papers*, II, 2404. This is Wolsey's own estimate of the sum.

[14] The garrison required 1500 men, at a cost of £21,120 a year (*Letters and Papers*, II, 1122; p. 1513; 4429). The repair of the fortifications took from £17,968 to £20,298 a year (*Letters and Papers*, II, 3065; III, 153; II, 4041; 4429; II, App. 45).

[15] *Letters and Papers*, I, 5755.

[16] Many of Wolsey's warrants are found in *Exch., Queen's Remembrancer*, 56/10. A typical one is written on the bill itself — "Fellow Master Daunce, the king's pleasure is that ye content and pay the parcells above written to Gunston or to the bringer thereof, T. Lincoln." (*Exch., Queen's Remembrancer*, 56/10 206). See also *Letters and Papers*, I, 5758, 5764, 5776, 5778 ; *State Papers, Henry VIII*, §27, p. 78 ; *Accounts, Exch., Queen's Remembrancer*, 58/7, 56/14.

[17] *Letters and Papers*, I, 3884.

[18] *Letters and Papers*, II, 1814.

The nation in Parliament was asked to contribute its share of the war expenses, which it did in three fifteenths and tenths and a poll tax of 1512, and the unsatisfactory grants of 1514 and 1515.[19] The nation paid these taxes "unwillingly with extreme complaint;"[20] but even so, their total yield was less than a third of the war and post war charges. Of these the greatest part was paid from the King's inherited wealth, upon which such drains were made that it seems to have been entirely used up in the process.[21] So depleted were the funds in the hands of the Treasurer of the Chamber who was keeper of the surplus, that in 1521, Mr. Myklowe, then Treasurer of the Chamber was reported as being "compelled to borrow money for his servants' wages."[22]

With the exhaustion of the surplus, the second war with France was begun in 1522 under more unfavorable circumstances than the first. As there was no money in the king's coffers to pay its charges, the nation was called upon to meet them in their entirety. The fact that Parliamentary taxation was a slow method of raising funds which were needed immediately, and not very productive at best, probably determined Wolsey to secure the funds necessary for the preliminary expenses, by resorting to forced loans. In June, 1522, the king sent to the city of London to borrow £20,000. "The mayor sent for none but men of substance; Howbeit the crafts sold much of their plate, the sum was paid," and the king and the Cardinal prom-

[19] In February, 1512, 2 fifteenths and tenths were granted (*Statutes of the Realm*, 3 Henry VIII, c. 22); in November 1512, one fifteenth and tenth and a poll tax (*Statutes of the Realm*, 4 Henry VIII, c. 19); in 1514 a subsidy of £160,000 was voted (*Statutes of the Realm*, 5 Henry VIII, c. 7); and because of the failure of this, a subsidy of £110,000 was granted in February, 1515 (*Statutes of the Realm*, 6 Henry VIII, c. 26). This too was unsatisfactory; and in November, 1515, a second levy was authorized and a fifteenth and tenth granted (*Statutes of the Realm*, 7 Henry VIII, c. 9). The convocation of Canterbury granted four tenths in February, 1512, and the convocation of York, three tenths (Wilkins, *Concilia*, III, 652, 657).

[20] *Venetian Calendar*, II, 456, 798; Brown, *Dispatches*, I, 320.

[21] This is asserted in Falier's report to the Venetian Senate, *Venetian Calendar*, IV, 694.

[22] *Letters and Papers*, III, 1650, Richard Pace, the king's secretary to Wolsey.

ised repayment.[23] In August commissioners were authorized to assess loans in all the counties in England in a way which showed the levy in its true character of a tax — rather than a loan. During 1522 and 1523 £352,231 were raised by forced loans,[24] but this amount had fallen £42,000[25] short of the money required for the military undertakings, the fruitless expedition of the Earl of Surrey into Picardy in 1522, and the invasion of France by the Duke of Suffolk, and the raids on the Scotch border under Surrey in 1523.

Meanwhile, the convocations of York and Canterbury had met in the spring of 1523, and made the unprecedented grant of one-half the value of one year's income of all benifices to be paid in five years.[26] Parliament had assembled too. For the purposes of the loan of 1522 Wolsey had had a careful assessment of men's wealth made. He now asked for a grant of £800,000 which would be realized, on the basis of the assessment of 1522 by a tax of four shillings in the pound. After the bitterest debate, and a threatening visit by Wolsey in state to the Commons' House, a smaller subsidy than was asked, was granted. In the country at large there were mutterings against the grant as soon as it was known, and resentment when the commissioners came to levy the tax.[27] Since the first payment of the new tax was not due until the spring of 1524 and the new forced loans in anticipation of the subsidy, in the autumn of 1523 (when the treasury was empty)[28] were a failure, England abstained from active operations during 1524, and contented herself with subsidizing the Duke of Bourbon with a second 100,000 crowns.[29]

During the past few years the tax-paying classes of the nation

[23] Hall, *Chronicle*, I, 258.

[24] *Letters and Papers*, IV, 214, 417. See also *Letters and Papers*, IV, App. 37 and III, 2483.

[25] This sum was paid out by the Treasurer of the Chamber for war purposes to make good the deficits (*Letters and Papers*, III, 2750).

[26] Wilkins *Concilia*, III, 698, 699.

[27] *Letters and Papers*, III, 3082; IV, 377; IV, App. 6.

[28] *Letters and Papers*, III, 3433, a letter from Wolsey to Henry VIII. Wolsey needed £10,000 to complete the next payment to Suffolk's army in France. "He has used all pains to bring in whatsoever is leviable that more cannot be done."

[29] *Letters and Papers*, IV, 365, 510. The first 100,000 crowns had been given him in 1523, *Letters and Papers*, III, 3288, 3307; IV, 510.

had contributed more largely than ever before to the support of the state and its enterprises, especially in the loans of 1522 and 1523. They had met practically the entire expenses of the campaigns of 1522 and 1523, and already in the Parliament of 1523 their discontent showed itself in opposition to further aid to the king. Their opposition hardened, until it became refusal, in 1525, when the battle of Pavia and the capture of Francis I by the Emperor led Henry VIII to decide to invade France and recover his crown of France.[30]

Pavia was fought in February, 1525. If advantage were to be taken of it, money was necessary at once. Commissioners were sent out in March and April, 1525, to raise an Amicable Grant from the laity and clergy, "to conserve the honor of the realm and recover the crown of France," the king intending a personal invasion.[31] Wolsey was chief commissioner to London. The London men refused to pay even though Wolsey threatened that resistance might cost some of them their heads.[32] At Reading the people refused one sixth of their property (the amount asked for) but granted one twelfth, to Wolsey's anger.[33] The Bishop of Lincoln found that the priests of his diocese alleged poverty, though willing to satisfy the king to the best of their ability, while the landlords of the district claimed they could get no rent from their farmers.[34] In Essex, the Earl of Essex assembled the townships before him, but could not induce them to grant any money, as they said they had not even enough to pay the subsidy. Just a few days before this, a thousand persons had assembled in the borders of Suffolk, near the town in which the Earl was holding his sessions; which caused even those who would have been willing to pay, to refuse to do so, for fear of being hewn to pieces.[35] In Kent, Archbishop Warham warned Wolsey when the commissions were first sent out that it would be hard to raise money at this time, especially as the

[30] *Letters and Papers*, IV, 1212, Henry's assertion of his intentions.

[31] *Letters and Papers*, IV, 1200, 1284, App. 34.

[32] Hall, *Chronicles*, II, 36.

[33] Hall, *Chronicle*, II, 36.

[34] *Letters and Papers*, IV, 1330, a letter to the Bishop of Lincoln, May 12, 1525.

[35] *Ibid.*, IV, 1321, a letter of the Earl of Essex to Wolsey, May 9, 1525.

other parliamentary grants were now payable, and reported to him the dissatisfaction prevailing among the people. They spoke " 'cursedly' saying that they shall never have rest of payments so long as some liveth." Some of the commissioners merely announced the king's command without pressing it; the promise that the money would be repaid was discredited because the promise made in regard to the former loan had never been kept; the people were sorry at the captivity of Francis I and no longer desired the conquest of France, since if the king won France he would be obliged to spend his time and his revenues there; and finally all the sums (so said the people) already spent in France had not gained the king more land in it than his father had, "which lacked no wisdom or riches to win the kingdom of France if he had thought it expedient." It seems that even where there was a willingness to contribute there was lack of money, and poverty, or fear of "the multitude who persecute all who comply." [36] Warham and his fellow commissioners did not show themselves at any time over enthusiastic for the loan; they do not seem to have pressed for payment and they constantly excused the people to Henry VIII and to Wolsey, saying that they seemed minded to accomplish their demands but could not, because there was great poverty.[37] In Norfolk the mayor of Norwich answered the Duke of Norfolk that although an invasion of France would be timely, they could not raise the money required, but they offered their plate. The Duke wrote that though the Norwich people behaved well there would be great difficulty

[36] *Letters and Papers*, IV, 1243, 1266, 1267, 1305, 1306, 1311, letters of Warham and other Kentish commissioners.

[37] *Ibid*. It is not known how much money was in circulation at this time in England among the people, but the per capita circulation was probably comparatively small, especially in the country. A good bit of the opposition to taxes and other payments to the government especially in 1525 was due to the real lack of money among the people. Cromwell, in 1523, estimated the coin and bullion of the realm at not over £1,000,000 and opposed the subsidy because it would bring all the money of the kingdom into the king's treasury. Perhaps this was not merely a figurative statement. The payments of 1522 and 1523 for the loans, had perhaps stripped the country of ready money, and large payments in 1525 were a physical impossibility. The Commissioners of 1525 repeatedly mentioned the scarcity of money.

in raising the money throughout the country.[38] The situation in Suffolk was complicated by lack of employment in the woolen industry in that county; and early in May the men in Suffolk, Essex and the scholars of Cambridge combined to the number of 20,000 men. The Dukes of Norfolk and Suffolk took prompt measures; the insurrection was checked at the outset; the leaders were arrested and the rest sent home.[39]

Henry VIII finally yielded to the opposition, and even though he took it "unkindly" that the commons pleaded their poverty and their lack of money so that they would not grant anything, he gave instructions by letters missive to the commissioners to proceed "doulcely" rather than by violence, to reform them if possible.[40] Wolsey now made an effort to collect a "benevolence" from the Londoners. Though the aldermen by vote of the common council urged the men in their wards to grant a benevolence, this was refused; and the aldermen and the lord mayor, when summoned into Wolsey's presence refused to name any sum which the city would give.[41]

It is worth noting that no mention was made in these years of dissatisfaction with the unparliamentary character of the king's devices for obtaining money from the people. They alleged their poverty, that is, their unwillingness, rather than any illegality of method. They were chiefly disgruntled that money was obtained from them at all. They desired not to bear the burdens of the state, which was the king's business.

When the costs of the wars with France in Henry VIII's reign, or even the costs of single campaigns in these wars be compared with the costs of wars in the fifteenth century, — for example, Henry VII's war with France in 1492, — a vast increase is found. The upward curve of war costs probably equalled, and even surpassed the accelerated increase of national wealth. But the experiences of 1522 to 1525 showed that direct

[38] *Letters and Papers*, IV, 1235, a letter of the Duke of Norfolk, April 1, 1525.

[39] *Letters and Papers*, IV, 1323, a letter of Norfolk and Suffolk to Wolsey.

[40] *Ibid.*, IV, 1318, a letter of Henry VIII to the commissioners, May 8, 1512.

[41] Hall, *Chronicles*, II, 39.

taxation, parliamentary or arbitrary, was too inelastic and too much opposed to the self-interest of the predominant classes of the state to make it possible to use taxation to divert large enough portions of the country's wealth to the government, to pay the costs of wars under modern conditions. Until taxes could be made more elastic and productive, and the prevailing popular attitude towards them changed, they were merely contributions in aid to the king in extraordinary times, so small now compared with the new extraordinary expenditures, that, contrary to the situation in the fifteenth century, but little dependence could be placed in them. If an active foreign policy continued to be followed involving the danger of war, it would soon become essential that the revenue system be radically extended.

Even in times of peace, the existing revenue system was showing occasional signs of inadequacy. There was a steady decline through the decade of the 1520's in the Exchequer revenues, while the expenditures of the government for ordinary purposes continued slowly to rise.[42] After the first war with France, there are a few indications of financial stringency, which was probably temporary.[43] In the years after the second French war, the situation was more disturbing.[44]

There was however, no serious inadequacy in the revenues for ordinary purposes as yet, and the foreign situation was not threatening. The pressure was not great enough to induce Wolsey, — the conservative reformer — perhaps even to suspect the need of any radical extension of the revenue system in the

[42] Accounts of the Exchequer and of the Treasurer of the Chamber.

[43] In 1517, Guistinian, the Venetian Ambassador wrote ''that those in authority here . . now think it prudent to husband their resources, contrary to their previous custom'' (Brown, *Dispatches*, II, 127). In 1519 it was necessary to send out letters missive to rich churchmen and nobles for loans (*Letters and Papers*, III, 562). In 1521 Pace, the king's secretary noted that the Treasury of the Chamber was empty (*Letters and Papers*, III, 1650). A little later Henry VIII wrote to the Earl of Surrey that he did pot propose to appoint a new lieutenant in Ireland with like retinue ''as ye now have,'' ''because of the expense'' (*Letters and Papers*, III, 1718).

[44] At the beginning of the year 1528 the outlook was so dark that in an estimate drawn up in January of all possible sums that might be levied, it seemed advisable to levy the unpaid portions of the loan of 1523, and to practice for the anticipation of the subsidy due in the spring.

near future. For what deficiencies there were, he trusted first to reform and retrenchment, and the removal of abuses in the existing order. In 1515 it was realized that grants of land had been made too lavishly to royal favorites; and an act of resumption of all the grants with certain exceptions was passed by Parliament.[45] In 1519 more frequent accounts by the regular treasurers were under consideration, together with the appropriation of fixed sums for various purposes and the reform of the Exchequer.[46] It was probably in connection with this reform of the Exchequer that the accounts of the wool subsidy collected at Calais by the Society of the Staple, and the accounts of the Clerk of the Hanaper ceased to be rendered there after 1519; and that many of the offices in the two branches of the Exchequer were filled with new men in 1522 and 1523.[47] Royal officials were warned at the same time to use extreme care that all the revenues and profits to which the king was rightly entitled should come to his hands.[48] In 1526 a great reformation of the household was affected by the Statutes of Eltham "which some said were more profitable than honorable." [49] Schedules of officials and servants, with their assigned wages were drawn up, the purchase of provisions was placed under the supervision of the treasurer and controller of the household; disbursements were to be entered every day and the accounts audited quarterly; superfluous servants were discharged and the number of the yeomen of the guard decreased.[50]

Wolsey also, characteristically, endeavored to turn to best advantage his master's foreign policy. From the wars themselves, and the international situation he reaped whatever financial benefits were to be gathered there for the rehabilitation of

[45] *Statutes of the Realm,* 6 Henry VIII, c. 25. These resumptions and later confiscations like those of the Duke of Buckingham's lands, worth £6,045 a year, raised the crown lands to even greater value than they had been in Henry VII's time.

[46] *Letters and Papers,* III, 576, Memorandum of the administration of king's affairs, drawn up by Wolsey; *ibid.,* III, 576 (II); IV, 5749, 5750.

[47] *Exch. of Receipt, Declarations of the State of the Treasury,* VIII, IX, X.

[48] *Letters and Papers,* II, 4547; III, 3692.

[49] Hall, *Chronicle,* I, 56-57.

[50] The Statutes of Eltham, *Letters and Papers,* IV, 1939.

the royal revenues, in the form of the pensions from France and their increase. Upon Henry VIII's accession, Louis XII had acknowledged the obligation of the French pension which Charles VIII had granted to Henry VII.[51] The old principal of 745,000 crowns was nearly all paid when the first war with France began.   In 1514, Louis XII was forced to increase the principal still owing, to one million gold crowns, to be paid at the rate of one hundred thousand francs a year, just double the former payment.[52] Beside providing revenue, the pension flattered the king. Henry VIII chose to regard it as a tribute paid to him as rightful sovereign of France, by the king in possession.[53]   In 1518 Francis I was so eager for the return of Tournai that he consented to pay 600,000 gold crowns for it, to be paid as a pension of 25,000 francs, each half year in addition to the other pension. The French indemnities were thus increased to 150,000 francs a year.[54] In 1522, as one of the conditions for securing the English alliance, Charles V was compelled to guarantee the French pensions, should they be stopped as a result of the war.[55] The humiliation of Francis I in 1525 gave Wolsey an opportunity to drive a very hard bargain with him in the Treaty of More. Francis bound himself for the payment of 2,052,631 crowns to Henry VIII. This sum represented 631,579 crowns of the unpaid portion of the 1,000,000 crowns, agreed upon in 1514; 500,000 crowns still due of the 600,000 crowns for the restoration of Tournai; 30,000 francs owing by the citizens of Tournai to Henry VIII, 462,000 crowns in repayment of a loan of 378,960 crowns which Henry VIII had made to Francis I in November, 1520, and an indemnity of 299,542 crowns for the rupture in Italy. Payment was to be made in half yearly payments of 50,000 crowns of gold or 47,368 crowns of the sun, each. If all was paid before Henry's death, the same sum was to be paid each year during the rest of his life.[56]

[51] *Letters and Papers*, I, 14, 318, 626, 1027, 1181.

[52] *Letters and Papers*, I, 5280.

[53] Brown, *Dispatches*, I, 237.

[54] *Letters and Papers*, II, 4476; III, 199

[55] *Ibid.*, III, 1508.

[56] Rymer, *Foedera* O. XIV, 58-68.

In April, 1527, there was a new opportunity to increase the pensions from France. The league of Cognac had been formed, and Francis was willing to pay high for an English alliance. The new treaties provided for the payment of a perpetual pension of 50,000 crowns of gold a year and 15,000 gold crowns worth of black salt, as a tribute in recompense of English claims to the French crown. The perpetual pension was to begin on Henry VIII's death and be paid in perpetuity to his successors; the black salt pension was granted for the term of Henry's own life. It was never paid in black salt, and was later commuted to a money payment of 10,000 crowns.[57] Wolsey's own opinion of the treaty, and his regard of its financial advantages is seen in a speech of his reported by Hall, which he made on the occasion of the peace of Amiens a few months later. "Therefore now my lords, be merry, for the king shall nevermore charge you with wars in France . . so that with exactions for wars of France you shall be no more charged, for the king shall have no need, because that he by this league shall be the richest prince of the world. For I assure you he shall have more treasure out of France yearly than all his revenues and customs amount to, yea and count his wards, forfeits and all such casualties."[58]

Finally, at Cambrai in 1529, Wolsey further increased the payments from France by persuading Francis I to assume the debts of Charles V to Henry VIII. Francis assumed these obligations of the Emperor as part consideration to the Emperor, for the release of his two sons, the Dauphin of Vienne and the Duke of Orleans, held as Hostages by Charles V.[59] But long before the treaty of Cambrai was signed, the simultaneous ap-

[57] In December, 1530, the black salt pension was converted into a money payment, with 30,000 crowns for arrears and 10,000 crowns yearly tribute (*Letters and Papers*, IV, 6755, 6775).

[58] Hall, *Chronicle*, II, 105-106.

[59] These obligations were various loans made to Charles since the beginning of the reign, with a debt of £100,000 owing by Maximilian to Henry VII, and an advance on the security of fleur de lys pawned by Maximilian with Henry VII; the indemnity for the loss of the French pensions between 1522 and 1525, and a penalty of 500,000 crowns for Charles's breaking his agreement to marry Mary (*Letters and Papers*, IV, 5881, 6231). Fancis took these obligations at an enormous discount.

pearance of the divorce question in England and the capture of Rome by Charles V, had ruined Wolsey's plan to augment the royal income by pensions from France. A French alliance was absolutely essential,[60] and for that alliance England paid, not only in remitted pension payments, but in actual cash subsidies.[61] During the years from 1531 to 1534 the payment of pensions was resumed; but after the May or November payment in 1534, Francis took advantage of the situation of England at home and abroad, on account of the divorce question, to cease payment.[62]

Wolsey was supremely great in diplomacy and very skilled in administration. He did not however, grasp the trend of the financial problem. Reforms and retrenchments temporarily relieved pressing situations; the increase of the French pensions precariously enhanced the royal income. But he did nothing which indicates that he saw that, since the small margin between income and disbursements gave the king no opportunity to save much money, and taxation could not be depended upon to provide rapidly and abundantly enough the money needed for wars or other sudden contingencies, the normal royal revenues would have to be vastly increased for the public safety, in the not far distant future. But even the greatest statesmen seldom cross bridges until they come to them.

[60] The necessity of the French Alliance is recognized in a letter of Knight to Wolsey (*Letters and Papers*, IV, 5771). See also a later statement of the recognition of the situation, in a report of Henry VIII's remarks to Chapuys, the imperial ambassador (*Ibid.*, XX, part I, 1197).

[61] Between August 18, 1527, when the Treaty of Amiens was signed, and May 1, 1529, £112,437 was paid to France; £49,148 in money, £10,000 in the form of a jewel, and £53,289 in remitted pensions (*Letters and Papers*, IV, 5515). See also *ibid.*, IV, App. 183; IV, 1604 (3).

[62] In 1531 and 1532, 15,000 crowns was paid each year for the arrears of the salt "tax;" 10,000 crowns for the commutation of the salt "tax;" 100,000 crowns for the debts of Charles V, and 94,736 crowns for the regular pension. In November, 1532, the last payment of the arrears of the pension of black salt, and the last payment for the debts of Charles V were made; so that in 1533 and 1534 the payments were reduced to 10,000 crowns for the salt "tax" commutation, and 94,736 crowns of the regular pension (*Letters and Papers*, V, 222, 1065, 1504). The November payment in 1534 is described as taking "the road of Germany to make a brewing" (*Letters and Papers*, VII, 1554, Chapuys to Charles V).

CHAPTER IX

CROMWELL'S EARLY ADMINISTRATION

Without question Cromwell's rapid rise to power was due to his services to the king in his "grete matier" of the divorce. But if we may believe one of the contemporary stories, in his first interview with Henry VIII, Cromwell promised to make him the richest king who had ever ruled in England. Henry was so struck by this promise that he at once made Cromwell a member of his council.[1] Certainly he was early interested in government finance. As early as 1531 he issued orders which show that he controlled financial officials;[2] in 1532 he began to act as a special treasurer for new revenues,[3] and from 1533 to his fall, every financial measure is noted in his remembrances, in a way indicating that he was personally occupied with planning and carrying it through. The "Remembrances" are short disjointed jottings on slips of paper, or on the backs of letters or important documents, which are the best source for a study of the things with which Cromwell was busied.

The financial situation was not serious or critical on Wolsey's fall. There were occasional difficulties, but no pressing urgent necessity for a radical reorganization. But several developments in the early years of Cromwell's adminstration brought the problem nearer the point where it must be solved. First, there was continued decrease in some of the old sources of income. As already noted, the French pensions ceased, except in the years 1531 to 1534. The Customs revenues, which averaged £42,643 a year during the first decade of the reign, and £35,305 a year from 1521 to 1529, fell to £32,195 for an average year during

[1] Merriman, I, 17, 76. The story is told in a letter of Chapuys, to Granvelle describing Cromwell, November 21, 1535.

[2] *Letters and Papers*, V, 277.

[3] *Ibid.*, V, 1639; VI, 228, 717; VII, 430.

the period 1530 to 1538.[4]   The loss was due to a sharp fall in
the wool subsidy revenues.[5]   Of greater effect than the ''decay''
of the revenues were increased expenditures.   Reference has
already been made to the rise in the expenses of the household.
Another most important increase after 1529 was the king's outlay
for the erection of new palaces and the purchase of new manors.
This became so great that Cromwell in 1534 wrote in one of
his remembrances, ''What a great charge it is to the king to
continue his buildings in so many places at once . . if the
king would spare for one year, how profitable it would be to
him.''[6]   Harbor improvements were begun at Dover; and extensive works were carried out in the fortifications and harbor
of Calais, at the cost of many thousands of pounds each year.[7]

Troubles on the Scotch borders and insurrections in Ireland
brought new charges.   The support of an army against Scotland
to prevent a repetition of the forays of 1532 cost £24,800 during
the year following.[8]   Irish revenues scarcely covered the costs
of the Irish government in ordinary years.   When Kildare's
rebellion broke out in 1534, and an army of two thousand foot
and three hundred horse were sent over to subdue the country, a
deficit of £38,000 for the first year's campaign had to be met
from the English treasury.[9]   Next, though of more interest

[4] Schanz, II, 12.

[5] The wool subsidy had yielded £15,231 a year in the first decade of
the reign; it fell to £5,701 a year in the period 1530-1538.   In other
customs dues there was a slight increase in these last years.

[6] *Letters and Papers*, VII, 143, Cromwell's Remembrances, January,
1534.   In 1536 Cromwell again referred to such expenditures in a paper of
''things done by the king's highness sythyn I came to his service''
(*Letters and Papers*, X, 1231).

[7] Works on a large scale at Calais were begun after Henry VIII's visit
in 1532.   See *Chronicle of Calais*, (Camden Society), App. 98, 123, 128;
Letters and Papers, V, 370, 1668; XVI, 303; VI, 228.   In May, 1533, the
mayor and citizens of Dover petitioned the king to ''have the harbor dug
out,'' since it had been filled up by small stones cast up ''by violent rages
of the sea.''   Work was begun in 1535 (*Accounts, Exch., Queen's Remembrancer*, 58/13; *Letters and Papers*, X, 102; XI, 1254; XII, part I, 92;
XIII, part II, 223).

[8] *Letters and Papers*, VI, 664, 1162; accounts of Sir George Lawson,
Treasurer of the Scotch Wars, September 14, 1532, and September 27,
1533.

[9] *Letters and Papers*, VIII, 788; IX, 217, Receipts of William Brabason,

than importance, in the series of new and enhanced expenditure during the first years of Cromwell's administration, were payments directly connected with the divorce of Queen Catherine. On the divorce itself, Henry VIII spent very little money, and that chiefly in salaries of ambassadors and special agents to Rome, bribes to high officials of the Curia and gratuities to University doctors for subscribing to opinions favorable to Henry's position.[10]

Though the divorce itself cost little, the foreign situation created by the divorce had tremendous effects on the financial history of the Tudor period. The Emperor Charles V bitterly resented Henry's attempt to divorce his aunt, Catherine of Aragon. Not only did he prevent the Pope from giving a decision favorable to Henry VIII, but there seemed to be danger all through the period from 1529 to 1536 that the Emperor would wage war on England in his aunt's behalf. To offset this danger, the English alliance with France was carefully cultivated, at great cost in remission of pensions; the Potestant princes of Germany were approached with a view to an alliance, and Jürgen Wullenwever of Lübeck was subsidized, in his efforts to secure the election of a Danish king opposed to Charles V.[11] The fear of an imperial attack was especially strong in the summer of 1533, after the passage of the Act of Appeals, the final sentence of divorce by Cranmer's court, the coronation of Anne and the papal bull excommunicating Henry. In the memoranda of Cromwell many notes are found which indicate his concern for measures of defence, — "To remember the king for the reparation of his navy;" "a bill to be drawn up for granting money for fortifying the frontiers;" "The Pope is only Bishop of Rome . . Devices to be made for repairing the fortifications, especially on the frontiers of Scotland . . The King's navy, ordnances and munitions of war, bows guns . . to be

Treasurer of the Irish Wars. To May, 1535, he had received £34,628 from England and £3,373 from the king's revenues in Ireland. In August, 1535, he received an additional £4,438 from England.

[10] *Letters and Papers*, IV, V, VI, passim.

[11] Henry VIII loaned Wullenwever 20,000 guilders in 1534; in 1535 he sent a sum rumored to be 90,000 ducats; and in 1536 he sent £5,000 (*Letters and Papers*, VIII, page XIX; IX, 287; X, 376).

repaired and provided for."[12] The works at Calais were most carefully surveyed, the ships of the royal navy were ordered to be got ready and orders were issued to erect block-houses and forts at various places in defence of sudden invasions — which Chapuys, the imperial ambassador said showed that "they are beginning to be afraid."[13]

During these years of stress foreign observers in England constantly refer to a new development in Henry VIII's character or policy, which they did not quite understand. From being liberal, he had become avaricious, in the words of Lodovico Falier to the Venetian senate,[14] and Chapuys showed in his letters to Charles V that he had the same general feeling. Cromwell even encouraged him in this simple belief; in the early summer of 1535 he took Chapuys aside privately and assured him, "to be frank, his master (Henry VIII) had become very greedy; and unless some other way were found to spend his money, he would collect in his treasury all the money of the kingdom to the great injury of private persons. He (Cromwell) and the other councillors wished to find means to make him spend it for the general good, thinking this would also moderate his greediness."[15] But simple greediness does not explain the king's desire to fill his coffers. When Carlo Capello wrote to the Signory of Venice, "he is amassing money and hastening the fortifications of the Tower of London," he was joining the process, with a clue to the cause in one sentence.[16] Cromwell's note "What necessity there is to cause treasure to be laid up for all events;" suggests the true explanation, and in many of the numerous schemes drawn up by him for adding new revenues to the crown, the reason given is the fear of an attack by the Emperor.[17]

In 1525 the lack of money, and the impossibility of getting any quickly from the nation had compelled Henry VIII to withdraw from the war with France. The situation which now

[12] *Letters and Papers*, VI, 997, 1381, 1487, Cromwell's Remembrances.

[13] *Letters and Papers*, VI, 1460, a letter of Chapuys to Charles V.

[14] *Venetian Calendar*, IV, 694, Lodovico Falier to the Senate.

[15] *Letters and Papers*, VIII, 826, a letter of Chapuys to Charles V, June, 1535.

[16] *Venetian Calendar*, IV, 788.

[17] *Letters and Papers*, VII, 143.

faced him was the possibility of a war not of his own choosing or volition. He would be on the defensive, and could not withdraw when he pleased. It was therefore essential for the safety of England and his own security as king, to accumulate a sufficient surplus to enable England to carry on a war vigorously as long as the enemy might attack. To fill up the War Chest, without which the security of the throne and the national safety was endangered, new revenues were necessary. Experiments with taxation again were made, but they only complemented the results of Wolsey's and Henry VII's experiences. The very rumor, current in 1531 that the king meant to draw from the Commons a large sum on the ground that they were involved in Wolsey's praemunire, as had been done in the case of the clergy, led the House of Commons to demand a free exemption from the charge. "As the king would not listen to them for some days, there was great a murmuring among them in the Chamber of Commons, where it was publicly said in the presence of some of the privy council, that the king had burdened and oppressed his kingdom with more imposts and exactions than any three or four of his predecessors, and he ought to consider that the strength of the king lay in the affections of his people. And many instances were alleged of inconveniences which had happened to Princes through the ill treatment of their subjects. On learning this, the king granted the exemption . . without any reservation."[18] In the next year fortunes were again essayed in Parliament. The necessity of the grant was intimated to the Commons in January, 1532;[19] but nothing was done by the Commons. Finally, on April 16, 1532 the king sent the Chancellor, the Duke of Norfolk and other lords to the House of Commons, to show the need of making a harbor at Dover, of fortifying the Scotch frontier, and making preparations for war during the peace. Two weeks later, two men arose in Parliament and boldly spoke against the fortifications of the Scotch frontier, for which Henry had asked aid, saying that it was the best fortification to maintain peace with the Emperor and take back Catherine. The words were well taken by

[18] *Letters and Papers*, V, 171, a letter from London, April 2, 1531.

[19] *Letters and Papers*, V, 762, a letter of Chapuys to Charles V, January 30, 1532.

I

nearly all present and nothing was concluded. "The king was displeased and sent for a majority of the deputies, and made them a long speech in justification of his conduct in the divorce." Parliament granted a fifteenth. The king was so displeased at the smallness of the grant, that he was not present at the last meeting of the session and eventually rejected it.[20]

Cromwell soon learned to render Parliament more docile by controlling the election of members; and later Parliaments could be got to vote taxes without difficulty.[21]   But the grants were never commensurate with the needs of the state, even when voted by subservient Parliaments; and worse, there was never any guarantee that the people would pay even the moderate taxes without murmuring.[22]   The medieval forms and notions of taxation were equally unfitted either to cover the growing deficiencies in the state disbursements, as the experiences of the fifteenth century showed; to finance wars directly, as Wolsey found; or to help the king to lay up a large surplus against a threatening war in the future, as was now discovered.

Since taxation was ineffective in aiding the king to accumulate treasure; "against all events," and even to meet the increasing expenses of the government, and make good decreasing revenues, the normal permanent revenues of the crown had to be increased, without infringing the self interest of the middle class whose alliance with the crown formed the Tudor Commonwealth. Cromwell's general problem was the same as that which Henry VII had coped with. The reduction of the nobility and the conversion of its wealth to the purposes of the crown by forfeiture or escheat of lands, and by way of great fines was Henry VII's solution. What the nobility was to Henry VII, the Church was to Cromwell. His work was simply the historical evolution of Henry VII's policy, under certain different conditions and circumstances. The permanent crown revenues were about to

[20] *Letters and Papers*, V, 941, 989, 1046, letters of Chapuys to Charles V, April and May, 1532.

[21] Merriman, *Life and Letters of Thomas Cromwell*, I, 91-92.

[22] While the tax of 1532 was being discussed in Parliament, many men in London believed that attempts to collect the tax would lead the people to mutiny. *Letters and Papers*, V, 762, 941, letters of Chapuys to Charles V.   The same was true in 1534 when a large grant was actually voted. *Ibid.*, VII, 1554.

receive their second great increase of Tudor times; and as in Henry VII's day, the large part of this increase came in the form of land or revenues from lands.

Diversions of the wealth of the church from the church to the crown were no new thing in England. Quite apart from the use of the revenues of the great ecclesiastical benefices as salaries for the great officials of the crown, of which Wolsey furnishes a striking example,[23] and apart from the tenths voted by the Convocations to the Crown, were the actual seizures of Church property in times past. Edward II dissolved twenty-three preceptories of Templars and only partially restored their lands to religious uses;[24] the Commons in 1410 petitioned for the confiscation of all the property of the church — a petition which was remembered in Parliament in 1529[25]—, and Henry V seized the property of the alien priories in England.[26] And that perhaps some further plan was on foot toward the end of Henry VII's reign is suggested by Dudley's warning to Henry VIII, "Restrain yourself from appropriation of benefices or to unite any house of religion to another, for if this do continue it shall by all likelyhood destroy the honor of the Church of England."[27] Moreover, "William of Wykeham and Chicele, Wayanflete and Fisher, Alcock of Ely, and Smith of London had all diverted wealth from monastic into educational channels, and this idea of utilizing conventional revenues for the promotion of learning and culture had been carried out on a large and impressive scale by Wolsey," who had suppressed more than twenty conventional houses for his school and colleges at Ipswich and Oxford.[28]

The newer and larger appropriations of the wealth of the Church now begun were quite in the current of the events of the day. Sequestration of church property into lay hands was in the air all over Europe. In Norway the spoliation of the treas-

[23] Cavendish, *Life of Wolsey*, p. 95. He was Archbishop of York, Bishop of Winchester and held the Abbey of St. Albans in commendam, and the Sees of Bath and Wells, of Worcester and of Hereford in ferme.

[24] Fisher, *Political History of England*, 369.

[25] *Letters and Papers*, IV, 6043.

[26] Fisher, *op. cit.*, 369.

[27] Dudley, *Tree of Commonwealth*, 5.

[28] Fisher, *op. cit.* 369, 370.

ures and wealth of the churches and monasteries was carried out to the benefit of Frederick I, and others.[29]   In Switzerland the monastic property had already been turned over to the purposes of education and poor relief.[30]   In Germany, Landgrave Philip and the Estates of Hesse — to give but one example — had suppressed the majority of religious houses by the regulations of the Diet of October, 1527.   From the property, compensation was given to the inmates, the University of Marburg was founded, the nobility were provided for, and the remainder of it was constituted a fund for the use of the prince, the nobles and the cities under the control of the estates.[31]   Even in Catholic Europe, the property of the Church was menaced.   The Austrian government went far in claiming secular administration of the episcopal domains, and the papist junkers were more Lutheran than the Lutherans themselves in the scramble for conventual lands.[32]

The confiscation of all Wolsey's property after his fall in 1529 was the preliminary act to the "great sacrilege" in England.[33]   In December, 1530, it was conveniently discovered that the whole clergy of England was involved in the Praemunire of Wolsey.   The spiritual lords were called in by process into the King's Bench to answere to that charge.[34]   The Convocation of Canterbury was quickly called, and the clergy offered the King 160,000 ducats for a pardon by act of Parliament.   This sum, the King refused to accept; saying he would have 400,000 ducats (£100,000) or he would punish everyone with extreme vigor.[35] The Convocation was so thoroughly cowed that it refused to allow the Papal Nuncio to address it, when he appeared offering to intercede with the King, "for they had not the King's leave to

[29] *Cambridge Modern History,* II, 618.

[30] *Ibid.,* II, 321.

[31] Ranke, *Deutsche Geschichte im Zeitalter der Reformation,* in Sämmtliche Werke, II, 317.

[32] *Ibid.,* II, 313-314.

[33] Du Bellay the French ambassador valued this at 500,000 ducats or £125,000 (*Letters and Papers,* IV, 6030), a merchant in England at 900,000 angelots or £150,000 (*Letters and Papers,* IV, 6057).

[34] Hall, *Chronicle,* II, 183.

[35] *Letters and Papers,* V, 62, a letter of Chapuys to Charles V, January 23, 1531.

speak with him." [36]   On January 24,[37] they voted £100,044 8s. 8d., only to find on February 7, that there was another condition to the royal pardon, — that they acknowledge the King as Head of the English Church.[38]   It may be, as one scholar asserts,[39] that the object of prime importance in the mind of the King and Cromwell, was to secure the recognition of Henry VIII as Head of the English Church; but certainly the circumstances which led to action just at this time were the need of money to make up the probable shortage in funds, and to provide revenue in case of a war with the Emperor.   That the King himself had this last point very much in mind is seen in his demand, probably made at the same time that the recognization of the King as Head of the Church was insisted upon, that in case he or any of his allies made war, the clergy should be bound to advance the money promised by them at once, without waiting for the regular times of payment spread over five years as offered by the Convocation.[40]   This the clergy refused; they even seem to have withdrawn their offer of money for a moment,[41] but it was finally agreed that the King should accept £100,000 to be paid in five yearly installments, and that he should not press for payment before the expiration of five years.[42]   The Convocation of York accepted the terms made between the King and Canterbury, and granted to the King £18,840 0s. 10d.[43]

But though the king could thus cow the Bishops in the Convocations, payment of the sums was not secured without disorder. The Bishops assessed contributions to these grants on their clergy; Bishop Stokesley of London called the curates to London at St. Paul's to have their benefices assessed; some eighteen noblemen among the priests assembled riotously and made an assault on the Bishop's Palace at St. Paul's where they continued

[36] *Letters and Papers,* V, 62.

[37] Wilkins, *Concilia,* III, 724.

[38] *Ibid.*

[39] Merriman, *Life and Letters of Thomas Cromwell,* I, 93-96.

[40] *Letters and Papers,* V, 105, a letter of Chapuys to Charles V, February 14, 1531.

[41] *Letters and Papers,* V, 105.

[42] *Ibid.*   See also *Letters and Papers,* V, 149, a letter of the Archbishop of Canterbury to the king, notifying him of the grant.

[43] Wilkins, *Concilia,* III, 744.

for an hour and a half. Eighteen or twenty persons were arrested and jailed in connection with the disorder.[44]

The payment of £118,800 was not the only exaction made from the clergy in 1531. Many individual churchmen were excepted from the pardon for praemunire, and had to make their peace separately with the King. The Bishop of Bangor paid £333 6s. 8d., the Bishop of Dublin, £1,466 13s. 4d., the Dean of Arches, £133 6s. 8d. Moreover, the great Churchmen seem to have been very heavily fined for offences of which there is no record since the reign of Henry VII. For the escape of seven prisoners, the Bishop of Bath paid £700; the Bishop of Lincoln for a similar offence £666 13s. 4d., and the Bishop of Hereford for an untrue certificate of non-bigamy which he had issued, £666 13s. 4d.[45] Three years later, in 1534, the Bishop of Norwich was accused of having fallen anew into praemunire, on the ground that he had cited the Mayor of Thetford before him in a spiritual case, although the town of Thetford enjoyed exemption from the Bishop's jurisdiction. The Bishop was arrested, and finally pardoned by the King and in return, made the King a "free gift" of £10,000. Chapuys suggested that his great wealth was as important a cause for his accusation as the alleged offense.[46]

In 1532, despite the fact that the clergy were now paying £24,000 a year to the Royal Treasury as the annual installments of the £118,800 promised by the Convocations, they were called upon for additional contributions. The Convocation of Canterbury sat during April and May 1532. When Parliament granted the fifteenth, the Duke of Norfolk so informed the Convocation "and warned the prolocutor and others, that they show themselves not less prompt and ready to assist the royal needs."[47] The Convocation practically refused the Royal command, much to the King's displeasure, and Chapuys writes that he was therefore determined to succeed, either "in a friendly way or other-

---

[44] *Letters and Papers*, V, 387, a bill filed in the Star Chamber by Christopher Hales, the Attorney-General. See also Hall, *Chronicle*, II, 200 ff.

[45] *Letters and Papers*, V, 637, "fines made with divers persons by the king's commandment."

[46] *Letters and Papers*, VII, 171, 270, 296.

[47] Wilkins, *Concilia*, III, 748 f.

wise.'' [48]   The Convocation of York, however, granted a tenth to the King. [49]

But already the minds of the King and his ministers were beginning to busy themselves with large plans for the annexation of the temporal estates of the Church to the Crown. The idea was in the air as early as 1531, when Falier the Venetian Ambassador reported to the Senate that Henry seemed bent on detaching himself from the Roman Church and annexing the ecclesiastical revenues to the Crown. [50] Rumor had it in January, 1533, that Cranmer, newly elected Archbishop of Canterbury, would renounce all temporalities of his See to the King — as a good way to force the rest to do the same. [51] In the next month, Chapuys understood that the King intended to raise a regiment of horse and was going to take the goods of the Church to pay them, [52] and a month later, these rumors of intended confiscation of Church property received confirmation from the lips of the King himself. In a long personal interview with Chapuys, he said that he was going to repair the damage done by John in making England tributary to the Pope and ''also to reunite to the Crown the goods which Churchmen held of it which his predecessors could not alienate to his prejudice and that he was bound to do this by the oath he had taken at his coronation.'' [53] A little later we have a suggestion written in the hand of Cromwell's clerk, which points to Cromwell as the author of it, that Cranmer write a book defending the King's marriage and abolition of Papal power, exhorting the clergy to avoid all ambition, all delicate fare, and ''to be ready with heart and mind to depart and dispose among the people of this realm, lands, goods and money.'' [54] In October there is a note of an act ''to be made at the Parliament'' ''that if war against the

[48] *Letters and Papers*, V, 1046, a letter of Chapuys to Charles V, May 22, 1532.

[49] Wilkins, *Concilia*, III, 748.

[50] Falier's report to the Senate in 1531 (*Venetian Calendar*, IV, 694 [p. 299]).

[51] *Letters and Papers*, VI, 89, a letter of Chapuys to Charles V, January 27, 1533.

[52] *Ibid.*, VI, 180.

[53] *Ibid.*, VI, 235.

[54] *Ibid*, VI, 738.

King is attempted on the Pope's occasion, the King shall have for his defence the moiety of the temporal lands of the Church,"[55] and a document drawn up in November, 1534, shows the plan finally contemplated.   All the temporal possessions of the Church both of the secular and of the regular clergy, except property of specific yearly value for the payment of the income of the clergy "were to be made sure to the King and his heirs for the defence of the realm and the maintenance of his royal state."   The Archbishop of Canterbury was to have 2,000 marks yearly, the Archbishop of York, £1,000 and the other Bishops 1,000 marks.   Lands and possessions of all monasteries of which the number of inmates was under thirteen persons were to go to the King, and in other monasteries every monk being a priest should have 10 marks a year; every novice not a priest £5; the Abbot was to have as much as all the others together and the residue was to go to the King.   The King was to receive one-half the revenues of every Cathedral Church and one-third of those in each Archdeaconry.   The Commander of the Knights of St. John was to have 1,000 marks; the rest of his possessions went to the King and at his death the whole; and likewise the lands of every Commandry, at the death of the knights in possession.   Moreover, Parliament was to grant a temporal subsidy of 2s. in the £ to be paid in two years, and a clerical subsidy of 4s. in the £ to be paid in two years "for charges of the present wars, for defence of Ireland, for making of Dover Haven and other fortresses against Scotland." [56]

Chapuys, and John Hussee, the well informed London agent of Lord Lisle, Deputy Governor of Calais, had expected some such measure to be introduced into Parliament, when it reassembled in January, 1534,[57] and they wrote of rumors that some of this confiscated property would be distributed among the nobles.   No bill was presented at the session of Parliament which began in January, 1534; but during the summer Chapuys

[55] *Ibid.*, VI, 1381

[56] *Cott. Mss., Cleopatra E. IV*, 174.   The clerical subsidies would be voted by the Convocations, but Parliament would have to pass a validating act since Convocations had lost the right of independent actions in 1533 by *Statutes*, 25, Henry VIII, c. 19.

[57] *Letters and Papers*, VII, 24, 114.

was convinced that some such measure would be taken up in November when Parliament reassembled,[58] and later, in September, Cromwell seems to have mentioned the matter to him.[59]

But even the Parliament which had just severed the relations between England and Rome was scarcely ready for so sweeping a change, and there is no record that a bill for the purpose was introduced. Instead, Cromwell and the King satisfied themselves with obtaining the first fruits of all benefices vacant after January 1, 1535, and the annual tenths of all benefices, while on the other hand, the last payments of the £118,800 granted by the Convocations in 1531 were excused.[60] A new assessment of the value of all benefices in England was to be made by Royal Commissioners. The assessment of 1291 which had been in force up to this time (except for the grant of £100,000 in 1523) was finally overthrown, and the clergy were to be taxed on the annual value of their benefices. The new revenue was expected to yield £30,000[61] per year, a sum equal to about one-fifth of the revenues in 1529; and to administer it, John Gostwike was soon after appointed Treasurer and Receiver-General and Commissioner of First Fruits and Tenths.[62]

As the year 1535 opened, Cromwell seems to have been very proud of his achievements in finance, and to have expected very much from them. Both he and Henry VIII declared to foreign ambassadors the wealth and authority of the Crown and the quiet of the Kingdom, and spoke enthusiastically of the new increases in revenue.[63] It is of course impossible to know how far these statements were made for effect, and how far they

[58] *Ibid.*, VII, 871.

[59] *Ibid.*, VII, 1141. Chapuys wrote to his master Charles V, ''Cromwell understands that at the said Parliament the King will distribute among the gentlemen of the Kingdom the greater part of the ecclesiastical revenues to gain their goodwill.''

[60] *Statutes of the Realm*, 26 Henry VIII, c. 3.

[61] *Letters and Papers*, VII, 1490, a letter of Brian Tuke, Treasurer of the Chamber, to Cromwell.

[62] *Ibid.*, VIII, 802, 820.

[63] *Letters and Papers*, VIII, 174, Palamedes Gontier, the French ambassador to Admiral Chabot, reporting a conversation of Cromwell. A draft letter of Henry VIII to De Brion with the same purport is calendared in *ibid.*, VIII, 339.

revealed the real thoughts of Cromwell and Henry VIII. But if they expressed a genuine conviction, it was one destined to be disappointed. There were troubles in Ireland, the French pensions were no longer paid, the new ecclesiastical tenths did not come in rapidly, and the subsidy granted by Parliament could not be collected in many places, owing to the surliness of the people and the failure of the crops.

The government added to its perplexities by the criminal execution of Bishop Fisher and Sir Thomas More, together with the Carthusian Monks, in the summer of 1535. A thrill of horror went through Catholic Europe; and the papacy was forced at length to proceed to formulate the bull of privation and deposition of Henry VIII. Probably there was no real danger that the Emperor would carry it out; but the fear that he would do so was almost a panic in England in the latter part of 1535, and this was heightened by the rumor of an understanding between the Emperor and the French King in February and again in December of 1535,[64] even though nothing came it. The Venetian and other foreign merchants expected to leave England and refused Cromwell's very generous concessions of customs privileges, offered to induce them to stay.[65] The French and German alliances were again sedulously cultivated. But above all, in the imminent danger of war, in case of invasion, money was necessary. It was under these circumstances that the conversion of a new portion of the wealth of the Church to public uses was necessary. In July, 1535, just a few days after the execution of Sir Thomas More, Cromwell began the royal visitation of the monasteries;[66] and the first step in the suppression of the monasteries had been taken.

[64] Fisher, *op. cit.* 357.
[65] *Letters and Papers*, IX, 965.
[66] *Letters and Papers*, VIII, 1127, 1130.

CHAPTER X

THE DISSOLUTION OF THE MONASTERIES

The plan for the secularization of all church property which Cromwell had been considering in 1534 was dropped in November of that year, when the annual tenth of the value of all benefices was granted to the king. As early as January, 1535, new plans seem to have been under deliberation for diverting more money from the Church to the Crown. There exist draft commissions for a visitation of all churches and monasteries, and other draft commissions for the visitation merely of all monasteries to find the value of their rents and lands among other things, dated in January 1535.[1] The plan as finally worked out, for the suppression of the smaller houses took shape slowly. In March, Cromwell made a note "to remember all the jewels of all the monasteries in England and especially the cross of emeralds at Paul's."[2] Later during the spring or the summer, the king advised with his council on the question of suppressing the monasteries, and the proposal was seriously opposed by at least one member of the council.[3] All that we know definitely is that at the beginning of June the visitation of the monasteries had been decided on,[4] and very early in July Cromwell began to visit the monasteries in person by virtue of his authority as Vicar-general. What his plan was when he began his visitation is nowhere hinted at; perhaps it was still not yet worked out in his own mind. Chapuys heard a report in September that the King intended to allow the religious of all orders to be free to leave their habits

[1] *Letters and Papers*, VIII, 73, 76, January 1535.

[2] *Ibid.*, VIII, 475, Cromwell's Remembrances.

[3] Lord Herbert, *Henry VIII*, 424-425.

[4] This we learn from a letter of Richard Layton to Cromwell, dated June 4, 1535, asking that he and Dr. Legh, be appointed visitors at the "approaching visitation." *Letters and Papers*, VIII, 822.

and marry. If, however, they wished to remain in their houses they must live in poverty since Henry VIII intended to take the rest of their revenue.[5] The plan is somewhat similar to the one suggested in the previous year, and differs materially from the plan finally evolved.

The task of visitation was of course too great for Cromwell alone, and he soon brought to his assistance a group of visitors; Dr. Richard Layton, Dr. Thomas Legh of "satrapike countenance," John Ap Rice, Dr. John London, John Tregonwell and Thomas Bedyll. These men armed with eighty-six articles of inquiry and twenty-five articles of injunction[6] visited monasteries in Kent, Oxfordshire, Northamptonshire, Leicestershire, Norfolk, Nottinghamshire, Yorkshire, Cheshire, and Cumberland and in many other counties. Their articles of inquiry concerned themselves with all sorts of details of monastic life; but the information most desired was clearly the value of the monastic revenues, property, jewels and lands. The injunctions "contain the core of a stringent and salutory reformation,"[7] but they were administered, especially by Legh, in a way to promote disobedience or surrender.

In connection with the administration of the injunctions, we find a hint of the development of the plan for dealing with the monasteries. Towards the end of September, two weeks after his letter last quoted, Chapuys came to feel that the object of the severe injunctions, one of which forbade the monks to leave the precincts of their houses was to force the monks to surrender; so that the King might seize their property without causing the people to murmur,[8] and a letter from Legh and Ap Rice to Cromwell in November confirms Chapuys' surmise. Legh wrote in the body of the letter "they will not need to be put forth, but will make instance to be delivered and so the deed shall be imputed to themselves," and Ap Rice added in a postscript, "though it were well done that all were put out yet to avoid calumny it were well that they were dismissed upon their own

---

[5] *Letters and Papers*, IX, 357, September 13, 1535.

[6] The articles are printed in Wilkins, *Concilia* III, 786.

[7] Fisher, *op. cit.*, 373.

[8] *Letters and Papers*, IX, 434, a letter of Chapuys to Charles V, September 25, 1535.

suit. They will all do this, if they are compelled to observe these injunctions; and the people shall know it the better that it cometh upon their own suit that they be not straight discharged while we are here; for then the people will say that we came for no excuse except to expel them."[9] The regard for public opinion is interesting and important. When Cromwell drew up the injunctions, he perhaps had in mind the restoration of the monasteries to Benedictine simplicity and rigor; their surplus wealth being confiscated by the state.[10] But Legh conceived the idea of using the injunctions in a way to bring complete surrender of their houses by the monks. At first, the other Commissioners protested to Cromwell against Legh's severity and strictness,[11] and Cromwell ordered him to be less rigorous.[12] But he explained in answer, how Cromwell might "advantage" himself in gratifying those houses that appealed to him for release from the strictness of the injunctions,[13] and Cromwell was satisfied; for nothing further is said on the matter. Shortly afterward, the other Commissioners, especially Ap Rice who had made the chief complaint against Legh's severity, were administering the injunctions as zealously as Legh himself. During the next months many monasteries appealed to Cromwell for leave to be free from the galling injunctions, always to Cromwell's own great profit of course; while other houses, too poor or too obstinate to purchase temporary reprieve in this way, were compelled to struggle along until from very weariness they were ready to surrender themselves to the King, even before the act of suppression had passed through Parliament.

Besides making their inquisitions and giving their injunctions, the visitors endeavored to get possession of the monastic jewels and ornaments. Thus Layton wrote, "I have crosses of silver and gold, some of which I send you not now because I have more that shall be delivered me this night by the Prior of Maiden Bradley himself. Tomorrow, early in the morning I

[9] *Ibid.*, IX, 708, a letter of Legh and Ap Rice to Cromwell.

[10] This was partly the plan in 1534, and is the plan indicated by Chapuys in his letter of the middle of September.

[11] *Letters and Papers*, IX, 139, a letter of Ap Rice to Cromwell.

[12] *Ibid.*, IX, 265, a letter of Legh to Cromwell.

[13] *Ibid.*, IX, 265.

shall bring you the rest when I have received all, and, perchance I shall find something here'' (at St. Augustine's Bristol).[14]

The commissioners or visitors finished their visitation near the end of February, 1536, having covered the last part of their tour, including the diocese of Coventry and Lichfield and the entire province of York in about six weeks. Really very rapid traveling. But hurry was necessary since Parliament had reassembled on February 4, 1536. Its only business of importance was to legalize the surrenders of monastic houses into the king's hands which had already been made at various times since the preceding November,[15] and to deal with the question of the monasteries as the king and Cromwell wished. Since the letters of Chapuys and Legh and Ap Rice in September and November 1535, there had been no indication, so far as the existing records show, of the development of the government's plan of procedure against the religious houses. Cromwell was perhaps not quite sure as to how much he could safely take; and it was not until March 3, that a rumor of his intentions appeared when it was ''bruited (in London) that abbeys and priories under 300 Marks by year and having not twelve in convent shall down.''[16] Unfortunately, all the records of the Parliament of February, 1536, are lacking; but from various scraps of letters and tradition, it is clear that the king presented the bill for the dissolution of the smaller monasteries having a clear yearly income of under £200, to the Commons in person on March 11, stating that on Wednesday next he would be there to hear their minds.[17] From the preamble of the act of disso-

[14] Wright, *The Suppression of the Monasteries,* (Camden Society), 59, August 24, 1535. The jewels were taken by the visitors probably from the fear that the monasteries suspecting dissolution would sell their jewels and ornaments and thus cheat the crown. In March of the next year Cromwell received a report that the prior and four or five monks of St. Swithin's Winchester were taking their jewels and selling them to a London jeweller who had been in divers religious houses for the purpose (*Letters and Papers,* X, 472, March 14, 1536, Thomas Parry to Cromwell) and the same thing may have been done earlier.

[15] For a list of surrenders between November, 1535, and February, 1536, see *Letters and Papers,* IX, 816.

[16] *Letters and Papers,* X, 406, a letter of Sir Richard Whetthyll to Lord Lisle, March 3, 1536.

[17] Gairdner, *Lollardy and the Reformation in England,* II, 80; Wright, *Suppression,* 38, 39, a letter to Thomas, Earl of Dorset.

lution and from a sermon preached many years later, by Bishop Latimer,[18] it seems that the enormities and crimes of the monks brought to light by the visitors, were stated to the house, in order to arouse the members against the monasteries; but even with this, it was March 18th before Chapuys wrote of the passage of the act.[19] The preamble of the act speaks of a great deliberation, before the Lords and Commons were finally resolved, and Sir Henry Spelman records the tradition that "when the bill had stuck long in the lower house and could get no passage, he (the King) commanded the Commons to attend him in the forenoon in his gallery, where he let them wait till late in the afternoon, and then coming out of his Chamber, walking a turn or two among them and looking angrily at them, first on one side and then on the other, at last, 'I hear' (saith he) 'that my bill will not pass; but I will have it pass, or I will have some of your heads,' and without other rhetoric or persuasion returned to his Chamber. Enough was said, the bill passed, and all was given him as he desired."[20] With this brief outline of the events leading up to the passing of the act for the dissolution of the smaller monasteries in mind, it will be possible to examine the causes of the dissolution.

The official cause of the dissolution may be gathered very well from Henry VIII's own words. "As to the suppression of religious houses . . none was suppressed but where most abominable living was used as appears by their own confessions signed with their own hands in the time of our visitations."[21] In 1539 an "Official Account of the Reformation" appeared in England, which put the matter more fully. After the King had taken the title of Supreme Head, he caused visitations to be made and finding the lives of the monks and friars, especially in small houses, to be vicious, all houses under £200 a year were suppressed and the revenues annexed to the crown.[22] And in the *Pilgrim* this cause is still more fully elaborated. The King

[18] Latimer, *Sermons*, (Parker Society), 123; cp. 117-122.

[19] *Letters and Papers*, X, 494, a letter of Chapuys to Charles V, March 18, 1536.

[20] H. Spelman, *History of Sacrilege*, (Ed. of 1853), 206.

[21] *Letters and Papers*, XI, 780 (2), a letter of Henry VIII to the Duke of Suffolk, October 19, 1536.

[22] *Ibid.*, XIV, part I, 402.

was aroused by the falsehoods of the monks and "for the better discovering of these hypocrites, (he) sent forth Commissioners into all the provinces of his realm, to examine particularly the manner of living that these ribalds used. Now came the matter fully to light . . hypocricies, murders, idolatries, miracles, sodomies, adulteries, fornications, pride and not seven, but more than seven hundred thousand deadly sins." The King at once called Parliament and Parliament resolved that these monasteries should be extirpated and the goods and revenues disposed of.[23]

There can be no question that the monastic life had sunk to a low standard, and that in many places, drastic reform was greatly needed. This is clear from the accounts of the visitation of Archbishop Warham of the monasteries in his diocese in 1511;[24] of the visitations of the diocese of Norwich[25] and those of Southwell Cathedral.[26] Some years earlier, in 1489, Archbishop Morton wrote to the Abbot of St. Albans, specifically accusing "him and his monks of 'defiling the very Church of God by infamous intercourse with nuns.' He names the very men and the very women, and tells how the monks 'live with harlots and mistresses publicly and continuously within the precincts of the monastery and without.' " [27] At the same time, care should be taken in accepting the reports of Cromwell's visitors as true to fact in every case. The characters of Layton and Legh and the great rapidity with which the investigation was made make it extremely possible than an honest investigation was not made. The tone of the reports of Layton and Legh, and of Ap Rice and London who accompanied them is not sustained by the reports of John Tregonwell and Thomas Bedyll, two other

[23] The *Pilgrim*, by William Thomas, clerk of the Council to Edward VI. Edited by J. A. Froude, London, 1861, pp. 43-45.

[24] Mary Bateson, *Archbishop Wardham's Visitation of Monasteries*, *E. H. R.*, VI (1891), 18-25.

[25] *Visitations of the Diocese of Norwich, A. D. 1492 to 1532*, Ed. by Rev. A. Jessop, D. D., (Camden Society).

[26] *Reports of the Historical Mss. Commission*, Report XII, App. part 9, visitations of Southwell Cathedral in the years 1481 to 1514.

[27] *Norfolk Antiquarian Miscellany*, II, 443, Editor's note by Walter Rye, quoting from Morton's letter in Morton's Register in the library at Lambeth palace.

visitors of 1535, and it is quite out of harmony with the reports
of Commissioners who were sent out in the spring of 1536 to
make surveys and valuations of the goods of suppressed houses.[28]
The houses of which we have the commissioners' reports, were
in most cases not the same as those visited by the visitors, but
in two cases where they visited houses previously visited by
Legh and Layton, they found only good conversation and living
where Layton and Legh found sodomy, incontinence and desire
to be released from the monastic vows.[29]   At Folkstone, to give
another illustration, Layton declared the house to be in utter
decay, the prior's monk maximus sodomita, and the prior an
apostate and runagate.   The commissioners sent to suppress the
house found the place in good repair and the prior a good husband, beloved by his neighbors.[30]

After all, the government had little primary concern about
the true condition of life in the monasteries, bad as it actually
was, but it did want a lurid picture of monastic living, such
as Layton and Legh supplied, with which to inflame popular
opinion against the monks.   For though the secular clergy were
disliked, the monasteries still held a very popular place in public
opinion, due probably to their charities.   Dr. Savine has shown
in his *English Monasteries on the Eve of Dissolution* that the
monastic alms, imposed upon them by legal obligations, amounted
to less than two and one-half per cent of the gross income
of the monasteries, and it is his impression that the voluntary
alms did not exceed this amount.   Probably, as he points out, the
monks did very little by their alms to relieve the acute distress
of their time, they did not perform any great economic service;[31]
but it is certain that the people thought that they were doing a
great deal for their welfare, and that is the important consideration in studying the reason for the popularity of the monasteries.   This feeling is reflected in the reports of the com-

[28] *Letters and Papers*, X, 857, 858, 916, 917, 980, 1166, 1191, reports
and letters of the commissioners of 1536.

[29] The houses were Garendon and Grace Dieu in Leicestershire.   The
commissioner's report is in *Letters and Papers*, X, 1191; Layton and
Legh's report on the same houses, *ibid.*, X, 364.

[30] *Letters and Papers*, IX, 669, 829.

[31] Alexander Savine, *English Monasteries on the Eve of the Dissolution*,
239, 241, 265.

missioners appointed to take the suppression of the houses in 1536. They were generally local gentlemen and represented local sentiment. The commissioners of suppression in Northamptonshire wrote to Cromwell that the nunnery of Catesby was a great relief to the poor and that by his alms the abbot of St. James, in Northampton, relieved three or four score folks in town and country round about daily.[32] The prior of Pentneye, other commissioners wrote, relieved the quarter wondrously where he dwelt, and it seemed a pity not to spare a house that fed so many indigent poor.[33] Lord Audeley the Lord Chancellor himself moved Cromwell to spare St. John's monastery at Colchester, because many poor people of the town depended upon it for relief.[34] Finally, Aske, the leader of the Pilgrimage of Grace, in his examination at London after he was taken into custody, declared he grudged against the statute of suppression and so did all the country in the North in the first place, because the abbeys in the North gave great alms to poor men.[35] The monastic alms possessed for the neighboring poor a very real value, which even the Lord Chancellor saw. At a distance of four centuries, we are inclined perhaps to minimize the benefits conferred, in the mind of the recipient at least, by a very small aid.

Another form of monastic charity of greater economic service than the alms was that vague and undefined thing known as "hospitality." This meant intermittent entertainment to travellers and merchants, especially in the wilder and more inaccessible parts of the country. On this ground Edward, Archbishop of York, begged that the monastery of Hexham be spared. "Wise men who know the Borders think the lands even if they were ten times the value would not countervail the damage that would ensue if it were suppressed. Some way there is never a house between Scotland and the lordship of Hexham and what comfort the monastery is, especially during war, is well known."[36] Aske also drew attention to the economic service

[32] *Letters and Papers*, X, 858, 916, 917.
[33] *Ibid.*, X, 563.
[34] *Ibid.*, XIII, part II, 306.
[35] *Letters and Papers*, XII, part I, 901, page 405.
[36] *Letters and Papers*, X, 716.

of the monasteries in the North. "Strangers and baggers of corn as betwixt Yorkshire, Lancashire, Kendal, Westmoreland, and the Bishopric was in their carriage of corn and merchandise greatly succoured both horse and man by the said abbeys; for none was in those parts denied neither horse-meat nor man's meat, so that the people was greatly refreshed by the said abbeys where now they have no such succour." [37] The North was less advanced economically than the other parts of England, and there the monasteries still performed a real economic function by furnishing accommodation to travellers and merchants, and making business and trade easier. But in the other parts of England, monastic hospitality no longer needed to be depended on, and the sentimental hold of the monasteries on the people could be destroyed by reports of evil living in them. It is interesting to note that just in the North, where the monasteries still did the realest service, and where public opinion would be hardest to influence, the reports of the visitors were filthiest and foulest. That the reports of the visitors were but a means to the suppression, and not at all the cause, appears further in a letter of Henry VIII when he was urging the King of Scotland to suppress the monasteries there. "The extirpation of monks and friars requires politic handling. First, the Governor should send commissioners as it were to take order for living more honestly . . with a secret commission to groundly examine all the religious of the conversation and living, thereby if it be well handled the governor shall learn all their abominations." This and other things arranged, "the suppression of them will be easy." [38]

A second cause assigned for the suppression of the monasteries is that the monks were the chief supporters of the papal authority, and that to succeed in asserting the royal supremacy over the church, it was necessary to break their power.[39] It is true that this cause is always stated in conjunction with other causes, but it is always placed as the first cause and far too

[37] *Letters and Papers*, XII, Part I, 901, page 405.

[38] *Letters and Papers*, XVIII, part I, 364, a letter from Henry VIII to Ralph Sadler, his ambassador in Scotland.

[39] See *inter alia*, Lord Herbert, *Henry VIII*, 424, 425; Gasquet, *Henry VIII and the English Monasteries*, 75; J. Gairdner, *Lollardy and the Reformation*, 45.

much emphasis is laid upon it. The main evidence for the statement that the monks were the chief supporters of the papacy and weakened the control of the crown is the story of the Friars Observant and the Carthusian monks, and their opposition to the royal supremacy in the church. The Friars Observant had preached against the king's marriage to Anne Boleyn, and now, in the spring of 1534, they refused to take the oath to the royal supremacy, as required by the act of succession of 1534. Before August 29, 1534, they had been turned out of all their seven houses in England and distributed in several monasteries where they were virtually prisoners.[40] Their houses were given to the Austin friars. The monks of the London Charterhouse also refused to take the oath. On account of their influence, very great efforts were made to induce them to yield and finally, on June 6, all the members of the London house subscribed the oath under conditions. In the early part of 1535 when the new title of Supreme Head was incorporated into the royal style by a decree of the privy council, the heads of three of the English Charterhouses, and the head of the Briggittine monastery of Sion resisted. Eary in May, 1535, these four, with John Hale, vicar of Isleworth, were publicly executed in London, and a few weeks later three more Carthusians were burned. For two years after this no further arrests among these monks were made, though great pressure was placed upon them to submit. It was not until May, 1537, that the monks who still refused to submit were imprisoned, and not until June 10, 1537, that the surrender of the London Charterhouse was taken. The story of the suffering and fortitude of these heroic martyrs for conscience sake, is very moving, but it does not show that the monks in general resisted the succession and the royal supremacy, and it does not show that the king suppressed the monasteries because they did resist. It is true that the Friars Observant were taken out of their houses; but their houses were not taken by the king, but given to another order of friars. The Carthusians and the inmates of Sion on the other hand were not even turned out, and their houses continued to stand until as late as 1537 and 1538. If the king suppressed the monasteries because of the opposition of the

[40] *Letters and Papers*, VII, 1057, 1095; Wriothesley, *Chronicle*, 25.

monks to the royal supremacy, why were not the London Charterhouse and the monastery of Sion, the great centers of opposition, suppressed at once? The punishment for the small number of monks and friars who are known to have resisted the
royal supremacy was imprisonment and death, not the suppression of all religious houses into the hands of the king.

An important part of the argument for this cause of the
dissolution is the assumption that the opposition of the London
Charterhouse, and the other Carthusians, the inmates of Sion
and the Friars Observant is typical of general opposition among
the monks to the royal supremacy and the succession. There is
no positive evidence of this. So great an authority as Canon
Dixon believes that "the oath was taken in almost every chapter
house where it was tendered." [41] Again, nowhere in the Remembrances of Cromwell, nor in other memoranda which relate
to the suppression of the monasteries, is there, so far as I have
found, the slightest hint of the opposition of the monks to the
royal supremacy and succession as the cause for the dissolution. Finally a comparison of dates still further weakens the
case for this cause of the dissolution. The first rumors of the
suppression of the monasteries were in the air in 1531, and
the confiscation of all church endowments including the wealth
of the monasteries was under consideration in 1533, a year
before the Observants and the Carthusians opposed the oath
required by the king.

While the opposition of the monks to the royal supremacy
and the succession cannot be taken as a very potent cause of
the suppression, it is true that Henry VIII, who was very
anxious, when once he separated from Rome, that the
work be not undone, saw very clearly that the dissolution of
the monastic houses made a breach with Rome which was almost
irreparable. When he was endeavoring to win other sovereigns
from the Papacy in order that he might not stand alone without
allies among the great rulers of Europe, he tried to effect the
breach between them and Rome by urging them to plunder the
church. Thus when Henry VIII tried to win France from the
church in 1535, he tried to persuade Francis I to increase his

[41] R. W. Dixon, *History of the Church of England*, I, 213. The whole
matter of monastic opposition to royal supremacy is here discussed.

revenues at the expense of the Church,[42] and Sadler sent to
Scotland in 1540 to detach James from Rome in order to close
Scotland to catholic fugitives from England, was instructed to
urge on James, the dissolution of the Scotch monasteries.[43]

The chief cause for the dissolution was a financial one. This
is already suggested by the circumstances and events in England
previous to the dissolution already sketched. There are further
indications of the same thing. In the bill drawn up in November, 1534, for the confiscation of all the church estates, the
cause given and repeated several times is "the increase and
augmentation" of the king's revenue, "for the maintenance of
the King's estate," defence against invasion, enterprises against
the Irish and the Scotch, and the making of Dover haven. A
secondary motive is "the taking away the excess which is the
great cause of the abuses in the church," but not a word is said
of the opposition of the monks to the royal supremacy and the
succession. Again, the great emphasis placed upon finding the
true values of the goods and property of all the houses in the
articles of inquiry of the visitors in 1535 and the fact that after
the act for the dissolution of the smaller monasteries, many
houses coming under the terms of the act, which could pay liberally enough purchased exemption from suppression, strengthens
the feeling that the financial motive was uppermost. When
Sadler went to Scotland in 1540, he was instructed to say that
it was bruited in certain quarters that James V gathered into
his hands "numbers of sheep and such other vile and mean
things in respect of his estate," "therewith to advance his
revenue." Henry thought this undignified and suggested "that
James, seeing the untruth and beastly living of the monks who
occupy a great part of his realm should rather increase his
revenue by taking such houses as may best be spared and convert
the rest to better uses as Henry himself had done. Thus he
might easily establish his estate so as to live like a king and
yet not meddle with sheep and mean things."[44] Is it not

[42] *Letters and Papers*, VIII, 537, a letter of the Bishop of Faenza to
Mons. Ambrosio.

[43] *Letters and Papers*, XV, 136, instructions of Henry VIII to Sadler,
ambassador to Scotland.

[44] *Letters and Papers*, XV, 136.

possible that Henry VIII reveals the motives on which he himself acted?

Finally in Ireland no attempt was made to conceal the purely financial reason for the dissolution of the monastic houses. Conditions in England and Ireland were quite different, but in each country there was a shortage in funds to meet the expenses of the government. Owing to the disorders and rebellions in Ireland, the subsidies granted by the Irish Parliament, were collected in only a small part of the country, and the customs were remitted to the towns.[45] The revenues had fallen so low, and the need of money was so great that there was fear that the King's army would break up for want of money, or even mutiny.[46] Henry VIII having spent £40,000 to repress the Geraldines, was anxious for a "revenue to repress such attemptates" in the future, to stop the drain on the royal treasury.[47] In June, 1536, as a result of such conditions the Irish Parliament passed bills to increase the revenues, granting to Henry VIII the first fruits of benefices, the twentieth part of the yearly income of the clergy and a subsidy, and with these, the suppression of the abbeys.[48] In the face of the disordered condition of the country, the suppressions could not be carried through immediately. But in 1538, when the wages of 300 soldiers in the garrison were increased, the Irish commissioners were authorized to suppress abbeys to the yearly value of 2,000 marks, and also to suppress abbeys in Kilkenny, Tipperary, Wexford, and Waterford and assign the revenue for the administration of justice there.[49] The circumstances attending the suppression of the abbeys in Ireland and the use to which the money was put indicate clearly that it was a financial measure. The dissolution of the English monastic houses was analagous.

The act for the dissolution of the smaller monasteries[50] gave into the hands of the king, the lands and goods of all monastic houses with a clear yearly value of less than £200, on the ground

45 *Letters and Papers*, XI, 521, notes given by Brabazon, Under-Treasurer in Ireland to Wm. Body, to be declared to Cromwell.

46 *Letters and Papers*, X, 267; XI, 351.

47 *Letters and Papers*, X, 1051, Cromwell's Remembrances.

48 *Letters and Papers*, X, 897, 1030, June, 1536.

49 *Letters and Papers*, XIII, part I, 641, March, 1538.

50 *Statutes*, 27, Henry VIII, c. 28.

that "manifest sin, vicious, carnal and abominable living is daily used and committed commonly," "whereby the governors of such religious houses and their convent spoil, destroy, consume and utterly waste" their goods, property and ornaments of their churches. In the preamble of the act, it is interesting to note, it is in houses of less than twelve members that vicious, carnal and abominable living is found; but in the enacting clause the possession of a yearly income of less than £200 is made the proof of vice. The reports of the visitors give absolutely no reason to distinguish between houses, either on account of their wealth or numbers — they are as bad for the large and rich houses as for the smaller and poorer ones. The pretense that the king was chiefly actuated by a desire to reform the evil life of the monks is kept up in the clauses which direct that the inmates of the smaller monasteries are to be sent to live, for their reformation, at the "great solemn monasteries, wherein (thanks be to God) religion is right well kept and observed." If, however, any monk wished to leave his habit, he was to be provided with a pension. Furthermore, though "his highness may lawfully give, grant and dispose them (the monastic properties) or any of them, at his will and pleasure to the honor of God and the wealth of his realm," the new possessor was bound to provide hospitality and service for the poor, in like manner as the houses had previously done. By such meaningless clauses did the king and Cromwell make the act less obnoxious.

In 1535 there were 372 monasteries and priories in England which had an income of less than £200,[51] besides 27 in Wales.[52] To administer the lands and properties of the monasteries, Parliament provided for the establishment of a new revenue court of record, called the Court of the Augmentations of the Revenues of the King's Crown. Its accounts begin April 24, 1536.[53] On this same day commissions were issued to commissioners to take the surrenders of the monastic houses coming within the terms of the act of suppression.[54] They visited the house

[51] Savine, *op. cit.*, App. 270-288. The list here given is worked out from the returns of the commissioners of the Tenth of 1535, found in the Valor Ecclesiasticus.

[52] *Letters and Papers*, X, 1238.

[53] *Letters and Papers*, XIII, part II, 457.

[54] *Letters and Papers*, X, 721.

to be suppressed and made a careful survey of the value of all goods and property, often enhancing slightly the values found by the commissioners of 1535, who had assessed the values of all church property in 1535 for the payment of the annual tenth. It was on the basis of this new and higher valuation, by the way, that all leases and sales of monastic lands were made by the crown.[55] The survey completed, an inventory was made of all the goods of the monastery, the plate and furniture, live stock, grain and provisions on hand, and debts owing to the house. The lead was strippd from the roof and cast into sows, and the bells were taken from the church tower to be kept to the king's use and sold later. The movables, furniture, crops and stock were sold "at days" and the money used to pay the debts of the house. The jewels and ornaments and plate were sent to the jewel house in London and the house and grounds given over to a royal farmer or to the king's beneficiary. The monks in the house who desired to remain in their profession were sent to other houses, while those who desired to go into the world were sent to Cranmer or to the Lord Chancellor for capacities. The head of the house was sent to the Court of Augmentations for his pension.[56]

The suppression of the religious houses once begun, it is hard to see how the process could have stopped with the smaller houses. Yet the dissolution of the larger houses was probably hastened by the Pilgrimage of Grace in 1536 and the beginning of the peace between France and the Empire in 1537 which showed the desirability of even greater revenues. To increase further the endowment of the crown, the remaining religious houses were attacked. The part taken by the abbots of Brid-

[55] *Letters and Papers*, part I, 530.

[56] *Letters and Papers*, V, 721, 1191; XI, 165, 274, 347; XIII, part I, 764, 776; XIII, part II, 168; XIV, part I, 1190. At first all walls of churches, steeples etc. were pulled to the ground, leaving only houses necessary for a farmer (*Letters and Papers*, XI, 242). But it was soon found that the walls were very thick and there were few to buy materials, to "help the charges of plocking down of them." To follow the commission, wrote John Freeman, would cost the king at least £1,000 in Lincolnshire (*Letters and Papers*, XI, 242). In June, 1539, the order was changed. The commissioners were to make inventories of all superfluous buildings, but pluck down nothing unless commanded by the King or the Chancellor of the Augmentations.

lington, Jervaulx and other northern monasteries in aiding the Pilgrims of Grace in the fall of 1536, at once laid them open to the charge of treason; and in the early part of 1537 the charges were investigated, the abbots condemned and hanged, and the houses confiscated into the king's hand, because of their abbots' attainder.[57]   At the same time, in April, 1537, the beginning of the surrender of other larger houses into the king's hand was effected. The surrender of Furness Abby, with £900 a year in rents was much desired; and on the king's personal instructions the Earl of Sussex closely examined the monks. When "nothing much" could be found against them, Sussex, "according, having considered if one way would not serve, by what other means the monks might be rid from the said abbey," assayed the abbot of himself, and found him "very facile." [58] A few days later, Sussex received a letter of thanks from the king, for his "prudent proceedings in the conducing of the house of Furness to the king's hand." [59]   In June, 1537, the London Charterhouse submitted itself to the king's mercy,[60] and other large houses did so before the end of the year.[61] In December, 1537, Cromwell took the question up in earnest and noted in his Remembrances the sending of Dr. Petre, Dr. Lee and Dr. Leighton, with Sir Thomas Straunge on a new visitation.[62] This they began early in January, 1538, and during the next two years they, with John Tregonwell, John Freeman, Robert Southwell, John Gostwick and others were busied taking the voluntary surrenders of the larger houses.

It is of considerable interest to note in passing how consistently the delicious farce that the monks were surrendering their houses voluntarily was played, in deference to public opinion, and especially from fear that if it became known that the larger houses were being dissolved, they would squander and waste their goods.[63] As soon as Layton, the king's commissioner ar-

---

[57] *Letters and Papers*, XII, part I, 127, 130, 490, 491, 590, 666, 1172.
[58] *Ibid.*, 840.
[59] *Ibid.*, 896.
[60] *Letters and Papers*, XII, part II, 27.
[61] *Ibid.*, 1119, 1274.
[62] *Ibid.*, 1151.
[63] The alienation of their property by the monasteries in view of a probable suppression was extensive in 1538 and 1539. See *Letters and*

rived, it was bruited in Cambridge that he was on a tour of suppression, and that the king was determined to suppress all the monasteries. "To stop this bruit" he wrote to Cromwell "I went to the Abbeys and priories, and calling to me all honest men dwelling near, openly in the chapter houses, charged the abbots and priors that they should not, for any such vain babbling of the people, waste, sell, grant or alienate any of their property; I said that babblers slandered their natural sovereign, and if they were knaves that did so report, I commanded the abbots and priors to put such in the stocks, and if gentlemen, to certify your Lordship and the Council of their reports. This digression has hindered us at Westacre, but if I had not sped it before the dissolution of the same, the abbots and priors would have made foul shift before we could have finished at Westacre. Your command to me in your gallery in that behalf was more weighty than I then judged." [64]   The king himself promised that if the monks used themselves as faithful subjects he would not in anywise interrupt their mode of living; and when this did not quiet the rumors, Cromwell declared in what seems to be a circular letter, addressed to various abbots, "that unless overtures had been made by the houses that have resigned, he (the king) would never have received them. He does not in any way intend to trouble you, or devise for the suppression of any religious house that standeth, except they shall desire it themselves with one consent, or else misuse themselves contrary to their allegiance." [65]   Finally, when the whole business was nearly over, and Parliament passed the statute 31 Henry VIII, c. 13, (which is often referred to because of its incorrect title as the act for the suppression of the larger abbeys, but which is really an act intended to confirm legally the king's possession of such monastic lands as had already or should in the future come to him) the preamble was made to tell how the abbots and priors and convents had surrendered their property "of their own free will and voluntary minds and assents, without constraint, coaction or compulsion of any manner, person or persons."

Papers, XIII, part II, 528; Letters and Papers, XIV, part I, 946, 1094, 1539.

[64] Letters and Papers, XIII, part I, 102, a letter of Layton to Cromwell.
[65] Letters and Papers, XIII, part I, 573.

The method which the king's commissioners used to obtain these voluntary surrenders, without constraint, coaction or compulsion, was to examine the abbot and monks of a house, perhaps accuse them of divers crimes, enormities, and even high treason, and then exhort them to surrender their property to the king's mercy. The monks, sometimes abjectly admitting the "enormities of their past living," "or stricken with sorrow" in most cases gladly subscribed the instrument of their surrender, sealed it with their seals and delivered it to the commissioners.[66] At the same time the monks were often considerably influenced in their action by the promise of the commissioners that the debts resting on their houses should be paid, and that they should have pensions, and in some cases, solemn covenants were drawn up between the monks and the commissioners to this end.[67] Lest the activities of the commissioners should be insufficient, a subtle kind of pressure was exerted directly from London by Cromwell himself in the form of requests, which the abbots and convents scarcely dared ignore, for grants to Cromwell's favorites of lands and manors which were essential to their continued existence as monastic houses.[68]

Occasionally, as at St. Oswald's, where the prior was in bed unable to move hand or foot, at Godstow, Vale Royal, Ambresbury and Henton, the commissioners met with a determination not to surrender that "which is not ours to give but dedicate to God," except on the king's own command.[69] Later it was admitted that all houses except a few which were to be converted into collegiate churches were to be dissolved. The commissioners were instructed to give life pensions to the inmates of every house where the surrender was freely made. In other cases they were to take possession of the house and lands "by force of the last Act for the alteration of ecclesiastical tenures."[70]

[66] Examples are given in *Letters and Papers*, XIII, part I, 42, 396, 956, 1340.

[67] *Letters and Papers*, XIII, part I, 405, 1073; XVI, part I, 349; *Reports of the Historical Mss. Commission, Report XIV, App. part IX*, 271.

[68] *Letters and Papers*,, XIII, part I, 478, 797, 912; part II, 100; XIV, part I, 205.

[69] *Letters and Papers*, XIII, part I, 409; part II, 314, 758; XIV, part I, 145, 269, 629.

[70] This refers to the *Statute 31 Henry VIII*, c. 13, which had no such force as is here implied.

Obstinate monks should have no pensions nor stuff, but should be committed to ward for future punishment.[71] Yet with all this, it required the judicial murder of the Abbots of Reading, Glastonbury and Colchester before opposition was broken down.[72] Even then the great houses of Christchurch, Canterbury and of Rochester held out until March 3, 1540, when a commission for their forcible dissolution was issued.[73]

During the same years in which Cromwell's commissioners most actively took surrenders of monastic houses, 1538 and 1539, the Bishop of Dover with several assistants was busy taking the surrenders of the friaries. They seem to have been very poor, because "the devotion of the people is clear gone," and they could not live on "the cold and small charity in these days." Many of the houses had already sold all their plate and implements, and were eager to surrender before their poverty compelled them to sell the stones, slate and lead of their houses,[74] though the Grey Friars so far resisted dissolution as to begin the collection of a fund for the purchase of the confirmation of their privileges from the king.[75]. If the Bishop of Dover can be trusted, the crown profited but little by the surrender of the friaries; the houses were scarcely sufficient in value to pay the debts and to dispatch the poor men.[76]

Other commissioners were also busy during this period razing the great shrines of England. Two years previously, in 1536, Chapuys had noticed the desire of the crown to abolish the festivals of saints and images, in order to spoil their shrines,[77] and at that time a draft for an act of Parliament against pilgrimages and superstitious relics had been drawn up.[78] In February and March, 1538, "Pilgrimage saints" began to go down apace, and beginning in September the great shrines of Canterbury, Winchester and Chichester were taken down and conveyed to

[71] *Letters and Papers*, XIV, part I, 1189.
[72] *Letters and Papers*, XIV, part II, 399, 427. Cromwell himself ordered and planned the details of their execution.
[73] *Letters and Papers*, XV, 378.
[74] *Letters and Papers*, XIII, part II, 32, 554; XVI, part I, 101.
[75] *Letters and Papers*, XIII, part II, 934.
[76] *Letters and Papers*, XIV, part I, 661.
[77] *Letters and Papers*, X, 601.
[78] *Letters and Papers*, X, 246.

London. The shrine of St. Thomas at Canterbury was esteemed
one of the wealthiest in the world; the author of the Pilgrim
says of it rather rhetorically "In the space of more than 250
years, I think, there have been few kings or princes of Christendom that did not either bring or send some of their richest
jewels thither . . (It was) so preciously adorned with gold
and stone that at midnight you might in some manner have
discovered all things as well as at noon day." [79] Winchester
shrine was a disappointment to the spoilers. "There was no
gold nor ring nor true stone in it, but all great counterfeits;"
the silver alone however, was worth 2,000 marks, and in addition,
there was a great cross of emeralds, with other ornaments.[80]
At Chichester there were 55 images of silver gilt, 57 pieces of
gold and silver work, and 3 caskets of jewels.[81]

Thus by the close of 1539 the great resumption was practically
accomplished. In the story of the suppression of the monasteries, friaries and shrines, as it has developed, the financial
causes of the movement stand out most clearly. Behind and
beneath all, however, were the great changes in thought and
the reawakening of spiritual forces which characterized the
Reformation. Henry VIII and Cromwell may not have been
deeply and genuinely affected by them; but it was only because
they had come into being, and by playing upon them, that Henry
VIII and Cromwell succeeded in carrying through their undertakings.

[79] *The Pilgrim*, 33-34.
[80] *Letters and Papers*, XIII, part II, 401.
[81] *Ibid.*, 1049.

CHAPTER XI

The Revenues and Their Yield, After the Increases Made by Cromwell

English antiquarians have paid considerable attention to the question of the value of the monastic property at the time when the dissolution began. The best figures give a net yearly value of £135,000[1] These figures have however, little value for the purpose of this essay. Henry VII's income from the monasteries consisted not only in the rents of their lands but in the value of their goods and buildings which he confiscated and sold and in the money received from the sale of their lands. Moreover, he never had all the monastic lands in his hands at any one time, for much of the property and lands of the first monasteries to be suppressed had been alienated before the houses dissolved later came to the king's hands. The value of the monasteries to Henry VIII can only be found by a study of the records of the court of Augmentations, where all their revenues were received. Further the concentration on the effort to find the king's profits from the dissolution has drawn attention from Cromwell's total increases in the revenues, of which the dissolution was only a part. Besides the monastic revenues there were the First Fruits and Tenths and the new clerical subsidies. Finally, owing to the change in the value of money and commodities, any absolute sums which may be named are almost meaningless. It is only when such sums are compared with the older income of the government that the relative importance of the dissolution of the monasteries, the annexation of the first fruits and tenths to the crown, and the clerical subsidies appears.

Before 1540 the entire income at the Exchequer was generally

[1] *Cott. Mss., Cleopatra E.* IV, 446-456. For a discussion of the pre-dissolution value of the English monasteries, see Savine, *Valor Ecclesiasticus,* 77-79.

137

less than £40,000 a year, and after a change in the Household and Wardrobe assignments in that year it dropped to £30,000 a year and less. These sums were derived from the *firma comitatus,* such land revenues as were assigned to the Household and Wardrobe (before 1540), the fee farms of cities, the farm of the ulnage, the moiety of forfeited merchandise, and especially the customs. The wool customs at Calais and such customs assigned for the keeping of Berwick were not however, paid at the Exchequer.

The clear yearly value of the crown lands in the survey of the court of General Surveyors was £38,080 in 1542, and in addition to this there was paid and accounted in this court several thousand pounds each year of the profits of the Hanaper of Chancery, and several hundred pounds yearly of the returns of the butlerage.[2] The net annual revenue of the Duchy of Lancaster was about £13,000.[3] The wards' lands in the court of wards yielded £4,673 clear in 1534, and £12,346 clear in 1546.[4] If an average may be taken from these, the only available figures, there would be £8,500 a year from wards' lands. On the basis of these figures, the normal ordinary, recurring income of the crown from pre-Cromwellian sources, especially the customs and rents of crown lands, and other revenues based on land, excluding the extraordinary revenues like parliamentary taxes, and excluding the revenues collected and expended locally at Calais, Berwick and in Ireland, was about £100,000 a year.

With the new revenues came great increases. During the first five years in which the First Fruits and Tenths were received by the crown, they yielded an annual average of £16,000; but from 1540 on, the yield fell to £9,700 a year owing to the suppression of the larger monasteries.[5] Cromwell himself was concerned about "the decay of first fruits by suppression of the monasteries;"[6] but it was impossible to have it both ways. The

---

[2] *Add. Mss.*, 32,469. No accounts of the General Surveyors' court for many years previous to 1542 have been found; but as the income of this court was not a fluctuating or increasing one, £38,000 probably represents the average income for the decade before 1542.

[3] *Duchy of Lancaster, Accounts Various,* bundle 24.

[4] *Court of Wards, Misc. Books,* 361, 362.

[5] *Treasurer's Accounts, Court of First Fruits and Tenths.*

[6] *Letters and Papers,* XIII, part I, 187.

annual tenth granted by the clergy averaged £29,400 a year from 1535 to 1538 inclusive; but after the suppression of the larger monasteries it was reduced to £18,400.[7] These revenues were received by the treasurer of First Fruits and Tenths. To him Cromwell also turned over in 1535 more than £130,000, probably money received from the clergy for their fine for praemunire, and from other sources. The treasurer of First Fruits and Tenths likewise received the new clerical subsidies. Although the annual tenth granted by the clergy and confirmed by Parliament in 1534 was intended to take the place of the occasional dismes or tenths voted by the convocations in earlier times, the government soon called upon the clergy for special subsidies. Such grants were made in 1540 when a subsidy of four shillings in the pound of the value of all benefices after the annual tenth had been deducted, was granted, payable in two years;[8] in 1542 when a similar grant of six shillings payable in three years was made,[9] and in 1545 when six shillings, payable in two years was granted.[10] The clerical subsidy due in 1540 was estimated at more than £24,000; accounts of the years from 1542 to 1544 show that more than £18,000 a year was received from the clerical subsidies in these years; and probably a like amount was received in every year from 1540 to the end of the reign. All in all, the Treasurer of First Fruits and Tenths, including the £130,000 turned over to him by Cromwell, received an average of £52,200 for every year between 1535 and 1546, with an additional sum of more than £18,000 for every year from 1540 on, from the clerical subsidies.

In the study of the income from the dissolved monasteries, a distinction must be made between rents and issues of the lands, which were true revenues, and the money derived from the sale of land, which was in essence the alienation of capital for pressing emergencies. The net receipts of the Court of Augmentations in Henry VIII's reign were:

August 24   1536   to   Michaelmas   1538   £ 71,616[11]

---

[7] *Treasurer's Accounts, Court of First Fruits and Tenths.*

[8] *Statutes, 32 Henry VII, c. 23.*

[9] *Statutes, 34-35, Henry VIII, c. 28.*

[10] *Statutes, 37 Henry VIII, c. 24.*

[11] *Letters and Papers, XIII, part II, 457.*

L

Michaelmas	1538	to	Michaelmas	1539	108,028[12]
"	1539	to	"	1543	465,684[13]
"	1543	to	"	1544	253,312[14]
"	1544	to	"	1545	200,511
"	1545	to	"	1546	139,152
"	1546	to	"	1547	66,186[15]

In addition to these sums, the gold and silver plate and jewels seized at the shrines in the monastic churches and elsewhere, and delivered into the Jewel House of the King were valued at £79,471.[16] The average net receipts from monastic sources were thus about £130,000 a year from 1536 to the end of the reign. Of this amount however, only £61,300 a year, derived from the rents of land together with small sums from the sale of goods, plate and bells, may be considered true normal recurring revenues. The balance, an annual average of £82,300 was derived from the sale of land and represents the alienation of capital funds.

From these figures, it appears that the net normal income of the crown had been more than doubled by Cromwell. Large parts of the additions which he made, were however, at once required for the business of the king and state. Work on the royal palaces and at Dover and Calais went forward with increased vigor.[17] After 1538 a remarkable increase in the expenditures in the royal household began. The expenditures there rose from less than £25,000 a year in 1538-1539 to £45,700 a year in

[12] *Letters and Papers*, XIV, part II, 236.

[13] *Letters and Papers*, XVIII, part II, 231.

[14] *Letters and Papers*, XIX, part II, 328.

[15] *Augmentations Office, Treasurer's roll of Accounts*, 3.

[16] *Account of Monastic Treasures confiscated by Sir John Williams, late Master and Treasurer of the Jewels.* Published by the Abbotsford club, Edinburgh, 1886.

[17] *Declared Accounts, Pipe Office*, no. 3199, Account of Robert Lord, paymaster of the king's works, showing the expenditure of £59,490 10s. 6d. at Hampton, Nonesuche Oatlande, Mortlake Syon, Oking, Windsor Hanworth and Asshere (1536 to 1539). For general repairs the Treasurer of the Chamber paid £100 a month on a warrant dormant; and the Court of Augmentations paid considerable sums for building at Westminster (*Letters and Papers*, XIII, part II, 457). For works at Dover, see *Letters and Papers*, XI, 1254; XII, part I, 92; XIII, part II, 223; works at Calais, *Letters and Papers*, XIII, part II, 381, 842.

1545-1546.[18]   The suppression of the Pilgrimage of Grace in 1536 cost probably £50,000.   Coming at a time when the new revenues were not yet all in hand, the revolt was particularly ill-timed for the government, and much ado was made to get the necessary funds to pay the king's soldiers.[19]

In Ireland, though the rebellion of the Geraldines was technically subdued, much money continued to be needed; and during the four years after 1536 the king complained constantly that revenue was being consumed to no purpose.[20]   The Irish revenues were increased by the suppression of all the monastic houses in 1538 and 1539 and by other means, from a gross average of £4,812 a year between Michaelmas 1534 and Michaelmas 1537[21] to over £8,000 a year from 1542 to 1547,[22] and the net amount annually available to pay the Irish army rose from £1,823[23] in 1534-1537 to £3,285 between 1541 and 1547.[24]   But these sums continued to be insufficient to pay the entire expenses of the army and repeated appeals were made by the deputy and council in Ireland to the king and to Cromwell for money, for lack of which the army at times became mutinous and was in danger of breaking up.[25]   With the new revolt in 1540, even greater sums had to be sent from England, Henry and the council having decided to exhaust great treasure to bring the inhabitants to civility and obedience, and so "redubbe" the great charges already made, and turn the island into a source of profit as conquered countries should be.[26]   Despite the recent

[18] *Exchequer, Lord Treasurer's Remembrancer, Wardrobe Enrolled Accounts,* roll 8, membranes 43-47 inc.

[19] For accounts of the various treasurers with the king's commanders, see *Letters and Papers,* XI, 930, 950, 1093. See also *Letters and Papers,* XIII, part II, 457; XI, 624, 724; *Rot. Reg.,* 7c XVI, 73/104; *Letters and Papers,* XI, 769, 788, 800; *Declared Accounts, Pipe Office,* no. 2074; *Letters and Papers,* XI, 823, 1124, 1152, 1220.

[20] *Letters and Papers,* X, 105; XI, 1149; *Carew Mss.,* no. 98.

[21] *Letters and Papers,* XII, part II, 1310, accounts of Brabazon, the under treasurer.

[22] *Record Office, Ireland, Folios* V, no. 4.   The revenues in 1544 reached to £10,124; in 1545 and 1546 they fell to £8,500, but rose to £12,056 in 1547.

[23] *Letters and Papers,* XII, part II, 1310.

[24] *Ireland, Folios,* V, nos. 3, 4.

[25] *Irish Calendar,* III, 47; *Letters and Papers,* XI, 267, 351; XVI, 42, 43, 70, 1119; XVII, 665, 688; XX, part II, 562.

[26] *Letters and Papers,* XVI, 1194, 1284.   Between Michaelmas 1540 and

great additions to the revenues, complaints of shortages in the various revenue offices are found as early as the spring of 1537, with a state of embarrassment, almost chronic, during 1537 and 1538. "The Treasury of the Chamber is often without money. The Jewel House, Augmentations, and First Fruits is as ill, and the Chequer is worse." [27] Cromwell chose to pretend that the stringency was genuine; and attributed it to the expenses of the suppression of the Pilgrimage of Grace, the continued costs of the suppression of disorders in Ireland, the works at Calais, Guisnes and Dover and the maintenance of garrisons at Berwick and Carlisle.[28] A study of the accounts of the various revenue departments shows that this condition was only apparent. The total expenditures of the government for all purposes were at least £60,000 less than the royal income, and though the various treasurers may often have been without ready money, as contemporary letters assert, the king himself had large supplies. For he drew upon all the treasurers constantly for their surplus funds, and stored them up in his own coffers. The Treasurer of First Fruits and Tenths delivered £59,139 to the king between January 1, 1535 and Christmas 1540;[29] the Exchequer delivered £15,533 6s. 8d. between Michaelmas 1535 and Michaelmas 1539;[30] and the Treasurer of the Chamber contributed something; but since his account books for these years are only fragmentary, no total sum can be given. The Court of Augmentations paid £45,731 4s. 8d. directly to the king's coffers between the date of the establishment of the court in April 1536 and March 1540[31]

Michaelmas 1547 Henry VIII sent £46,835 to Ireland, which added to the surplus of the Irish revenues for these years made up £65,894 paid to the army in Ireland during this period (*Ireland, Folios,* V, no. 3).

[27] *Letters and Papers,* XIII, part II, 434, a letter of John Husee to Lord Lisle. See also *ibid.,* XII, part I, 116; XII, part II, 69, 90, 274; XIII, part II, 222.

[28] *Letters and Papers,* XIV, part I, 869, a memorial drawn up by one of Cromwell's clerks, and corrected by Cromwell himself April-June, 1539. The same reasons are urged in the draft preamble for an act for subsidy in 1540 (*Ibid.,* XV, 502.).

[29] Lansdowne, Mss., 124 f. 137.

[30] *Exchequer, King's Remembrancer, Misc. Books,* 69; *Exchequer of Receipt Declarations of State of Treasury,* 17, 18, 19.

[31] *Letters and Papers,* XIII, part II, 457; XIV, part II, 236, Accounts of the court of Augmentations.

and £73,538 13s. 4d. between March 1540 and April 1541.[32]
The subsidy and the fifteenth and tenth, granted in 1534, and
collected in 1535, 1536 and 1537, yielding in all at least £77,000,
likewise found their way to the king's coffer in all probability,
since there is no record of their use in any of the revenue courts.[33]
Not only were the royal revenues now sufficient for all the purposes
of the government, but a new surplus was rapidly being gathered.
Before long however, the international political situation became
so portentous, that more rapid progress in the accumulation of
treasure was believed to be necessary and desirable. The royal
purpose to achieve this were masked behind a plea of the king's
great expenses and the inadequacy of his supplies.

[32] *Ibid.*, XVI, 745.

[33] Edmund Denny, the keeper of the king's palace at Westminster had
charge of these surplus funds at least from 1541 onward. His account,
extending into the reign of Edward VI is found in the British Museum,
Lansdowne Rolls, No. 14. His functions were somewhat analagous to
those of John Heron in Henry VII's reign, but he did not become a new
permanent treasurer.

CHAPTER XII

The War with France and Scotland, 1542-1547

By Henry VIII's own statement, he feared no one so long as there was not perfect accord between the Emperor and the Most Christian king.[1] For as long as these two catholic sovereigns were at odds, no effect could be given to any papal bull of privation. But once at peace, they might unite to carry out the provisions of such a bull which was actually promulgated in Rome, December 18, 1537, and divide England between them. While Francis I may have entertained such a thought,[2] it is certain that Charles V never did, because of his multitudinous other activities. Yet Henry VIII thoroughly believed in the possibility of a combined attack upon his throne, and his foreign policy during the last decade of his reign was a long series of attempts to keep his rivals hostile towards each other, and one of them friendly to himself.

The beginning of the new period in Henry VIII's foreign policy came in July, 1537, when a truce of ten months was concluded between France and Flanders. The cordiality between Francis I and the Emperor thus begun, ripened, despite Henry's efforts to the contrary, into the treaty of 1539 by which both Francis and Charles bound themselves to make no new alliances, agreements or accords with the king of England without mutual consent.[3] The direct result of this treaty, and the growing

[1] *Letters and Papers*, XX, part I, 1197, a letter of Chapuys to Charles V.

[2] In 1539 Francis I went so far as to tell the imperial ambassador in France that he was willing to let the bull of privation be published and obey it, if the Emperor would do the same, and suggested that the island might be conquered by three armies and divided (*Letters and Papers*, XIV, part I, 115, Latino Juvenale to Charles V).

[3] *Letters and Papers*, XIV, part I, 62. During 1538 English diplomatists had endeavored to make either Charles or Francis more favorably disposed

hostility which was being shown to Henry VIII in France,[4] was a series of negotiations between Henry VIII and possible allies — the princes of northern Germany, the Duke of Urbino and Christian III of Denmark. There were also great preparations to put the country into a state of defence against invasion. Bulwarks and blockhouses were built on all parts of the coast from Berwick south; men and money were sent to Calais and Guisnes; musters were ordered and not less than ninety ships of war equipped and made ready.

Though nothing came of the rumors of war in 1539, the irritation between France and England was increased by friction over a disputed passage and fort at Calais, and by renewed references to the pensions, so long unpaid.[5] Though amity continued between France and England throughout 1540 and 1541, relations became more and more strained, especially because Francis not only did not pay the pensions, but made "no honorable offer of satisfaction," while in the affair at Calais, he "showed a desire to pick a quarrel with England."[6]

On the other hand, relations with the Empire were constantly improving. Katherine's death in 1536 had removed the chief source of discord between Charles V and Henry VIII, while the growing hostility between France and England made greater friendship with the Emperor desirable. In 1541 a ten months truce was arranged between Henry and the Emperor, that

toward Henry than toward each other. The Emperor was offered a strict alliance; it seems to have been suggested to Francis that here was an opportunity to do away entirely with the pensions which had not been paid since 1534. *Ibid.*, XIII, part II, 914, 915, 1087, 1163.

[4] Throughout France, Henry VIII was reviled as a heretic. At a meeting of the Council of State the Cardinal of Paris reproached him as a tyrant for his latest judicial murders; while Henry's new bibles printed in Paris were sequestered by the University of Paris. See *Letters and Papers*, XIV, part I, 37, 92, 371.

[5] There were rumors in France in the summer of 1539 that Henry VIII had asked Parliament to help him recover his pensions in France (*Letters and Papers*, XIV, part I, 1230). When the French protested against the construction of their bridge at Calais, Henry VIII asserted "we have suffered great unkindness at their hands as the nonpayment of our pension, to which they were bound by oath" (*Letters and Papers*, XVI, 174).

[6] *Letters and Papers*, XVI, 851, a report of Marillac's, of a conversation with the Duke of Norfolk held with him in May, 1541.

neither should treat anything to the other's disadvantage, and Henry even proposed a treaty of closer amity.[7]

When war again threatened between France and the Empire, over the murder of two French ambassadors, Fregoso and Rincon, Henry VIII was in negotiations with both Charles V and Francis I, each of whom was suddenly made willing for a close English alliance. The negotiations with France turned on the French pensions, and the unpaid arrears since 1534. Francis at first impugned their validity; but finally consented to acknowledge his obligation for 600,000 crowns of arrears and accept its acquittance as a dowry with the Princess Mary, provided that Henry would commute the future annual payments due during the course of Henry's life to 40,000 crowns, and give this to Mary as part of her dowry as well. In exchange for these releases, Francis would assign lands to Mary worth one million crowns a year. The perpetual pension claimed by Henry by the treaty of 1527 was to be left as it was, and Henry's successors might dispute as to its validity. But as Henry VIII's greatest concession was the remission of 300,000 crowns of the arrears negotiations were broken off.[8]

Henry VIII's rejection of the French terms was probably hastened by the development of his Scottish policy. Of late years Henry VIII and his nephew James V had not been friends. James V harbored adherents of the old religion who escaped from the north of England; he had refused to follow Henry VIII's example by breaking with the Pope. His country might be an open way for the entrance of Papal legates into England to preach revolt, and it added one more to the number of countries which might join in an attempt to carry out the Papal Bull. War between England and Scotland broke out in 1542, with an unprovoked border raid led by Sir Robert Bowes on August 24, 1542. On his way home he was ambushed at Haddon Rig. Henry was furious. Negotiations with Scotland which had been proceeding were broken off by the king's order "until at notable exploit had been done upon the Scots toward expurging the national dishonor done the realm by the reports

---

[7] *Letters and Papers*, XVI, 910, 1291.

[8] *Letters and Papers*, XVI, 1351; XVII, 164, 167, 185, 208, 270, 286; instructions of Francis I to Marillac, and dispatches of Marillac.

of the Scots, that Bowes and his men had fled before an inferior force of Scots.'' [9]   France of course aided her old ally.   The French refused to renew their negotiations over the pensions, with the sacrifice of Scotland.   When the ship which carried Cardinal Beaton to Scotland was captured by the English, the French ambassador in London was so passionate in demanding its restoration, and became ''so wilful, so proud and so glorious'' that Henry asked his recall.[10]   A few days later, Henry signed a treaty of alliance with Charles V,[11] and in the summer of 1543, Henry actively entered the war with France by the dispatch of a small force under Sir John Wallop to serve with the imperial army in Flanders.   In 1544 the great invasion of France, led by the king in person, was begun.

The war with France and Scotland cost in all £2,134,784 1s. 0d. between the time of the first alarms and the end of Henry VIII's reign.[12]   An anticipation of the great charges of war as it would now have to be waged was given by the costs of the new works at Calais and of the blockhouses which had been erected along the English coast in 1539,[13] while the little border raid into Scotland of 1542 cost £60,129.[14]   As early as 1539, Cromwell seems to have been conscious that the new war, when it came, would pale expenditures in all previous wars.   At the existing rate of accumulation the royal treasure would be inade-

---

[9] *Letters and Papers*, XVII, 925.
[10] *Letters and Papers*, XVIII, part I, 63, 91, 92.
[11] *Letters and Papers*, XVIII, part I, 144, February 11, 1543.
[12] The expenditures were made up:-

The siege of Boulogne	£586,718	12s.	3d.
The keeping of Boulogne	426,306	19s.	5d.
Fortifications and extra garrisons at Calais and Guisnes	270,765	9s.	6d.
War against Scotland including fortifications and garrisons on the border and at Berwick	350,243	2s.	2d.
Charges of the navy	265,024	4s.	3d.
The expedition in aid of the Emperor in 1543, under Sir John Wallop	26,500	0s.	0d.
Fortifications and blockhouses within England from March 1, 1539 onward	203,205	12s.	11d.

State Papers, Edward VI, XV, no. 11.
[13] In the preliminary period 1539-1542 these had cost at least £74,000.
[14] *Declared Accounts, Pipe Office*, no. 212.

quate to finance it. He felt it advisable not to meet the extraordinary expenditures for that year, for the new fortifications, from the existing revenues, since such a procedure would be a potential drain on the surplus. It was moreover, desirable to build up the surplus more rapidly by finding new supplies of ready money. This seems to be the explanation of the ''device'' which Cromwell drew up at this time for the fortification of the realm, according to which every man was to contribute according to his ''behavor,'' and the names of all wealthy men were to be collected. Although Cromwell took care to appoint Richard Morison to defend his plan for a subsidy in the House of Commons,[15] and Norfolk explained the king's necessity in the House of Lords, the session was prorogued before a grant was made.[16]

It was however, soon demonstrated there was a ready market and a great demand for land, and that money could be raised in vast sums quickly and easily by selling the monastic estates. Cromwell had not confiscated the monasteries to alienate their lands in lavish grants or by sale. During the three years following the dissolution of the smaller monasteries, from April 1536 to March 1539, the alienations of crown lands were comparatively small. Estates valued at £11,633 a year, only one-eighth of the entire confiscated domain were alienated during this period, by way of sale at small prices, or as free gifts, chiefly to men in the service of the crown, like Pope, Sadler,

[15] Morrison drew up a draft of his speech in Parliament reciting the king's need. Of late his Majesty's charges had been wonderfully great. Less would serve him, but for his tender love which he bore his subjects which daily enforced him to new charges. Especially costly had been the commotion in the North. Now the whole country was in jeopardy. Much money was being spent in the repair of the fortresses and much treasure had been bestowed on Calais, Guisnes and Dover, on the rebels in Ireland and the garrisons at Berwick and Carlisle. ''Let us,'' he suggested ''lay up our sweet lips for three or four months (which Cromwell in revising the draft altered to ''years'') giving the overplus of our accustomed monthly charges to the present necessity of the commonwealth. It will be better spent than in belly cheer.'' (*Letters and Papers*, XIV, part I, 869).

[16] Norfolk himself, on the plea that shortness of time prevented a grant at this session moved the prorogation to another time ''at which each would make satisfaction to his majesty for his expenses and labors as far as he could.'' (*Lord's Journal*, I, 111).

Wriothesley, Seymour, Gostwick, and Cromwell whose aid alone had enabled Henry VIII to carry through the changes of the past years.[17]   In March, 1539, a new policy was adopted of selling monastic lands to any purchaser at the good price of "twenty years purchase," that is for twenty times the annual rental.   In the year ending at Michaelmas 1539, £80,622 were received from the sale of lands.[18]   To expedite matters, in December, 1539, Cromwell and Sir Richard Riche were given a general commission to sell lands up to a clear yearly rental value of £6,000, for ready money, at twenty years purchase. Throughout the remainder of the reign great extents of monastic lands were sold each year, at first to provide additional funds toward the surplus, and then to meet the costs of war directly. Before Henry VIII's death two-thirds of the monastic domain had been alienated,[19] with the return of £799,310 to the crown in sale money.[20]   This was one of the largest sources of income in the course of the war.   The alienation of so much land, however, really defeated the object of the sequestration of the monastic properties, in order to provide for the temporary exigencies.

In the opening months of 1540 Cromwell returned to the task of finding new funds against future contingencies, with

[17] The value of lands alienated between April 1, 1536, and March 1, 1539, is constructed from the patents of grants, in the *Letters and Papers*. The sum of £46,000 in money, together with certain lands in exchange was received by the crown, from the grantees.   The character of the grantees as servants of the crown appears from a tabulation of all grantees between April, 1536, and March, 1539, constructed from a study of the patents of the grants.

[18] *Letters and Papers*, XIV, part II, 236, accounts of the Court of Augmentations.

[19] Fisher, *Political history of England 1485-1547*, Appendix, table of total alienations, worked out by Dr. Savine.

[20]	April	1536	to	Michaelmas	1538	£ 29,847
	Michaelmas	1538	to	Michaelmas	1539	80,621
	,,	1539	to	,,	1540	91,986
	,,	1540	to	,,	1541	30,438
	,,	1541	to	,,	1542	36,122
	,,	1542	to	,,	1543	105,322
	,,	1543	to	,,	1544	164,495
	,,	1544	to	,,	1545	165,459
	,,	1545	to	,,	1546	72,826
	,,	1546	to	,,	1547	12,284

renewed vigor. The Parliament of 1540 assembled April 12. Ten days later on the seventh day of the session, the first revenue bill of the session, was read in the House of Lords, "for the reduction of the possessions of the Hospitalers of St. John in England into the king's hand." [21] The houses of the knights of St. John had not been touched during the confiscation of the monasteries; but a quarrel in 1540 between an English knight, Sir Clement West and the Grand Master of the order, and West's imprisonment at Malta for appealing to Henry VIII in the matter, gave Henry an excuse to act.[22] The bill met with no opposition, and passed both houses by May 10.[23] Just three days previously, the prior of the order in England died, and the king at once took over his house in London worth £3,385 a year.[24] The priory at North Allerton surrendered soon after; but the house at Bristol continued to stand until March, 1544.[25]

On May 8, the second revenue bill of the session was passed, granting a subsidy to be paid in two years, and four fifteenths and tenths, payable in four years.[26] Still later, the third revenue bill was passed, confirming the action taken by the clergy in their convocations, legalizing their "spontaneous offer" of four shillings in the pound of their income payable in two years, in addition to the annual tenth.[27]

In these years of preparation against the future war, there was also a kind of recrudescence of the measures by which Henry VII had enriched himself at the expense of his nobility. In 1540 Cromwell was attainted of treason, and his property and goods assured to the crown.[28] In 1541, Lord Leonard Grey,

[21] *Lords' Journal*, I, 132.

[22] *Letters and Papers*, XV, 490, 491, 522, 523, 531, 532.

[23] *Lords' Journal*, I, 136; *Statutes, 32 Henry VIII*, c. 24.

[24] The figure is given in Stowe's *Survey of London*, (Ed. by Kingsford), II, 84. *Letters and Papers*, XV, 646.

[25] *Letters and Papers*, XIX, part I, 157.

[26] *Statutes*, 32 Henry VIII, c. 50.

[27] The convocation of York made the grant in consideration of their deliverance from the yoke or Rome, and the king's excessive charges upon havens, blockhouses and fortresses (*Letters and Papers*, XVI, 64). For the grant of Canterbury see Wilkins, III, 850. The enabling act is *Statutes*, 32 Henry VIII, c. 51.

[28] Though these included £7,000 in money and as much more in plate, crosses and chalices, they were not of such value as people thought;

the Countess of Salisbury, Sir John Neville the leader of the abortive revolt in Yorkshire, with 60 of his followers, Lord Dacre of the South with 5,000 ducats a year, and a Mr. Mantell with 12,000 ducats a year, as Chapuys remarked with a sly dig at the real reason for their fate, were executed on various charges and their lands added to the royal estates.[29] Lord Dacre's lands were found to be entailed, and the king's justices and learned council agreed that they ought not to be forfeited, but that the king should have the wardship of the heir and the custody of the lands until he became of age, because part of the lands were held *in capite*. But the king thought that the will of Lord Dacre's grandfather ''should not be so perfect'' but that he might confiscate that part of Dacre's lands held in fee and still have wardship of the rest and have the entail avoid all escheats.[30] At the close of the year, when the misdemeanors of Queen Katherine Howard brought more worthy people to their end, the council showed an indecent haste and eagerness — to say the least — to seize their goods. They feared, for instance, that as the Duchess of Norfolk was old and testy she might take her commital so hard as to endanger her life. And so it was better to indict her and the others at once, ''whereby Parliament shall have better ground to confiscate their goods if any of them should die before the attainder.''[31]

The collection of the lay subsidy and of the fifteenths and tenths in February, 1541, and February, 1542, had netted £153,500;[32] very large sums were received from the land sales and the clerical subsidies. But ''to furnish the treasure requisite in the event of war,'' in March, 1542, it was determined to practice a benevolent loan. Renewed emphasis was put upon the king's expenditures for the fortifications of the realm and the great amount needed to complete them. True a subsidy had just been collected, but this was much less than the king's charges. The

although too much for a ''compaignon de telle estoffe,'' according to a letter from Marillac, the French ambassador in London to Montmorency, June 23, 1540 (*Letters and Papers*, XV, 804).

[29] *Letters and Papers*, XVI, 954.

[30] *Letters and Papers*, XVI, 978, 1019.

[31] *Letters and Papers*, XVI, 1433. For other instances of the same spirit see *Letters and Papers*, XVI, 1422, 1437.

[32] *Exchequer, Lord Treasurer's Remembrancer, Subsidy Rolls*, 43, 44.

commissioners were even to admit that the king had considerable treasure, but considering the daily preparation made by the Emperor and France, "and the motions threatened by the Turks," they were to disclose the "unwisdom" of drawing upon that at this time, lest "he might be disfurnished against any sudden event by outward parts or otherwise." [33] Both Chapuys and Marillac wondered greatly about the purpose of the new levy, "considering the great accumulations of money he has from the spoils of the abbeys, the confiscation of the goods of so many lords for treason, the long time he has been exempt from war and the imposition of the above mentioned tax" (the subsidy of 1540).[34] Neither of these ambassadors with all their experience saw so clearly the probable costs of the next war as did Henry and his council.

The success of the subsidies in the past two years and of the loan of 1542 led Henry to resort to them again in 1543. Parliament granted a lay subsidy and confirmed a clerical subsidy without any opposition.[35] The lending of 40,000 ducats to the Emperor in the summer of the year was used as a reason for asking for a new loan, under the name of Devotion money, from the people. The king gave orders at this time that for six weeks all curates preach and exhort contributions to aid against the Turks, in place of what used to be given for bulls and indulgencies. Chapuys wrote to his master that it was expected that three or four times 40,000 ducats would be raised. If there was any such hope, it was disappointed, for the entire collection of the "Devotion money" was only £1,903 8s. 3d.[36]

As the plans for the invasion of France in the summer of 1544 with 42,000 men were maturing, Wriothesley and Paget, members of the council, assumed the chief burden of responsibility for finances. They took careful survey of the situation at the beginning of the year. They estimated that the campaign in France would cost £250,000. There was immediately

[33] *Letters and Papers*, XVII, 194.

[34] *Letters and Papers*, XVII, 235, 338, Marillac to Francis I, *Ibid.*, 280, Chapuys to Granvelle.

[35] *Lords' Journal*, I, 213, 215.

[36] *Exchequer, Lord Treasurer's Remembrancer, Miscellaneous Rolls*, 2/23. See also *Letters and Papers*, XVIII, part I, 955; XVIII, part II, 315.

available from the revenues without considering the money in the king's chests or the loan of 1542 in Mr. Pekham's hands, but including £50,000 which could be borrowed in Flanders, £134,000. The sum lacking, £116,000, they hoped to raise by various extraordinary means, so as not to have to draw on the surplus. The sale of land, the sale of lead from the monastic houses or the pledge of lead for loans, levies on English and foreign merchants and on those in the king's fee, the profits of the mint and of the issues of debts due the crown were suggested by Wriothesley as satisfactory for his purposes.[37]

On March 1, 1544 to take the first plan for bringing in more money, a commission was issued to William Paulett, Wriothesley, Riche and Robert Southwell to sell the king's lands and the lead from the roofs of the conventual houses which had been lying in storage since the dissolution of the monasteries, and to conclude with subjects for fines and "incombes" for leases, for manumission of bondmen and for the sale of wards.[38] The number of sales was expected to be so large, that power was granted to sign patents with the king's stamp. In April, Sir Anthony St. Leger received a commission to sell and lease the royal possessions in Ireland,[39] in order to relieve pressure for money from that quarter; and in July, Wriothesley and others were commissioned to sign grants of land to citizens of London who had advanced certain money to the king on condition that the king might redeem the lands within one year.[40] The old acts of Henry VII that all who had grants of land from the king or who held any crown office or annuity must attend the king in person on his military expeditions were again enforced; but persons desiring to compound for such attendance were

37 *Letters and Papers*, XIX, part I, 272, a memorandum of finances drawn up by Wriothesley in 1544.

38 *Letters and Papers*, XIX, part I, 278 (4), (5), (67). The commission began "For the accomplishment of this enterprise (of a war against France) it is expedient to prepare a mass of money by sale of the king's possessions because he will not at present molest his loving subjects for money unless thereto caocted." This commission was resumed in June and re-issued in a slightly different form to Sir John Baker and others (*Letters and Papers*, XIX, part I, 812 [77]).

39 *Letters and Papers*, XIX, part I, 443 (7).

40 *Letters and Papers*, XIX, part I, 1035 (87).

enabled to do so.[41]   All these opportunities were taken advantage of by the English people.   Before Michaelmas, 1544, £5,776 had been received at the court of Augmentations as composition for exemption from attending the king, and £22,616 from the sale of mortgages to the citizens of London, while £164,495 was realized from the sale of lands from Michaelmas, 1543, to Michaelmas, 1544.[42]

But the sale of lands and privileges were not alone relied upon. Like governments of modern times, the English government resorted to loans from the rich bankers and merchants in Flanders and Germany.   Stephen Vaughan was the English agent in Antwerp for negotiating these loans, and he succeeded in borrowing 210,000 crowns in 1544.   Though the sum was small compared with the costs of the war during the year, it was more than a year's revenue at the beginning of Henry VII's reign.   It was used to provide for merely incidental expenses, like the wages of German mercenaries whom Henry VIII had hired and from whom he received practically no service, and the purchase of ordnance, gunpowder and grain.[43]

The third means taken to raise money in 1544 was the debasement of the currency.   Color of justification was sought in the excuse that the debasement of the coinage in Flanders and France caused money to be carried out of England notwithstanding the king's command to the officers of the ports to enforce the statutes against this, so that the only remedy appeared to be the enhancing of the value of silver and gold within the realm.[44]   This cause had probably been the valid ground for earlier changes in the value of gold and silver by Henry VIII, even as late as the alterations in the coinage of 1542.   The great sums of money needed by the king at this time however, together with two papers in Wriothesley's hand, counting upon the mint for a large portion of the money estimated to be needed for the

[41] *Letters and Papers*, XIX, part I, 1035 (86).

[42] *Letters and Papers*, XIX, part II, 328, accounts of the court of Augmentations.   In the next year £165,460 was received from land sales, and in the year ending Michaelmas 1546, £72,826.   Augmentations Office, *Treasurer's Roll of Accounts*, no. 3.

[43] The loans in Flanders are treated separately, in Chapter XIII.

[44] *Letters and Papers*, XIX, part I, 513, the proclamation of debasement, May 6, 1544.

year, and calculating the king's gain by the debasement, leave
no doubt about the real reason for the step.[45]   The mint was
reorganized, with Edmund Pekham already well known in connection with the loan of 1542, as High Treasurer of the Mint.
From this time forward for many years the profits of the mint
arising from the coinage of debased money became the great
"shot anchor" of the government, furnishing it with even more
money than did the sale of monastic lands.[46]

The campaign of 1544 belied Wriothesley's greatest expecta-
tions. It cost not £250,000, but nearer £650,000. It consumed
not only the new extraordinary funds and the revenues counted
upon as available early in the year, but it seems to have drained
the surplus as well. As the fall of 1544 came on, the king was
clearly ill-furnished with funds. When money was sent to the
army in the North in October, 1544, Shrewsbury the king's lieutenant was requested to use all the husbandry he might.[47]   At
this same time, Richard Riche, treasurer of the armies in France,
was compelled to borrow money in order to pay his soldiers the
wages due them. According to his letters, for lack of money
"the poor soldiers do here die daily at Calais of the plague
and also of weakness for lack of victual."

Since the king was determined to keep Boulogne, the financial
ministers, Wriothesley and Paget were compelled to turn their
hands to raising for the year 1545 enough money to meet the
entire costs of the year's campaign, without help from reserve
funds. But this was supposed to be an easy task, since the
expenditures of the year would be light. With a blind optimism
Paget estimated in November, 1544, that the war during the
first six months of the new year would take £90,000, to be expended chiefly at Calais, Guisnes and Boulogne. The subsidy
would yield £100,000, less £40,000 "for the debt" (in Flanders).
There would therefore be lacking £64,000 (sic), which must be
provided. A benevolence was much surer and quicker than a
new Parliamentary grant — and a benevolence would not only
provide the shortage of the first six months of 1545, but would
leave a balance of £50,000 available for the charges of the

[45] Wriothesley's papers are found in *Letters and Papers*, XIX, part I,
272 (2), 513 (5).
[46] The debasement is studied separately in detail in chapter XIII.
[47] *Letters and Papers*, XIX, part II, 510.

M

second half of the year.[48] What Paget did not foresee or cal-
culate on was that Boulogne would cost the country not £6,000,
but £13,000 a month; that the Scotch would inflict a severe
defeat upon Sir Ralph Eure in February, 1545, which would
make it necessary to send a great expeditionary force to Scotland under Hertford in September, to desolate their country
and to strike terror into their souls; or that France having
made peace with the Empire, would plan to invade England in
the spring of 1545, and that to face this invasion England would
have to make ready the greatest fleet which had ever sailed
under the flag and three armies of 60,000 men.[49]

All these causes necessitated the expenditure of £560,000
between Michaelmas, 1544, and September 8, 1545.[50] To meet
these very great payments crown lands were thrown upon the
market in even larger quantities than before. Stephen Vaughan
borrowed £128,929 Flemish from the Fuggers and Italian merchants.   A little more alloy and a little less gold and silver
were put into the coins. The practice was developed of borrowing from the mint. Merchants came with their bullion to have
it coined; for the coined money they were obliged to wait three
and four months; meantime it was being used by the government.
The mint was indeed "our holy anchor." Despite Pekham's
protests that no more be borrowed until all that had previously
been borrowed be repaid, and despite the councillors' fears
that if the news should come out that men's coming hither
be thus employed, it would make them withdraw their resort,
the loans from the mint were continued until they had reached
100,000 marks.[51] Part of the subsidy due in February, 1546,
was collected by anticipation.[52] The confiscation of the service
silver in the parish churches was even considered,[53] but Paget

[48] *Letters and Papers,* XIX, part II, 689, a paper in Paget's hand
November, 1544.

[49] *Letters and Papers,* XX, part II, 558. The charges at Boulogne from
September 27, 1544, to October 9, 1545, were £152,500 (*Letters and
Papers,* XX, part I, 1078, 986, 856, 926, 958).

[50] *Letters and Papers,* XX, part II, 324, Wriothesley to Paget, in a
letter commenting upon the reports of the treasurers he has just received.

[51] *Letters and Papers,* XX, part II, 746, 749, 453, 729.

[52] *Letters and Papers,* XX, part I, 675.

[53] *Letters and Papers,* XX, part I, 16, January, 1545. Hertford approved the plan (*Ibid.,* 1145).

stayed his hand. Finally the confiscation of the chantry wealth — logically the next of the church's accumulations to be attacked, was authorized by Parliament in November, 1545, with a frank recognition of the purpose of the measure.[54] During the year many of the chantries were taken over by the crown, even before the act was passed; but probably because they did not provide ready money most of them were left intact at the time of Henry's death.

Though vast sums were received from all these measures, money was spent more quickly than it came in; and Wriothesley and Paget more than once lost their tempers when ever new demands came to them from the Council. In September, for example, Wriothesley received a letter from the Council, noting the levying of 4,300 new men for the relief of Boulogne, desiring preparation of money for their coats and conducts. "As to money," he replied, "I trust you will consider what is done already. This year and the last, the king has spent about £1,300,000, his subsidy and benevolence ministering scant £300,000 and the lands being consumed and the plate of the realm molten and coined, I lament the danger of the time to come. There is to be repaid in Flanders as much and more than all the rest. . . Though the king might have a greater grant than the realm could bear, it would do little to the continuance of these charges this winter, most of the subsidy being paid, the revenues received beforehand and more borrowed from the mint than will be repaid these four or five months — and yet you write me still, pay, pay, prepare for this and that."[55] And again he wrote to Paget, after examining the very discouraging reports of the various treasurers — "Now what I shall do or how I shall divide this matter that all may yet be saved upright I cannot tell. I would you felt a piece of the care and I wene you would not write so often as you do, knowing the state of things as I, by the declarations of the treasurers. You bid me run as though I could make money. I would I had that gift but one year for his Majesty's sake."[56]

The situation was eased in 1546 by the very extraordinary yields of the first payment of the subsidy and of the payment

[54] *Statutes,* 37 Henry VIII, c. 4.
[55] *Letters and Papers,* XX, part II, 366, September 14, 1545.
[56] *Letters and Papers,* XX, part II, 746.

of the first fifteenth and tenth granted in 1545, which netted £135,000,[57] and by the conclusion of peace with France. On June 7, 1546, the Treaty of Camp was signed. France was to pay all pensions due to Henry VIII during his life and to his successors as it was directed by former treaties, that is 94,736 crowns a year during Henry's lifetime, and 50,000 crowns in perpetuity to his successors after his death, and 10,000 crowns a year for the commuted tribute of black salt to Henry and his successors if found to be perpetual. Within 15 days after Michaelmas, 1554, Francis I was to pay for the arrears of the pensions and for the fortifications of Boulogne built by Henry, 2,000,000 crowns; whereupon Francis should be released of the arrears of the pension due to May 1, 1546, and all charges of the war, and Boulogne should be restored to France.[58]

For these worthless pensions and eight years of the possession of Boulogne, Henry had squandered his resources. He left to his son a debt of £100,000 Fl. in Flanders; an empty treasury,[59] a debased currency, depleted estates and charges vastly increased by the necessity of maintaining a post war establishment, in France and against Scotland.

[57] *Exchequer, Lord Treasurer's Remembrancer, Subsidy Rolls*, nos. 42, 43.

[58] *Letters and Papers*, XXI, part I, 1014. The treaty made further provision that a debt of 512,022 crowns 22s. 6d. upon certain letters of Francis of January 29, 1529, for money lent to him by Henry VIII was to be submitted to commissioners.

[59] The Treasurer of First Fruits and Tenths made no declaration at the end of the fiscal year 1546, because he had nothing (*Letters and Papers*, XXI, part II, 34). See also *ibid.*, 134.

CHAPTER XIII

Direct Taxes, Loans and the Debasement of the Coinage, 1542-1547

The great dependence on direct taxes and loans, and on the profits of the debasement of the coinage to meet the exigencies of the war, appears very clearly in the history of the last years of Henry VIII's reign. A more detailed examination of their nature, and the method of their use forms the topic of this chapter.

Much greater success was achieved in the use of the direct parliamentary taxes, the fifteenth and tenth, and especially the subsidy, than had been met with in earlier periods. Though they bore only a part of the total war charges, they were, considered absolutely, vastly more productive than they had been in former periods. Whereas, Henry VIII had raised £253,000 by direct taxation during his first war with France, and little more than £150,000 during his second French war, the subsidies and fifteenth and tenths voted and collected from 1540 to 1547 (both years inclusive) netted £650,000.[1]

The Lancastrian and Yorkist kings, it will be recalled, attempted to supplant the fifteenth and tenth by a more flexible tax, under royal control. Their experiments were continued by Henry VII, who finally succeeded in abolishing the exemption of certain towns from taxation, in making a new assessment, in putting the assessment and collection into the charge of royal officers, and in introducing the alternate levy on either land or goods. Some progress was made towards these ends in the grant of 1497, and the precedents were firmly established in the tax of 1504. The alternate levy on either land or goods newly assessed for each grant by royal officials and

[1] L. T. R. Enrolled Accounts, Subsidies.

collected by them, with no exemption or remittances to favored towns or localities are the essence of the Tudor subsidy. The first three decades of Henry VIII's reign were a period of experimentation to find the most productive and least obnoxious and disturbing forms of the tax with such essentials. In 1512 a so-called "poll tax" was tried. A duke was levied for ten marks, a marquis, earl or countess, £4; a baron, baronet or baroness, £2, and a knight 30 shillings. Persons with freehold or other lands of the annual value of £40 or more were to pay 20 shillings; with lands worth from £20 to £40, ten shillings; with lands worth from £10 to £20, five shillings; with lands from £2 to £10, two shillings; and with lands worth under £2, 12 pence. Persons with personalty, goods, chattels and moveables paid 12 pence if their goods were worth from £2 to £10, and so in an ascending scale until they paid four marks if they had goods worth over £800. Persons paid on either their land or their goods, according to which was of the greater value, but never on both. Artificers and handicraftsmen without property, who had wages above 40 shillings a year were to pay 12 pence; if between 20 shillings and 40 shillings, six pence; and if below 20 shillings, four pence. [2] In 1514 a great simplification was introduced. The grant was a tax of six pence in the pound of annual value of land above 20 shillings, six pence in the pound on wages above 20 shillings or six pence in the pound on the value of moveable property above the value of 40 shillings. All natives except real beggars, above 15 years of age not coming under the other provisions of the act were to pay four pence.[3] The rate was very considerably increased to something like its later extent in the act which Wolsey forced through the hostile parliament of 1523. This granted a tax of one shilling in the pound of the yearly income from lands each year for two years, and one shilling in the pound on the value of goods and moveables above £20, and six pence in the pound on such values between 40 shillings and £20, each year for two years. Workmen with wages of 20 shillings a year or with goods of 40 shillings of value, paid four pence each year for two years. In the third year

[2] *Statutes,* 4 Henry VIII, c. 19.
[3] *Statutes,* 5 Henry VIII, c. 17.

landed gentlemen whose lands were worth £50 a year or more, were taxed an additional shilling in the pound, while in the fourth year a tax of one shilling in the pound was due from all who possessed moveables above the value of £50.[4] The levies of the third and fourth year in this act were rather accidental, being added to it by the jealousy of the country-gentlemen toward city-members,[5] while the tax of four pence upon all persons with more than 20 shillings a year in wages added comparatively little to the value of the grant and much to its unpopularity.

In later grants the "super taxes" of the act of 1523 were stripped off, and wide limits of exemption were created, to include eventually more than half of those who had paid under the act of 1523.[6] But even to the end of Henry VIII's reign the form of the subsidy had not become fixed. In 1540 £20 in value of lands or goods was set as the limit of exemption; the tax was one shilling in the pound of the value of land, and six pence in the pound of the value of movables, above this limit, payable each year for two years.[7] In 1543 the limit of exemption was only £1 in lands and goods. The tax was a graduated one; on the value of goods it ranged from four pence in the pound on values between one and five pounds, to two shillings in the pound on values over £20; on land it began at eight pence in the pound for values between one and five pounds, to three shillings in the pound on values above £20. Not only aliens, who had always done so, but guilds and corporations paid at a double rate. Payment was extended over three years; one half being due in 1544, and one quarter at each of the successive payments in 1545 and 1546.[8] In the subsidy of 1545 one pound was the limit of exemption for land, five pounds for moveables. In this grant the land tax was two shillings in the pound payable in two years (one shilling a year in each of two years), but

[4] *Statutes*, 14 and 15 Henry VIII, c. 16.

[5] Hall, *Chronicles*, I, 285.

[6] In 1524, 17,000 persons paid the tax in Suffolk, representing a very large part of all the heads of families. In 1568, only 7,700 persons paid. *Suffolk Green Books*, X, "*Suffolk in 1524, being the Returns for a Subsidy granted in 1523*," (Ed. by S. H. A. Hersey), page XXIV.

[7] *Statutes*, 32 Henry VIII, c. 50.

[8] *Statutes*, 34 and 35 Henry VIII, c. 27.

the tax on personalty was graduated from eight pence in the pound on goods worth from £5 to £10, to one shilling four pence in the pound on goods worth more than £20.[9] It was not until Elizabeth's reign that the final form was fixed, and the subsidy became a stereotyped institution.

The subsidy of 1540 yielded £94,000; that of 1543 £183,000 and that of 1545 £196,000.[10] The augmenting value of the yield of these subsidies may have been due to the wider incidence and higher rates of the later two; to the greater insistence of the crown upon its dues, which was especially emphatic as the war demands became more pressing, and to the increasing wealth of the people of the country. Besides these three subsidies six fifteenths and tenths were granted by Parliament in this period from 1540 to 1547, and netted £176,000, or a little more than £29,000 each. Fifteenths and tenths were used in conjunction with the subsidies now as earlier, and they continued in their old form without change. In most of the years from 1540 to 1547 the crown collected two parliamentary tax levies; in the year 1546, three. That it was enabled to do so means more than that the nation was committed to a foreign war, for which such taxes were justifiable measures, and that the crown had now organized its power so completely as to stamp out at their inception such revolts as had arisen in Henry VII's reign in 1489 and again in 1497 and such dissatisfaction as had greeted Wolsey's measures. The nation was stirring with life and prosperity, and taxes which would have dethroned a Yorkist could be paid without grudging, to further the personal ends of a popular king.

The subsidies and fifteenths and tenths represent but a part of the money taken from the nation in direct taxes during the war period. Despite the fact that the clergy had granted the perpetual tenths to the king in 1534, which it was supposed would take the place of the occasional tenths or dismes, voted all through the Middle Ages to the crown, new subsidies were now demanded. These took the form of the tenth part of the nine tenths of the clerical income which remained after the

---

[9] *Statutes,* 37 Henry VIII, c. 25.
[10] *Exchequer, Lord Treasurer's Remembrancer, Subsidy Roll,* 42.

perpetual tenth had been paid. They were voted by convocation, with parliamentary authority and permission, and payments were made in every year from 1540 to the end of the reign.

Taxes in reality, though not in name were the forced loans and benevolences of the war period. Henry VII observed a careful distinction between a forced loan and a benevolence; the first, he always repaid; the second was not intended to be repaid. But this distinction vanished in his son's reign, and forced loans and benevolences became nothing less than arbitrary taxes, levied by the king without parliamentary authority, sometimes made easier of collection by promises of repayment, which were repudiated by subservient parliaments in due time. Wolsey's failures in 1525, when bon-fires, reports of the destruction of the French army and the capture of the king of France, processions and ''other tokens of joy'' could not induce the people to pay the loan then demanded, and in 1528 when a new loan caused grave discontent among the people,[11] cast disrepute upon the forced loan; and no further resort was made to it until the war period at the end of Henry VIII's reign. On March 22, 1542, the keeper of the privy seal was commanded to deliever by indenture to Sir Thomas Wriothesley and Sir Ralph Sadler letters under the privy seal, in this form,— ''By the king, where our Councillor A. B. has upon great and earnest considerations * * * * advanced us in prest the sum of N. sterling, we promise to repay it in two years.''[12] Sadler and Wriothesley delivered these ''privy seals'' which were blank royal bonds, to royal Commissioners appointed in the several shires, to be filled out by them and given to the persons who lent to the king. With the blank privy seals were sent lists of the names of persons to be approached, compiled from the subsidy books, giving the rate at which they were assessed for the subsidy.

The commissioners were to declare to the people with whom they ''practiced,'' how the king had been at great charges in erecting and repairing castles and fortresses, both in England and at Calais and Guisnes, in making his haven at Dover, and in maintaining a great garrison in Ireland. It was not desirable

[11] *Letters and Papers*, IV, 3303, 3866, 4772.
[12] *Letters and Papers*, XVII, 188.

that the king should spend his own treasure, lest he be unprovided against a sudden need. For these reasons, the commissioners were to proceed, the king desired his nobles ''and others who may strain themselves'' to advance him money. The Commissioners were to first liberally assess themselves and then to consider the whole shire with reference to their lists of names of such as were thought meet to contribute. They might ''dismiss'' some, and take others at their discretion, pressing no man to contribute who had not £50 a year in lands or £100 in goods The least rate ''that can conveniently be levied of the hundred'' was ten pounds on the value of lands, and ten marks on the value of goods. If any person showed himself ''stiff'' in condescending to the loan at this rate, upon the allegation of poverty or other pretences which seemed insufficient, the Commissioners were to use what persuasion they could, and if ''all would not draw him to some reason and honest consideration of duty'' they were to charge him to keep secret what had been said to him, note his name, and send him home, ''and so pass him over in such a silence as he would be no impeachment or evil examples to the rest.'' [13] Repayment was promised in two years, but Chapuys, the Imperial ambassador wrote that it was more likely to be at the Greek Calends, like that in Wolsey's time, and none of the lenders expected their money back again.[14] To give encouragement to the faint-hearted and assure them that repayment would be made, the Customs officers were ordered to abate in payment of customs dues such sums ''of which they shall be advised'' to those who had lent money to the king.[15] But even those who were repaid in this way had little good of it, for parliament in 1543 remitted the king's obligation to repay the loan, and all those who had secured repayment were called upon to return it.[16]

The loan of 1542 was more productive than any single collection of any parliamentary tax had ever been, bringing

[13] *Letters and Papers*, XVII, 194, 189, 190. See also *Historical Mss. Commission, Report XII, App. IV*, 27.

[14] *Letters and Papers*, XVII, 280.

[15] *Letters and Papers*, XVII, 193.

[16] *Statutes*, 35 Henry VIII, c. 12; *Letters and Papers*, XXI, part 1, 1084.

£112,229 into the treasury.[17] It was followed by the unsuccessful scheme of the "Devotion money" in 1543, preached by the ministers in the churches as a free will offering to aid the crusade against the Turks and by a very small loan in 1544, part of which was actually repaid.[18] The chaotic financial situation at the end of 1544 resolved Wriothesley to attempt a levy without promise of repayment, called the "Benevolence money." The commissioners were given their instructions in January, 1545. The great charges made last year for the siege and capture of Boulogne and the preparations now being made "have and will exhaust more money than we (the king) can sustain without the help of our subjects" and knowing by experience our people to be so loving toward us that they will gladly contribute what is necessary, as if it were granted by parliament, we forbear troubling them to repair hither; and by our council's advice require contributions by way of benevolence. The Commissioners were to make a "frank example contribution" themselves, to encourage the rest to strain themselves as the necessity of the time required; they were to urge the defence of the realm, their wives and children, and to sound the note of ingratitude if need be. Every man with lands worth 40 shillings or more a year, or with goods worth five marks was to be forced to contribute. The least rate acceptable was eight pence in the pound on lands or goods being below £20 in value, and one shilling in the pound above £20. Those who would not contribute were to be sworn to keep secret what had been said to them, and sent home, not to be an evil example to the rest.[19]

The king's naive assumption that this contribution, which was assessed, levied and collected with all the machinery of a regular parliamentary tax, would be gladly paid, may be a piece of royal humor. The fact is, that the royal power was now so strong that fear of popular opposition did not need to be considered. The government could and did crush any protest promptly and effectively. Two examples were sufficient.

[17] *Exch., Lord Treasurer's Remembrancer, Misc. Rolls,* 2/23. Much of the payment was made in plate.

[18] The proceeds of the loan of 1544 were only £12,970 (*Letters and Papers,* XIX, part I, 368). Records of repayment are found in *ibid.,* XXI, part I, 775, 477; *Treasury of Receipt, Privy Seals,* bundle 4, no. 86.

[19] *Letters and Papers,* XX, part I, 17, 52, 125 (5); part II, App. 4.

When the Duke of Suffolk called the citizens of London before him at Baynard's Castle, one alderman, Sir William Roach protested the legality of the benevolence. He was sent to the Fleet prison until Passion Sunday, when he purchased his liberty from the king.[20] Richard Reed, another alderman, refused to pay, and "could not be persuaded to conform thereto." The fate of Reed deterred others from following his example. For, "as for the defence of the realm and himself he would not disburse a little of his substance, the king thought he should do some service with his body." He was sent North to fight the Scots; to serve under Evers as a soldier with his men at his own charge. Within three months he was taken prisoner and made to pay a heavy ransom.[21] Had Roach and Reed lived a century later, they would have been remembered as great defenders of constitutional rights in England. As it is, they live in the pages of Wriothesley's Chronicle and in one or two old documents as the despicable examples of men so lacking in patriotims that they would not willingly give of their substance to the king's necessity.

The Benevolence of 1545 was even more successful than the Loan of 1542, yielding £119,581,[22] the rate was lower, but the incidence was much greater. Its general lines were followed in the "Contribution" of 1546, levied on all who had lands of the value of 40 shillings a year or goods worth £15. Here the least rate was higher than in the previous year — four pence in the pound monthly for five months, or twenty pence in the pound on the value of lands, and two pence in the pound monthly for five months, or ten pence in the pound of goods. The provision that payment might be made in five monthly installments is rather novel. The account of this levy has not come to light, but it was probably as great in its returns as the Loan of 1542 and the Benvolence of 1545.

In addition to the £650,000 raised by parliamentary taxation during the war period, the king received £270,000 from arbitrary taxes, in addition to the Contribution of 1546, of which the return is unknown. If the Contribution of 1546 was as produc-

---

[20] Wriothesley's *Chronicle*, 151.

[21] *Ibid.*, 151, 153.

[22] *Exchequer, Lord Treasurer's Remembrancer, Misc. Rolls*, 2/23.

tive as the Benevolence of the previous year, more than a million pounds was taken from the nation in the war period of the last years of the reign, in the form of direct taxes. Though this is thirty times the national revenue in 1485, it was now merely a contribution in aid.

THE LOANS IN FLANDERS

Henry VIII's foreign loans during the last years of his reign are perhaps of more interest, than of preëminent importance. The activity of his agent in Flanders gives some glimpses into the practice of international banking and business in this earlier time. Stephen Vaughan was sent to Flanders in 1544, the year of the Boulogne campaign, to negotiate loans which would be necessary to meet the charges of the year. The regent, the Queen of Hungary, was much surprised to learn that he had come to raise 100,000 ducats monthly for Henry VIII, as she knew he was well furnished with money. She even instructed Chapuys, the Imperial ambassador in London, to tell Henry VIII that the levying of money in Flanders would hinder the Emperor's plans, and that she would pray Henry to levy it in his own realm.[23] No real opposition however, was made to Vaughan's operations. He fell in with a broker or intermediary, Jasper Douche, through whom he was brought into touch with the merchants and bankers who had money to lend. Things moved quickly, at first. Vaughan had arrived on May 23. On June 4, he had promises from Douche that Henry VIII should have 100,000 crowns in ten or twelve days, with interest at 14 in the hundred, or 14 per cent, for the year, to be repaid at the next Cold Mart, February 12 or 14. Douche would deliver a second hundred thousand crowns in July, but could not promise that the interest would be the same.[24] The security for the loans was curiously arranged. The royal credit was not sufficient. Some great London mercantile house sent a "bill of credence" to its factors or correspondents in Antwerp, with directions that they become bound to such persons as Vaughan appointed, for a certain sum. The London house was guaranteed against

[23] *Letters and Papers*, XIX, part I, 578, the Queen of Hungary to Chapuys.
[24] *Letters and Papers*, XIX, part I, 360.

loss by bonds or obligations in which Wriothesley, Suffolk, Sir Anthony Brown and other members of the Council, with the two Greshams, Sir Richard and Sir John, the two richest London merchants, bound themselves to pay a large forfeit to the house if the loan for which they stood surety was not promptly repaid.[25] The guaranteeing houses were perforce Italians, since the Staplers and Merchant Adventurers would not suffice; and of the Italian houses in London, merchants in Antwerp preferred the companies of the Vivaldi and the Bonvise as sureties.[26] Before long, Vaughan received his first bills of credence from England, and for some reason, these first bills were refused in Flanders, because the bankers suspected the Bonvise of underhand dealing; and it was necessary to send to London for new bills.[27]

In this same letter in which he first asked for the new bills, Vaughan sent the good news that the first hundred thousand crowns would be received from the Welsars, a house which had lent 800,000 crowns to the Emperor, "and was not yet empty." The first loan "would be a mean to practice with them otherwise." Vaughan wrote further that he had already "made a motion to them for lead," that is, he had suggested their purchase of some of the lead from the roofs of the monastery buildings which Henry VIII had on hand, and he had been promised an answer in fifteen days.

The new bills of credence arrived from London in due course; but a new difficulty arose when it came to receiving the money. The merchants refused to pay more than 36 stivers to a crown, although the rate in France was 38 stivers.[28] Vaughan soon came to the conclusion that he had "to do with foxes and wolves which are shrewd beasts, whose natures are well known to your (the council's) honors." Finally on July 2, the bargain for the first loan was concluded for 122,778 crowns at ten and one-half per cent interest for nine months, payable at the next Cold Mart.[29]

Even before the money of the first loan was in his hands,

25 *Ibid.*, 759.
26 *Ibid.*, 630, Vaughan to Wriothesley.
27 *Ibid.*, 725.
28 *Ibid.*, 733.
29 *Ibid.*, 822.

Vaughan began negotiations for further loans, and by the end of the year 1544, he had succeeded in raising altogether, 210,000 crowns. Most of the money was spent for the incidental expenses of the campaign of 1544, like the hire of wagons, advances to German mercenaries and the purchaes of gunpowder and other stores, while £14,000 Flemish was sent to Suffolk in July for the wages and charges of the solidiers in his division of the army invading France.[30]

In June, 1544, Vaughan had mentioned the king's lead to the Welsars. In July he advised the Council to send a good stock of lead to Antwerp, to remain there, ''the sight of which would get credence easier and cheaper than merchants' bills.'' The Council was eager to act on Vaughan's advice, and bettered it — they conceived the idea of sending lead to Flanders in great quantities, to sell it there, to provide money for the repayment of the loans. Vaughan cried out upon the plan, since the flooding of the market would surely drive the price down. It would be better, he thought, to extend the loans, rather than secure money for their repayment in this way. The loss on the lead would be 33 per cent, while the loans cost only ten and one-half per cent. Nevertheless as December came around, and the prospect of the coming day of repayment began to disturb the Council, Vaughan went to all the mercantile houses of Antwerp as salesman for the king's lead. But no one offered more than four pounds three shillings for a fodder of 2184 pounds, which was fourteen shillings sixpence below the market price in August, while one house at Aix-la-Chapelle offered to buy 3000 fodder a year at four pounds, with twelve months for payment and an agreement that the king would sell to no one else. The offers were not accepted. Eventually in July, 1545, Vaughan made a contract with Spanish merchants for the delivery of 30,000 hundred weight or quintals of alum, at sixteen shillings eight pence the quintal to the king at London or Southampton, in exchange for lead at four pounds thirteen shillings and four pence the fodder, with customs paid by the Spanish merchants on both the lead, and the alum which the King expected to sell to cloth manufacturers in England for cash.[31]

30 *Ibid.*, 822, 1099, 859, 887; *ibid.*, part II, 108, 160, 220.

31 *Letters and Papers*, XIX, part II, 119, 143, 743; XX, part I, 1261, 1265; part II, App. 41.

Some of the first loans were for only six months, and were due in December, 1544. Since Vaughan could sell no lead, and there was no money available in England, Vaughan got them extended until February 10, 1545.[32] At this time 210,000 crowns were due, and repayment was promptly made from the revenues in the Exchequer, the Augmentations, the Treasury of the Chamber, the First Fruits and Tenths, and the Mint through Sir Richard and Sir John Gresham.[33] The king's credit now stood very high. Before long, the "Fowkers" (Fuggers), acting through Douche, offered, among other things, to bargain for any sum the king pleased upon the credit of the Staplers and the Merchants. Much negotiation followed. Vaughan wrote: "We have much ado here with the Fowker for the making of his obligations. Wonderful tricks had a lawyer here devised to bind the king's Majesty and his city (of London) in, all of which we refused." Finally the Fowker agreed to accept the obligation of merchants of London and the king's promise *in verbo regio,* and lent him 300,000 crowns, of which 40,000 crowns was in jewels and the rest in money, at ten per cent on the money only. The low rate of interest was accounted for by the profits on the jewels. An extra two per cent was added to dispense with the obligation to repay in carolus gilderns and crowns.[34] As soon as the agreement was concluded came a new difficulty, about getting the money out of the country. The Flemings suspected that Vaughan was going to try to send "valued gold," money of good fineness, into England, to be melted down and minted into the king's new debased coins. This they felt would destroy the Low Countries. Vaughan denied any such intention; but at the same time he was planning with Paget and Wriothesley to smuggle the money out of Flanders to Calais in wagons, packed away under merchandise.[35] In September all the money in Vaughan's hands was arrested, to prevent its export; but permission was finally given to export under certain safeguards.[36]

[32] *Letters and Papers,* XIX, part II, 755.

[33] *Letters and Papers,* XX, part I, 154; XXI, part I, 716 (4), (5).

[34] *Letters and Papers,* XX, part I, 13, 892, 996, 1316; part II, 36, 114, 333, 362, 595, 707 (19).

[35] *Ibid.,* XX, part II, 262.

[36] *Ibid.,* 388, 407, 507, 550.

During 1545 Vaughan carried out other negotiations with Christopher Haller — who demanded impossible sureties, — with Douche on his own account, and with the Bonvise and Ancelyn Salvage. In all, he raised £128,929 Flemish during the year, of which he expended £77,066 for german mercenaries, paid £31,827 to Thomas Gresham to be taken to Calais, and carried 40,000 crowns in jewels to England, on his return thither at the end of the year.[37]

Early in 1546 he returned again to Flanders, bringing with him a letter of credit on Bartholome Compaigne and fellowship for £6,000 Flemish. He at once set about raising new loans. John Carlo Affaitadi, who had advanced 50,000 crowns in 1544, now wished to have the king take a great diamond in part payment of a new loan; the Fuggers raised the question of sureties, since those which the king offered were insufficient. In reply to Paget's importunities for more speed, Vaughan once wrote, — "I trust the king's Majesty doth not think that I am able to borrow his Highness £40,000, £50,000, £60,000, or £100,000 upon my credit only. As these be no wanton sums, no more be they to be found in every man's house. Ye have already had £100,000 upon the credit of London. If ye woll have me press men overmuch, ye shall too much discover that which were better not known. Men here be wise, have many eyes, great intelligence out of all countries. Think you that these men will disburse so huge sums of money before they can be honestly assured to be repaid again? If ye woll have me make haste, then can I certainly answer you I shall not speed * * * * I wot not what to say when such sureties will not be given as they desire. Prepare sureties to the contentation of men here and I will wage my life to serve the king's Majestey with £200,000 Flemish, but if that come not, I shall be able to do little. Think you that the merchants here woll take the bonds of noblemen in England? No, I assure you. And as to our merchants they are better known to strangers here than to ourselves. They woll not all be taken for 30,000 crowns, no, though ye lay them heaped all in one bond."[38] Vaughan succeeded at last in raising £30,000 Flemish in fustians from the Fuggers on the bond of the city of

[37] *Ibid.*, 957.
[38] *Letters and Papers*, XXI, part I, 241, February 18, 1546.

N

London, to be repaid in six months. Of this £30,000, £12,000 was used to repay the advances made in the previous fall by Diodati and Company, and Baldassar and Company on the letters of credit of Bonvise and Salvage. An additional £6,000 was used to repay the advances made in the previous fall for six months. To the loan from the Fuggers was attached the "hard condition" that the fustians be sold by the king at a price not lower than he had paid for them.[39] The sale of these fustians, as well as the exchange of lead and alum arranged somewhat earlier, was in charge of Sir John Gresham and Andrew Judd. The fustians were sold at little or no loss, but the alum received in exchange for £17,700 worth of lead brought only £7,700. The net loss to the crown on the two transacactions was £10,200.[40]

Vaughan further succeeded in the early part of 1546 in raising £27,125 on letters of credit of Italian houses in London, but he failed to carry through negotiations for 600,000 crowns or £200,000 Flemish needed to pay off the bonds that were to fall due in the summer and fall of the year. The most important part of these were the obligations held by the Fuggers for 300,000 crowns borrowed in 1545 and the £40,000 Flemish borrowed in February 1546, both due on August 15, 1546. In May, Vaughan who had a little unemployed money on hand tried to get the Fuggers to accept part of the debt due to them before time, on condition that they would respite the payment of the rest as long after the day. But the Fuggers' Antwerp agent refused to extend part of the loan in order to receive part of it beforehand, and no one was willing to advance any sufficient sum on the obligation of London, which was all that Henry VIII had to offer. The Council studied the problem and concluded that the smaller loans, owing to Italians, the greater portion of the debt due to the Fuggers which with interest amounted to £152,180 Flemish, should be repaid, but that the rest must be prolonged, if it were necessary to send a special agent to Anton Fugger himself in "Dowcheland," to do so.[41]

During May, June and July £94,000 were scraped together in the various revenue treasuries and made over by exchange by

[39] *Ibid.*, 367, 409, 410, 504 (24).

[40] *Declared Accounts, Pipe Office*, no. 11.

[41] *Letters and Papers*, XXI, part I, 1042.

English and Italian merchants to Flanders.[42]   Erasmus Sheetz, who was to figure very prominently in Edward VI's and Mary's reigns as a royal creditor, lent the king £20,000 Flemish, paying it directly to the Fuggers.[43]   Finally the tension was relieved by the consent of the Fuggers to an agreement that of their total debt of £152,180 payable on August 15, 1546, £92,180 should be paid, and the rest respited for six months at six and one-half per cent interest for the term, while the king should buy from them 8571 quintals, 13 pounds of copper, at forty-six shillings eight pence the quintal, at a cost of £20,000 Flemish payable without interest at Antwerp, August 15, 1547.   Both the unpaid portion of the loan and the debt for the copper were secured by the bonds of the Mayor and commonalty of London.[44]

But difficulties were not yet over.   The Emperor's preparations for war in Germany brought trade to a standstill in Flanders during the sumer.   English merchants could not sell their cloth, and were therefore unable to meet the payments of their exchanges in August.   Moreover, the king's debased money would not be accepted by Italian bankers in Flanders.   With only money at his disposal which the king's creditors refused to accept, and the time of payment passed, Vaughan was in an unpleasant position early in September.   ''The Fugger is never from me,'' he wrote; ''the house of Bonvyce whose day was the fifth instant pulls me hourly by the sleeve.''[45]   On September 9th the Bonvise having received only £3,000 Flemish of the £9,000 due them, sent to Vaughan demanding the rest.   Vaughan replied that he could only pay if a good part were taken in angels.   Then the Bonvise declared in a great heat, that he would take no more angels or British coin, and for his credit as a merchant, he must bring a notary to protest against him for non-payment.   Eventually however, during September and October the Italians and the Fuggers received what was due to them, and their receipts taken.[46]

[42] *Declared Accounts, Pipe Office*, no. 10; *Letters and Papers*, XXI, part I, 1380, 1421, 1535.   The amounts stated in these accounts vary slightly.

[43] *Letters and Papers*, XXI, part I, 1420.

[44] *Ibid.*, 1250, 1383 (98), 1537 (2).

[45] *Letters and Papers*, XXI, part II, 51.

[46] *Letters and Papers*, XXI, part II, 70, 154, 177, 317; *Declared Accounts, Pipe Office*, no. 9.

Henry kept faith with his foreign creditors even though he was a little slow in paying. He left no overdue loans unpaid at his death in January, 1547. The loan of £20,000 Flemish of Erasmus Sheetz and a debt of £80,000 Flemish to the Fuggers, (£60,000 for the extended balance of the loan due in 1546 and £20,000 for copper purchased) were left as a heritage to Edward VI. The new government paid Sheetz's loan and the £60,000 Flemish owing to the Fuggers, when payment fell due in February, 1547. When however, the payment of the £20,000 for the copper fell due in August, 1547, the debt was renewed and more copper purchased.[47]

DEBASEMENT OF THE COINAGE AND THE PROFITS OF THE MINT

The alienation of crown lands and monastic estates to provide war resources defeated the plan for a sufficient revenue system under the king's own control; the use of direct taxes on a large scale enforced national thrift in war time, and perhaps helped to familiarize the people with the idea of paying taxes. Ultimately the social effects of these measures were enormously beneficial — the Long Parliament would have been impossible had Henry VIII not sold so much of the monastic lands. But no good can be alleged for the most desperate of the war measures of Henry VIII's ministers, the debasement of the coinage, to provide immediate funds. The debasement of the coinage aided in enhancing the price of all commodities which the government was buying in great quantities to supply its armies. Prices were already rising in England before the debasement began, as a result of the price revolution, but the upward tendency was greatly accelerated by the debasement. The effects of the price revolution and of the debasement are so inextricably connected in Edward VI's and Mary's reigns that it does not seem possible to disentangle them. But the general rise in prices due to the two causes was serious for the government. Inasmuch as the crown lands were rented on long term leases, it was not possible for the government to increase its rentals at once to correspond with the lower value of money. Similarly for the other revenues. There was a kind of poetic justice in the situation. The crown cheated the people to get immediate funds; it had to take back

[47] *Declared Accounts, Pipe Office,* nos. 9, 14.

the poor money in payment of its revenues at its face value; it had to pay at increased rates for all its supplies; the real value of the revenue expresed in terms of purchasing power was seriously reduced.

The enhancement of the coinage was no new thing in Europe in the fifteenth and sixteenth centuries, and it had been effected several times in England since the beginning of Henry VII's reign. In 1489 Henry VII "let smite" a new coin called a royal valued at ten shilings, and groats and pence were coined lighter than they were before, while the value of the old noble was raised from six shillings eight pence to eight shillings four pence.[48] In 1524 Wolsey turned to a study of the English coinage and came to the conclusion that English coins were undervalued as compared with those of the continent.[49] In 1526, accordingly, the value of gold was increased from forty to forty-five shillings an ounce. The old angel, containing one-sixth of an ounce of gold was thus raised from six shillings eight pence to seven shillings six pence, and other coins proportionately. New coins, of lighter weight, the george noble and the crown of the double rose, worth six shillings eight pence, and five shillings, and lighter groats, half groats and pence were minted.[50] The measure was one of self protection to prevent the heavier and better coin from being drawn out of England to the continent. Inasmuch as the continental nations especially France, continued to debase their coinage, English coins were again altered in 1542. The weight remained the same, but the fineness was changed. The alloy in the gold coins was increased from one-third of a grain to one carat, while the alloy in the silver coins was increased to two ounces in the pound Troy. The legal value of the ounce of gold and silver remained unaltered, but the fineness of the metal in the coins was lowered. This debasement was not a financial expedient; it was defensible on purely economic

[48] *Three Fifteenth Century Chronicles,* Camden Society (1880), 80.

[49] *Letters and Papers,* IV, 956, notes in Wolsey's hand.

[50] *Letters and Papers,* IV, 2338, 2423, 2597, 2609; *Two London Chronicles,* 2; Grafton's *Chronicle,* II, 93; *Grey Friar's Chronicle,* 33; Hall's *Chronicle,* II, 77; *A Short English Chronicle,* 93. The two proclamations ordering the change in value were issued August 22, 1526, and November 5, 1526.

grounds, as a necessary measure to prevent the export of gold and silver from England.[51]

But the great debasement which began in 1544 has no such justification. The finanacial situation of the time, the pressing need of money and Wriothesley's caluculations of the king's gain and profit by the measure leave no doubt that it was adopted to supply sorely-needed ready money, and for no other purpose. Of course the real reason was masked behind the causes which were deemed valid for earlier cases of the same kind. The preamble of the proclamation ordering the debasement solemnly declares that whereas in Flanders and in France the value of money was so enhanced that coin was daily carried out of the realm notwithstanding the statutes, the only remedy appeared to be the enhancing of the value of the silver and gold within the realm.[52] First the value of gold and silver was raised; an ounce of gold was raised in value from forty-five to forty-eight shillings and an ounce of silver was raised from three shillings nine pence to four shillings. Almost immediately after, the standard of fineness was lowered. On May 28, 1544 the standard fineness of gold used in the coinage was fixed at 23 carats; a year later (March 27, 1545) at 22 carats; on April 1, 1546 at 20 carats. The silver coinage was even more debased. In 1544 nine ounces of silver to the pound Troy were used, in 1545 six ounces was prescribed and in 1546 only four ounces, with eight ounces of alloy.[53]

The king's profit came in the first place from the enhancement in the values of the gold and silver, since he was able to coin at a great profit great masses of plate in his jewel house, and to recoin money in his own hands. He also reduced the value of his debts. His greatest profits however, came from the debasement of the fineness of the coinage. He purchased gold bullion at twenty-four carats fine at the legal price; he issued it forth from his mints at twenty-three, twenty-two, twenty car-

[51] *Letters and Papers*, VI, 197; VII, 1332; XI, 45; XV, 791; XVII, 197; XIX, part I, page 61. *Accounts, Exch., Queen's Remembrancer*, 302/22. The profits to the crown in two years were only £23,189.

[52] *Letters and Papers*, XIX, part I, 513, the proclamation of May, 16, 1544.

[53] *Letters and Papers*, XIX, part I, page LV, account of Sir Martin Bowes, under treasurer of the Mint.

ats; and for this ounce of twenty carats of gold and four carats of alloy he received likewise the legal price, 48 shillings. On every pound weight of gold coined, the king gained from twenty-seven shillings six pence in 1544 to ninety-four shillings six pence in the early part of 1546; and on every pound weight of silver he gained from nine shillings one-half penny five mites in 1544 to twenty-nine shillings eleven pence in 1546.[54] The king's profits from his mints, arising from the recoinage and debasement were £363,000 from May, 1544, to the end of the reign. The evil practice begun by Henry VIII's government was bettered by his son's; between May 14, 1544 and January 1, 1551, the crown received £900,000 clear from the profits of the mint — more than the revenues of the court of Augmentations for the same period.[55]

[54] In detail the king's profits were June 1, 1544 to March 31, 1545
in every pound Troy of gold   27s. 6d.
in every pound Troy of silver   9s. ½d.   5 mites

April 1, 1545 to January 1, 1546
in every pound Troy of gold   53s. 6d.
in every pound Troy of silver   20s. 7d.

January 1, 1546 to March 31, 1546
in every pound Troy of gold   42s. 6d.
in every pound Troy of silver   20s. 7d.

April 1, 1546 to September 30, 1546
in every pound Troy of gold   94s. 6d.
in every pound Troy of silver   29s. 11d.

September 30, 1546 to March 31, 1547
in every pound Troy of gold   84s. 6d.
in every pound Troy of silver   29s. 11d.

The figures include the profits of the debasement and the ordinary profits of the mint. They are taken from the accounts of Sir Martin Bowes, Under Treasurer of the mint, *Letters and Papers*, XIX, part I, page LIII ff.

[55] *Declared Accounts, Pipe Office*, no. 2077, Declaration of the account of Sir Edmund Pekham, High Treasurer of the Mint.

CHAPTER XIV

THE SCOTCH AND FRENCH WARS, 1547-1550

The wars of Henry VIII with France and Scotland had seriously strained the government's resources in the last year of his reign in England. Besides the permanent reduction of the revenue by the great alienation of crown lands,[1] and the increased expenditures induced by the rise of prices, there was a debt of £100,000 owing in Flanders; Boulogne was a heavy burden on the state; the costs of the upkeep of the fleet, the garrisons, and the fortifications at Calais, Berwick and other places were large.[2] But the wars did more. By them the business of the state was so tremendously increased, that even if the king had not been growing old, it would have been a physical impossibility for him to guide and direct all of its manifold activities himself. As it was, the state was turned over to the official class, who as members of the council assumed more and more completely the management of affairs. Creatures of Henry VIII, as long as he lived they stood in fear of him, but the accession of a child king left them in absolute control of the state. They had been rewarded by Henry VIII, adequately at first, more richly in the latter years. They were rich, but not yet so rich as they were to make themselves. It must not be supposed that they crudely stole government money from the treasury. They solemnly and in all legal form conveyed to themselves the basic resources of the state, the crown lands, as fitting rewards

[1] In the years between 1540 and 1544, both inclusive, the average rental of monastic lands alone had been about £44,000. In 1545 it fell to £32,739; in 1547-48 the first year of Edward VI's reign, the entire rental of all crown lands, monastic and non-monastic, was only £51,058. *Augmentations Office Treasurer's Rolls of Accounts*, nos. 1-4.

[2] *Exch. of Rec., Misc. Books*, 259, Tellers' declarations of issues in the Exchequer, 1544-1560.

178

of the grateful boy king to themselves for their toils endured
in the onerous business of government. Before Henry VIII was
dead a week Paget produced a list of promotions and grants,
intended, as he alleged, by Henry. From year to year huge
blocks of land were thus voted by the council to themselves and
their retainers; throughout the reign of Edward VI lands to
the annual value of £27,000 were thus disposed of as free gifts.[3]
These lands, greater in extent than the land sold during the
reign, were permanently lost to the crown for practically no
return at all, and the revenues reduced. This was all the more
serious for the future, for as rents and values rose these lands
would have brought an ever increasing revenue. Another serious
evil was the promiscuous granting of annuities and pensions
and lands for life to royal favorites. Edward VI's government
was following a practice of Henry VII's and earlier reigns in
this; many of the pensions and annuities paid in Edward VI's
time had been granted by his father. To provide for such payments, more than £32,000 of the royal revenues was required in
1551.[4]

But the picture of graft and corruption must not be overdrawn. Certain very important reservations must be kept in
mind. There was no disintegration of the financial system, no
general breakdown of all restraints in a universal plunder of
the state. It was only to the masters of the state, the council
and its friends, that robbery was permitted, and then only in
legal form. In its dealing with the government agents and
officials who supervised the revenue and expenditures, the council
insisted upon a high standard of honesty and exactness. From
the very beginning of the reign of Edward the council devoted a
very considerable amount of its time to a consideration of finances, as the acts of the privy council show. Careful accounts of
the great treasurers were frequently ordered to be prepared and

---

[3] *State Papers, Domestic, Edward VI*, XIX. In the first year of the
reign gifts were made of lands to the annual value of £5721-13-8; in the
second year £3358-13-9; in the third year £1257-6-2; in the fourth year
£8804-19-10; in the fifth year £3991-10-8; in the sixth year £3442-13-10;
in the seventh year £4099-17-11. Rents to the value of £3619 were reserved
to the crown out of these grants.

[4] *Add. .Mss.*, 30198, report on the revenues for the year 1550-1551.
Annuities and pensions, £20,000; grants of land for life, £12,000.

laid before the council, or committees of the council were appointed to investigate the state of the revenues. Individual members of the council sat as commissioners for the auditing and passing of the accounts of the very large numbers of persons who had royal money in charge during the wars with Scotland and France.[5] These accounts seem to be carefully and accurately drawn. It is possible of course, that the crown was overcharged, that goods provided were inferior in quality, or that supplies intended for the government were diverted to private uses. But charges of this kind brought to the attention of the council are negligible.[6] On the other hand there were some notorious cases of embezzlement of government funds by important financial officials. Sir William Sharington, master of the mint at Bristol, one of the Lord Admiral's adherents, withheld certain sums from his books in every month and burnt the originals from which the indentures had been made up. He did not know how much had been stolen, but admitted that it was over £4,700.[7] Lord Arundel, the Lord Chamberlain, was charged with peculation at the time of Somerset's fall, which he confessed, and in punishment he was sentenced to forego his office and pay a fine of £12,000, "by £1,000 by the year."[8] In 1551, Sir Martin Bowes was contented to give unto his highness by the name of a fine, £10,000 to be clear of all demands.[9] In the summer of 1552 some of the most able of Somerset's adherents were brought to book. Whalley, the receiver of the crown revenues in Yorkshire, confessed that he had lent the king's money upon gain and lucre, that he had paid one year's revenues with arrearages of the last and had bought the king's lands with the king's own money.[10] The system of book-keeping in vogue made Whalley's

   [5] For orders to the treasurers to lay their accounts before the council see *Acts of the Privy Council*, n.s., III, 29, 130, 133, 228, 236, 314; IV, 12, 44, 62, 164, 183. For investigations of the revenue by committees of the council, see *Add. Mss.*, 30198; *State Papers, Domestic, Edward VI*, II, 9, 30, 31. For the audit and passing of accounts by commissioners see the preambles of the declarations of accounts of this reign, e.g., *Declared Accounts, Pipe Office*, 43, 17, 14.

   [6] *Acts of the Privy Council*, n. s., II, 492; III, 127.

   [7] *Historical Mss., Commission Reports, Hatfield Mss.*, I, 64-70.

   [8] *Acts of the Privy Council*, n. s., II, 398.

   [9] *Acts of the Privy Council*, n. s., III, 188.

   [10] *Journal of Edward VI*, 71.

practice easy for a dishonest man. It seldom happened that all the rents and revenues due in a district for the year were collected. Yet when the formal declaration of the account was made, the issues and rents for the year were set down in full on the debit side of the account. On the credit side were entered the payments of money to the crown's use, including all the actual receipts of the year. What had not been collected was then entered on the credit side of the account as "arrearage" for the year, to balance the two sides of the account. The arrearage of the year was added to the arrearages of past years, which formed an ever-increasing sum, in which little interest seems to have been taken when the accountant presented his account in the following year. Some arrears of rent were paid every year, but inasmuch as the records of the details were scattered in many books, it was easily possible for the accountant to conceal such payments and use them, as Whalley did, for his own purposes. Similar operations on a far greater scale than Whalley's were conducted by John Beaumont, receiver-general of the Court of Wards and Liveries. He concealed in his arrearages receipts of £9,763 in money, and £11,822 in obligations, more than £21,000 in all. These sums he had lent to purchase the king's own lands from him. He was further guilty of taking bribes as a judge in chancery.[11] Lord Paget was also found guilty at this time of great malefeasance in his office of Chancellor of the Duchy of Lancaster, for which he was sentenced to a fine of £8,000,[12] and in the same manner Sir John Williams, treasurer of the Court of Augmentations, spent some time in the Fleet prison. From his accounts it appears that he had kept back £28,445 received in his own time and in the time of his predecessor from the sale of lands.[13]

Punishment for illegal fraud was of the nature of political vengeance; there is therefore reason to suspect that the number of offenders included many who never lost favor, and went unpunished. And yet, when most has been made of the corruption of public life in Edward VI's reign, Froude's picture of "all

[11] *Journal of Edward VI*, 70. Court of Wards, Misc. Books, 365, ff 166-236. This is the account in which the concealment is admitted.

[12] *Journal of Edward VI*, 71, 86. *State Papers, Domestic, Edward VI,* XV, 58.

[13] *Augmentations Office, Treasurer's Roll of Accounts*, no. 8.

but universal fraud'' and the ''infinite'' ''expenses of universal peculation'' in which all classes of persons in public employment were contending with each other in the race for plunder and extravagance, is much overdrawn. It rests upon such false assumptions as an increase in the expenditures in the royal household from £19,000 a year in 1532 to over £100,000 a year in Edward's time; the disappearance of the chantry lands into private hands ''with small advantage to the public exchequer;'' and upon the hysterical overstatements of the popular revivalists, Lever and Latimer.[14] Public corruption heightened, but did not cause the serious financial difficulties of the reign. The frauds were cumulative, for even the effects of the plunder of the crown estates by the councillors did not show to the full until the last year of the reign, but the financial difficulties began almost at once. Of these the most obvious explanation is the renewal of the Scotch and French wars, and their aftermath.

The wars demanded great sums of money, at once available. During the first five years of the reign of Edward, his government was called upon to find a total of £1,386,687 in addition to the normal governmental expenditures, for war purposes, for the fleet, the armies in Scotland and France, the garrisons at home and in Boulogne and Calais, and for new fortifications.[15] There was no surplus on hand, as there had been in 1542; the situation was similar to that in 1522-1523, during the second of Henry VIII's French wars. At this time when Wolsey failed to get money by means of loans and subsidies, he had been compelled to advise the king to make peace. But since then Henry VIII discovered means of raising money quickly by the sale of lands and the coinage of debased money. In this way entered into by Henry VIII in his last years, the Edwardian government followed on to procure the ready money needed ''to go on with.''

With the first rumors of a renewal of war with France, and the beginning of war with Scotland, the confiscation of the accumulated wealth of the worn-out institutions of the church was consummated. In 1545 Henry VIII had received the power to visit and suppress colleges, hospitals, free chapels, chantries and

---

[14] J. A. Froude, *"History of England,"* V, chapters 26, 27.
[15] *State Papers, Domestic, Edward VI*, XV, 11.

other corporations of similar nature. Many chantries had been suppressed during Henry VIII's lifetime. The act lapsed at his death. In December, 1547, parliament renewed the statute in favor of Edward VI, vesting all the property of colleges and chantries in the king after the next Easter.[16] The council viewed the grant as made ''specially for the relief of the king's majesty's charges and expenses which do daily grow and increase by reason of diverse and sundry fortifications, garrisons, levying of men and soldiers which is at this present so chargeable and costly that without great help and aid of money his majesty should not be able to sustain the charges thereof.'' In April, 1548, when the approach of war with France made it necessary that his majesty should ''have in readiness all that should be for the defence of his majesty's realm,'' and the council noted that ''nothing (is) so much lacking as money to maintain the costs and charges thereof, without the which no defence can be had,'' it was decided, since there was at this present ''none other means without great difficulty, danger and grudge to make such a mass (of money) as might serve for this present necessity,'' to authorize the sale of chantry lands to the annual rental value of £5,000. Before the Michaelmas accounts of 1548 were made up, £110,486 had been received by the commissioners of the sales, and paid into the treasury of the Augmentations Court.[17] The sales not only provided the government with available funds for a time, but assured the support of the war by the wealthy merchants of London. The government's need furnished them further opportunity to purchase the land which was still the safest investment for surplus capital and the necessary basis for social distinction.

16 *Statutes*, 1, Edward VI, c. 4.

17 *Augmentations Office, Treasurer's Roll of Accounts*, no. 4. In 1549 there was received for the sale of lands £92,695; in 1550, £47,286; and in 1551, £7,856 (*Augmentations Office, Treasurer's Roll of Accounts*, nos. 5, 6, 7). Sales after 1551 are treated below. The receipt by the state of these sums effectively replies to Mr. Froude's assertion that ''the chantry lands, which if alienated from religious purposes, should have been sold for public debts, were disappearing into private hands with small advantage to the public exchequer'' (*History of England*, V, 154). As a rule the state received twenty years' purchase, or twenty times the annual value, a good price.

As was shown "for certain by divers motions in the late
parliament made," the king's loving subjects "were induced
the rather and franklier to grant" the chantries and other religious corporations to the king "that they might thereby be relieved of the continual charge of taxes, contributions, loans and
subsidies the which by reason of wars they were constrained
in the late king of famous memory his majesty's father's reign
to abide."[18] But the freedom of taxation which parliament had
sought to achieve by the transfer of the chantries to the king
was short-lived. The expenditures for war purposes were so
great that a new appeal to parliament was necessary in 1548.
The tax measure which followed was a curious one. Instead of
a direct tax on land, it provided an indirect tax on sheep and
wool, to the raising and production of which land was being
more and more devoted. For the inadequate subsidy it offered
a substitute which promised to yield £106,000 to £156,000 a year.
This estimate was based upon a calculation of the number of
sheep in England in Edward III's reign, arrived at from the
wool customs of that time.[19] In the measure is to be seen also
something of Somerset's spirit of agrarian reform, a design to
check conversion of arable to pasture land by indirect taxation.
With the new taxes on sheep, wool, and woolen cloth, were combined some of the older subsidy features of a tax on personalty
and a poll tax on certain aliens.[20] At the same time the clergy
made a grant of a subsidy of six shillings in the pound of the
yearly value of all their livings, payable in three years.[21] The
relief was not nearly so productive as the later subsidies of
Henry VIII's reign. The first payment, in 1549, brought in

[18] *Acts of the Privy Council*, n. s., II, 184.

[19] *State Papers, Domestic, Edward VI*, II, 13. This is a paper book
endorsed "Customs for Wools," addressed to my Lord Protector's grace.
It sets forth the project in several forms. See also *ibid.*, V, 20.

[20] *Statutes*, 2 and 3 Edward VI, c. 36. The tax, known as the Relief,
was taken at the rate of 1 shilling in the pound of the value of personalty
yearly for three years. Aliens were assessed at double rates; those of
them not paying the personalty tax, paid a poll tax of 8 pence. For
every ewe sheep kept in pasture was taken 3 pence; every wether 2
pence; every shear sheep on commons 1½ pence, or in lots of more than
ten, 1 penny yearly for three years. Each piece of woolen cloth made
was taxed 8 pence in the pound of its value.

[21] *Statutes*, 2 and 3 Edward VI, c. 35.

slightly less than £54,000; the second pyament, in 1550, only
£47,500. But before the second payment had been collected,
Kets' rebellion had broken out, and Somerset had been deprived
of his protectorship. In the parliament of November, 1549, Somerset's agrarian policy was reversed; with the repeal of the
Tudor agrarian legislation and the reënactment of the Statute
of Merton, there was also the repeal, on the initiative of the
commons themselves, of the final payment of the tax on sheep,
wool and cloth.[22] As a compensation the subsidy of a shilling
in the pound of the value of goods was extended for another
year.[23] On the whole, but little aid obtained from taxes of
parliamentary grant in Edward VI's reign. Their total yield,
including £120,000 granted in Henry VIII's time and paid in
April and June, 1547, was only £299,000. For the purpose of
the wars with Scotland and France the grant of 1548 was of
especially little consequence.

The chief reliance of the government, for its war finances,
was placed upon the mint, and the profits of coining debased
money. In the first two years of the reign, Henry VIII's standard of fineness, eight parts of alloy and four parts of silver,
and his dies, continued to be used. The coins of these years are
identical with those of the last years of Henry VIII's reign.
In 1549 a change was made. The gold sovereign was coined
22 carats fine instead of 20; but the new coin was lighter, containing 170 instead of 192 grains of metal, and only 156 grains
of pure gold as opposed to 160 grains in the older coin. In the
silver coins the silver content was raised to six parts, with six
parts of alloy; but as the new coins were only two-thirds the
size of the older coins which they replaced, they contained exactly the same number of grains of pure silver.[24] There was great
difficulty in securing bullion due to the prohibition of the export of bullion from Flanders, where large quanities were

[22] *Commons Journal*, I, 11. On Monday, November 18, 1549, it was
ordered that the speakers and others of the house should be suitors to
know the king's pleasure by his council, if upon their humble suit they
might treat of the last relief for cloths and sheep. On the 20th the
king's pleasure was announced that the house might treat for the act
of relief ''having in respect the cause of the granting thereof.''

[23] *Statutes*, 3 and 4 Edward VI, c. 23.

[24] C. W. C. Oman, *The Tudors and the Currency*.

purchased by loans.[25] Yet, with all the difficulties, the profits of the government were very great. Between the first day of Edward's reign and the first of January, 1551, covering approximately the war period, £537,000 was realized on the debasement of the currency.[26]

The confiscation of the chantries, the sale of their lands and goods, the new taxes, and the debasement of the currency provided notable sums, but not enough to meet the war bills. Further shift was made by using funds intended for normal charges, so that at the end of the war the various governmental departments were deeply in dept.[27] Finally heavy loans were made in Flanders, of the Fuggers, the Tuchers, the Sheetz and other bankers in Antwerp. At times to repay one loan another was made; or the original loan was extended on disadvantageous terms, generally involving the purchase of fustians, jewels or other goods by the king.[28] In this device of foreign loans, as

[25] *State Papers, Domestic, Edward VI*, VIII, 38.

[26] *Declared Accounts, Pipe Office*, 2077, Declaration of the account of Sir Edmund Pekham, high treasurer of the mints, to January 1, 1551.

[27] *Lansd. Mss.*, II, f. 125. A paper noted in Cecil's hand, drawn up before November, 1552. The Household owed £28,000; the Chamber £20,000; the Wardrobe £8,333; the Stables £1,000; the Admirality £5,000; the Ordnance £3,134; the Surveyor of the Works £3,200; the Treasurer of Calais £15,000; the Treasurer of Berwick £6,000; the Master of the Revels £1,000; the Treasurer of Ireland £13,128; and paymasters at Sicily, Alderney, Plymouth and the Isle of Wight £2,000.

[28] One bargain made March 23, 1551, between the council and Christofer Haunsell for and in the name of Anthony Fugger and his nephews provides: For the sale of one jewel containing four rubies marvellous big, as the boy king described it in his Journal, one orient, and one great diamond and one great pearl for £33,333-6s.-8d. Flemish to be paid in Antwerp without interest in eleven months. For the sale of twelve thousand marks weight of fine silver bullion at 50s. 4 4/5d. the mark, to be delivered at Antwerp by the last of August next. A clause protects the Fuggers in case of lawful impediment to the delivery. For the sale to the king of so many bales of fustians as shall amount to £14,000 Flemish, to be paid in Antwerp without interest April 30, 1552. All fustians will be sold in England and not conveyed beyond sea again. Provision is also made that where the king owes Erasmus Sheetz and Sons £42,090 Flemish, payable May 15, 1551, the Fugger shall pay the Sheetz this sum of £42,090, and the king shall repay one year later, with interest at 8 per cent. Finally where the king owes the Fuggers £38,976 Flemish, payable August 15, 1551, the sum is respited for a year at 12 per cent. *Treasury*

in all others, the Edwardian councillors were simply following, and perhaps bettering the examples of Henry VIII. They paid the same interest, 14 per cent, they renewed and prolonged as he had done. But their operations were on a larger scale and they created a heavier incubus of debt to burden the post-war period.

of Receipt, Letters Patent, bundle 4, No. 15/37. A letter of the council dated April 9, 1550, to Damosell agent in Flanders urges him to do the best he can for prolongation of the debt due in May, 1550, for a year longer. He is to accept an offer to prolong, purchasing 2400 kintalls of powder at 50s. a kintall, to be paid at the end of the year also. *Acts of the Privy Council,* n. s., II, 426. In his Journal Edward notes, ''debt of 30,000l, and odd money put over for a year, and there was bought 2500 quintals of powder'' (*Journal*, 18).

Other loans abroad during the war were, 13 October, 1547, of Anthony Fugger, 129,650 florins to be repaid March 31, 1548; April, 1548, of Lazrus Tucher 167,218 florins; 11 September, 1549, of Anthony Fugger 328,800 florins to be repaid August 15, 1550; 5 May, 1550, of Erasmus Sheetz, 107,520 florins to be repaid May 15, 1551. *Treasury of Receipt, Letters Patent,* bundle 4; *State Papers, Domestic, Edward VI,* IV, 5.

o

CHAPTER XV

NORTHUMBERLAND'S FAILURE, 1550-1553

Peace was made between France and England in 1550. Among the terms of treaty was a provision for the restoration of Boulogne, of which the capture, fortification, and keeping had cost the English state £1,342,550 in five and one-half years. Its surrender for nothing would have been a great financial relief to the English government; Henry II of France generously paid 400,000 crowns (£133,333) for its recovery. For months after the peace was signed the garrisons at Calais and in the north were continued at their full war strength, because "there wanted money to dispatch them," that is pay their arrears of wages and discharge them. Although there seems to have been an intention of keeping the 400,000 crowns as ready money available in emergencies — the first payment was ordered laid up in the Tower "for all purposes" — it was at last necessary to order payments to be made from it to discharge the soldiers and meet other charges.[1] Despite the discharge of the soldiers from Calais and in the north, there remained a large war establishment, which could not be, or was not at once, disbanded. At Calais the ordinary garrison had long cost £5,000 a year more than the rents of the town and the wool customs collected by the merchants

[1] *Acts of the Privy Council,* n. s., III, 93. Of the first (half) payment £10,000 were sent to Calais; £9,500 to Ireland; £15,166 to the north; £2,000 were assigned to the ordnance department; £1,000 to Alderney, and £1,000 to the Admirality. Of the second payment of 200,000 crowns, £8,000 were sent at once to Calais; £5,000 to the north and £10,000 "was appointed to be occupied to win money to pay the next year, pay the outward pays; and it was promised that the money should double every month" (*Journal of Edward VI,* 26). The scheme by which the money thus invested was to double every month is described by Froude, in *History of England,* V, 265.

of the Staple, while the cost of work on the fortifications and the wages of the extraordinary crew continued at over £19,000 a year in addition.[2] There were heavy charges for works and garrisons at Berwick, and on the Scotch marches, and in the various blockhouses or forts on the English coast;[3] there were the charges of the admirality and ordnance offices, and the expenditures in Ireland above the Irish revenues. The Irish revenues, after the costs of the civil government there had been paid were about £4,700 sterling a year. During the first years of Edward's reign the island had been aflame with insurrection; large sums had been sent to Ireland for military purposes which the Irish revenues did not meet. In 1550, however, it was resolved that Ireland should no longer be a drain on the English treasury; the situation was to be reversed, and Ireland was to contribute to the royal resources. To carry out the new policy, Anthony St. Leger returned as deputy.[4] He was as little successful in making Ireland "pay" as Henry VIII had been in a similar scheme; the charges of the necessary military establishment increased by leaps and bounds. Whereas in 1547 the charges of Ireland were £15,500, in 1551 and 1552 they rose to £42,000. The Irish revenue did not increase; the deficit had to be made good from London.[5]

Not directly due to the war, but certainly induced in part by causes connected with the war were the serious increases in the costs of the royal household. In the first years of the reign the household had required about the same amount of money as in the last years of Henry VIII's reign, about £38,000 a year. In 1550 and 1551 the expenditures increased to £50,000 and

2 *Add. Mss.* no. 30,198, a statement of the revenues for the year 1550-1551; *Declared Accounts, Pipe Office*, 2079, account of Sir Edward Pekham. In the year February, 1551, to March, 1552, Pekham paid out £25,500 for Calais causes.

3 These required £9733-17-7 for the year 1550-'51. *Add. Mss.*, no. 30, 198.

4 Froude, *History of England,* V, 392.

5 Add. Mss., no. 4767, f. 99; f. 160. The yearly charge in Ireland is given in the latter paper; anno 1, Edward VI, £15,958; anno 2, £21,024; anno 3, £27,113; anno 4, £20,566; anno 5, £42,986; anno 6, £42, 609. All sums are in sterling money.

£56,000.[6] This was in part due to increased luxury at the court, in part in all probability to peculation by officials, but in greatest part to the rise in prices. A similar increase, on a much smaller scale, is to be noticed in the wardrobe expenditures. And while the government was endeavoring to meet all these great payments and increases, in addition to normal state expenditures, it was constantly reminded of the unpaid debts in the household, wardrobe and chamber, and of the great loans raised abroad at 14 per cent interest, which somehow had to be paid.

Government finances were studied by the council between 1550 and 1553 with a zeal which shows how clearly the seriousness of the problem was realized. One investigation, carried out by Thomas Lord Darcy Lord Chamberlain, Thomas, Bishop of Norwich, Sir Richard Cotton Controller of the Household, Sir John Gates Vice-Chamberlain, Sir Robert Bowes Master of the Rolls, and Sir Walter Milday one of the General Surveyors of the Court of Augmentations, for the year Michaelmas, 1550 to Michaelmas, 1551, showed that the clear normal income from all sources, deducting fixed charges, grants and annuities, was £168,150. The fees of the royal officials, ministers and servants, the ordinary household and wardrobe assignments,[7] the expenses of the audit courts, the charges for decays and reparations, and the charges for certain garrisons, that is to say, the normal govern payments, were £131,600. There was available thus a balance of £36,550. From this sum the committee reported, there had to be met the charges of the admirality, of the ordnance, of the king's privy purse, the New Year's gifts, the charges at Calais

[6] *Declared Accounts, Pipe Office*, 1795. Household expenditures for the year

1547-48	£38,804- 6s.-6d.
1548-49	41,359- 3s.-4d.
1549-50	50,778-16s.-4d.
1550-51	56,806-13s.-8d.
1551-52	55,791-15s.-9d.
1552-53	51,903-10s.-2d.

The increase is not however nearly so great as has been alleged.

[7] From time to time each court was ordered to set aside and pay regularly a certain sum for the household. These sums amounting in all to £41,864 in 1551-52 were the household assignment. The expenditures in the household exceeded the assignment in every year of Edward's reign. See above, note 6 of this chapter.

and in Ireland above the revenues there, and the extra charges in the household above the assignment. The various military establishments alone — Calais, Ireland, the navy, the North and Berwick, the ordnance and so forth — took more than £112,000 from February, 1551, to Michaelmas, 1552, or at the rate of £80,000 a year.[8] The extra charges in the household in the year 1551 were £15,000 more than the assignment. Even with the addition of the subsidy of £43,260 paid in April, 1551, there was not enough money available from the revenues to meet the current charges. Then some way must be found to pay off the war debts of £250,000 owing in England and Flanders.[9] It was further deemed desirable to "get £50,000 of treasure money for all events," that is accumulate a new surplus,[10] and finally money had to be found for the new standing army, the bands of horsemen attached to Northumberland's most devoted partisans, organized in December, 1551.[11]

In the expedients which were used to remedy this alarming deficiency, resort was had to all the old devices, betraying a sterility of ideas and the failure to grasp the cause of the situation. Solemnly the council determined upon a policy of retrenchment. The garrisons at little blockhouses like Porland and Pendivis were reduced by from two to four men each, and several small forts were discontinued,[12] with a saving of £583 12s. 6d. a year.[13] The tables of the "young lords" and others in the household were discontinued, auditorships were abolished to save fees, and workmen discharged.[14] As early as 1551 at-

---

[8] *Declared Accounts, Pipe Office,* 2079; account of Sir Edmund Pekham, high treasurer of the mints.

[9] The amount of the debt is variously stated. An entry in Edward's Journal (p. 66) puts the sum at £251,000 at least in May, 1552; a paper of Cecil's, before November, 1552, puts it at £241,179 (*Lansd. Mss.,* II, f. 125); another paper of 1552 gives it at £235,700 and still another at £219,686 (*State Papers, Domestic, Edward VI,* XV, 13, 14). At least £132,372 was due to the money lenders in Flanders, and £108,800 was owed in England.

[11] *Acts of the Privy Council,* n. s., III, 339; IV, 4, 15, 132.

[12] *State Papers, Domestic, Edward VI,* XIII, 10, 11, 12; *Acts of the Privy Council,* n. s., IV, 130.

[13] *Acts of the Privy Council,* n. s., IV, 139.

[14] *Journal of Edward* VI, 79; *Acts of the Privy Council,* n. s., III, 316;

[10] *Literary Remains of Edward VI,* II, 543, note in the king's own hand.

tention was directed to the superfluous charges of the large number of revenue courts, with too many officers and too little business.[15]   They escaped pruning for the moment because an office in a revenue court was a vested interest, a property right, which could be abolished by the state only in return for the compensation of a life pension.[16]   In the spring of 1552 the reduction of the fleet was ordered, and it was even suggested that some of the king's old ships be let to rent, and hulks of no more value be sold.[17]   There was however, no mention of retrenchment or restriction in the plunder of the crown by the council in the form of grants of land to the councillors themselves, though it is true that the grants of the fifth, sixth and seventh years did not equal in extent those of the fourth year of the reign.

In all the revenue courts there were great arrears of overdue rents and revenues owing to the crown through many years. "My debts owing me" after this sort were estimated by Edward to be £100,000.[18]   In times of stringency in the middle period of Henry VIII's reign it was a much used practice "to call in the debts." So at this time. In February of 1551, the treasurer and chancellor of the Augmentations were commanded to bring in with all diligence a book of all such debts and arrearages as are due to the king's majesty in that court, and it may be that similar commands were sent to the other treasurers.[19]   Late in the same year and in 1552 commissioners were appointed to call in the debts.[20]   They succeeded in collecting £16,667 before Michaelmas, 1552.[21]   Something, too, was expected from the fa-

IV, 102, 115, 160, 260. See also *Journal of Edward VI*, 65, 83, for retrenchment in the mint and Ireland.

[15] *Literary Remains of Edward VI*, II, 500, 543.

[16] When the Court of the General Surveyors was amalagated with the Court of Augmentations, January 1, 1547, the officials of the older court for whom no place could be found were given pensions or annuities of more than £3,000 a year.

[17] *Acts of the Privy Council*, n. s., IV, 46; *State Papers, Domestic, Edward VI*, XIII, 10, 11, 12.

[18] *Literary Remains of Edward VI*, II, 550.

[19] *Acts of the Privy Council*, n. s., III, 228.

[20] *Journal of Edward VI*, 56, 58; *Literary Remains*, II, 500.

[21] *Augmentations Office, Treasurer's Roll of Accounts*, no. 10. All debts were ordered paid to Peter Osborne, who was to act as a special treasurer, keeping the money to the king's use.

miliar device of Empson and Dudley. For in March, 1552, a
committee of the council was appointed to examine the penal
laws and put certain of them into execution.[22] It seems to have
been decided to enforce those touching horses and plows, riots,
the planting and grafting of trees, the cutting of wood and
billets and forestalling and regrating.[23] The sale of the king's
gunpowder, fustians, and copper, which he had been compelled
to take as "fee penny" for the prolongation of the Flanders
loans, and the sale of "certain jewels," bell-metal and lead,
part of the spoil of the church was tried.[24] Next, the completion
of the confiscation of the church plate, and the sale of church
goods and ornaments was ordered and carried through. In 1549
commissioners had taken inventories of ornaments, plate, jewels,
bells, and vestments in all churches, forbidding the sale or embezzlement of any part of them.[25] On February 26, 1551, it
was decreed in the council that "forasmuch as the king's majesty
had need presently of a mass of money, therefore commissions
should be addressed into all shires of England to take into the
king's hands such church plate as remaineth to be employed
unto his highness' use." The first commissioners for the plate
and goods were sent out in the spring of 1552;[26] they were followed by others, who, still busy in the spring of 1553, were urged
by the council to greater speed.[27] From "church plate superfluous" being coined, it was estimated that £20,000 would be

[22] *Journal of Edward VI*, 62.

[23] *Literary Remains*, II, 543. Memorandum in the king's own hand,
entitled, "Matters for the council, October 3, 1552. How a mass of
money may be gotten to discharge the sum of £300,000 both for discharge
of debts, and also to get £50,000 of treasure money for all events."

[24] *Acts of the Privy Council*, n. s., IV, 108; *Literary Remains*, II, 543.
£49,133 was received from the sale of such goods, 1552-1553, *Augmentations Office, Treasurer's Roll of Accounts*, no. 8.

[25] *State Papers, Domestic, Edward VI*, VI, 25.

[26] *Acts of the Privy Council*, n. s., III, 228, 223, 467, 536; *Journal of
Edward VI*, 65.

[27] *Acts of the Privy Council*, n. s., IV, 219, 265, 270. For volumes of
the reports of the commissioners detailing their activities, and sometimes
excusing themselves for not being able to do more for the king's advantage and other interesting comments, see B. M. Stowe Mss., Vols. 147, 827.
The bulk of the reports is in the Records Office; those of certain counties
have been published. The best general account is in Dixon, *History of
the Church of England*, III, 448ff.

realized and from the sale of church goods £10,772 was received.[28]   Other developments however returned some of the plate to the churches in Mary's reign.   Finally in their quest for money, the council turned to the mint.

For many years the mint had been the great recourse of the government in times of storm and stress.   The evils of the debasement of the coinage, the exportation of all the good money, especially the gold in the country, and the adverse foreign exchange, together with the effect of the debasement on prices, were by now clearly recognized by writers, merchants, and the popular preachers.[29]   Even the council was convinced of the necessity of restoring the standard of the fineness of the coins. The first necessary step in doing this, as Lane, the London merchant, had pointed out to Cecil, was the "calling down" of the value of the testoun, groat and penny to their intrinsic silver-content value.   This was first considered in the council in April, 1551.   But fatuously enough, it was decided that there should be one last orgy of debasement before the proclamations for calling down were issued, "to get gains of £160,000 clear by which the debt of the realm might be paid, the country defended from any sudden attempt, and *the coin amended.*"   And so "for the discharge of debts and to get some treasure to be able to alter all," that is to meet the expenses of altering and bettering the standard, twenty thousand pounds weight of bullion was ordered to be coined three ounces of silver and nine ounces of alloy.[30] But before two months were out, the misgivings of the council were such that is was decided not to proceed after £80,000 of money of the standard of three ounces fine together with ten thousand marks weight of four ounces fine had been coined.   But because of the changes in the fortifications at Calais and Berwick,

---

[28] *Literary Remains*, II, 550, Edward's memorandum ; *State Papers, Domestic, Edward VI*, XV, 42, a paper by Cecil ; *Declared Accounts, Pipe Office*, 2080.

[29] *Cotton. Mss., Vespasian D.,* 18, papers of William Thomas, clerk of the council ; *State Papers, Domestic, Edward VI*, XIII, 3, a letter of William Lane, merchant of London, to William Cecil, January 18, 1551. This letter is printed by Froude, *History of England*, V, 266.   Latimer, *Sermons,* (Parker Society), 68, 95, 136, 137 ; John Hales, *A Discourse of the Commonwealth of this Realm of England,* (Edition of 1892), 104.

[30] *Journal of Edward VI,* 33, April 10, 1551.

it was agreed three weeks later to issue another £40,000 of a
standard of three ounces fine while five thousand pounds weight
of silver should be coined seven ounces fine at least.[31] Thus the
council vaccillated between regard for the opinion of the people,
and need for money. In July the mints were ordered to stop
coining,[32] not however until £114,500 had been taken from the
people of England in the profits of the recent debasement.[33] In
September, 1551, the council directed the mints to begin the coinage of good money of the standard of eleven ounces and one
pennyweight of silver and nineteen pennyweights of alloy. A
month later when the new coinage was actually being issued, the
council ordered the lord chancellor "to haste forth the proclamation of the coin for the satisfaction of the people." This last clause
probably carries the explanation of why the council did not
dare to issue any more debased money, although in the spring of
1552 the project was reconsidered.[34]

From all these sources large sums were received, but practically everything that came in from them was used for current
charges in Ireland, at Berwick and Calais, and for the fleet and
ordnance. But little was available for the payment of the bonds
held in Flanders by the Fuggers and the Sheetz. In March, 1551,
the Fuggers renewed a bond and accepted new obligations, provided that the king purchase bullion and jewels.[35] When the
time for first payment of the new bonds came, Sir Philip
Hobbey took £53,500 Flemish in French crowns over seas with
him — probably the last remaining portion of the Boulogne
ransom money, — but had to borrow £10,000 Flemish of Lazarus
Tucher at seven per cent for six months to make up the pay.
At the end of April, 1552, £14,000 additional was due the
Fuggers, which was paid possibly by a new loan.[36] In May

[31] *Ibid.*, 35, May 30; 37, June 18, 1551.

[32] *Acts of the Privy Council*, n. s., III, 316, July 17, 1551.

[33] *Declared Accounts, Pipe Office*, 2079, account of Sir Edward Pekham,
high treasurer of the mint.

[34] *State Papers, Domestic, Edward VI*, XIII, 47, directions for the new
standard, Sept. 25, 1551. Between October and December, 1551, 6543
pounds weight of silver worth more than £21,000 were coined (*Declared
Accounts, Pipe Office*, 2079). See also *Acts of the Privy Council*, n. s.,
III, 400; IV, 57, 102.

[35] See above, p. 186 note. See also, *Journal of Edward VI*, 33.

[36] *Ibid.*, 60, 62, 63, 65, 66; *Acts of the Privy Council*, n. s., IV, 27.

a debt of £6,180 Flemish due Jasper Sheetz was paid out of the money that came from the king's old debts.[37] But regarding another bond of £45,000 due to the Fuggers in May, 1552, "a letter was sent to the Foulcare," writes the king in his journal, "that I have paid £63,000 Flemish in February, and £14,000 in April, which came to £77,000 Flemish, which was a fair sum of money to be paid in one year, chiefly in this busy world, whereas it is most necessary to be had for princes. Besides this, that it was thought money should not now do him so much pleasure as at another time peradventure. Upon these considerations they had advised me to pay but £5,000 of the £45,500 I now owe and so put over the rest according to the old interest 14 per cent with which I desired him to take patience." [38] In August a bond for £56,600 fell due. Gresham, the government agent in Flanders, had no money to meet the payment; he secured an agreement for prolongation on the usual terms that the government purchase certain fustians and diamonds of the lenders. The council in Northumberland's absence refused the conditions. The king, Gresham was informed, would pay as soon as he could; until he did so the bankers must wait. Gresham insisted that the loan must not be defaulted, or the country would be brought to shame.

In the early summer months of 1552 the council register shows that the treasuries were often actually empty; in August payments by the government were actually suspended, "for that his highness is presently in Progress and resolved not to be troubled with payments until his return." [39] The acme of the crisis had come. It brought with it the failure of Northumberland's plan to seize the government. For at Michaelmas, 1552, the gens d'armes, the mercenary army which Northumberland had gathered in December, 1551, had to be disbanded for lack of money. Against money and metal, the weight of guns and mercenaries, Mary and her followers could not have raised up their heads. But without money, and hence without the mercenary soldiers, Northumberland had no chance against the divinity that doth hedge about a king, and the magic of the

[37] *Journal of Edward VI*, 68. *Acts of the Privy Council*, n. s., IV, 58.
[38] *Journal of Edward VI*, 66.
[39] *Acts of the Privy Council*, n. s., IV, 109, August 8, 1552.

Tudor name. With the discharge of the mercenaries North-unmberland disarmed himself, and all possibilities of his success were gone.

In the summer of 1552 Northumberland probably expected a longer reprieve than he was to have before the test. The government was bankrupt, but if there was time enough all might still be mended. Rather bravely Northumberland attempted to retrieve the situation by the use of heroic measures. The management of the finances he turned over to William Cecil, who in later years was to become the greatest master of governmental finances of the sixteenth century.[40] The mayor and aldermen of the city of London endorsed the new loans in Flanders;[41] the merchants of the Staple and the Merchant Adventurers advanced money to the government to meet its obligations, and took over the payment of loans as they fell due.[42] In these days, too, the accounts of Northumberland's political opponents who had held important financial offices were investigated, and

[40] A note book of June and June and July, 1552, in Cecil's hand (*State Papers, Domestic, Edward VI*, XIV, 53), shows him very much interested in all government business, especially disbursements of money. In the following months there were many memoranda from his hand, showing the debts, with fruitful suggestions for amending the situation (*State Papers, Domestic, Edward VI*, XV, 13, 17, 42).

[41] *Acts of the Privy Council*, n. s., IV, 29, 129, April and September, 1552.

[42] In July the merchants of the Staple were desired by the council to advance by way of prest or loan some good portion of money besides the sums as should be due for the wool custom at this shipping. In October, in anticipation of the ''pay'' of £48,000 to be made in December ''beyond seas'' the Merchant Adventurers agreed to lend the king £40,000 repayable in March, 1553. The sum was assessed by the merchants upon themselves at the rate of 20s. for each cloth exported. It was estimated that at this shipping they would carry 40,000 broad cloths. The grant was confirmed by a ''company'' assembled of 300 Merchant Adventurers, October 4, 1552. A month later the Staplers agreed to take over a loan of £21,000 due to the Fuggers on February 15, 1553, paying £10,000 before the day, and the balance ''on prorogation'' — ''for which they must pay the interest.'' In the spring of 1553 the Staplers and the Adventurers assumed responsibility for the payment of £43,771 due to the Fuggers, the Sheetz, the Rellingers and Francis van Hall (*Journal of Edward VI*, 80; *Acts of the Privy Council*, n. s., IV, 169, 267). Repayment was made to the merchants out of money from the land sales.

Beaumont, Whalley and Paget compelled to disgorge great sums. Northumberland contemplated going much further in these investigations, to discover whether the crown had been justly answered of the plate, lead and iron that belonged to the abbeys, the profit of alum, copper, and fustians appointed to be sold, and such land as Henry VIII had sold. He was minded to examine the accounts of the treasurers and receivers of the various revenue courts, and finally "to call on everyone who had received money in behalf of the crown since the year 1532 to produce his books and submit them to an audit." [43]

The sale of crown lands, which had almost ceased since the making of peace with France, possibly out of the realization that sales and gifts could not proceed concurrently without ultimate disaster, was renewed on a larger scale than ever before in the reign. In May, July and October new commissions of sales were issued for the sale of chantry and other crown estates, together with rectories, parsonages, advowsons and other spiritualities.[44] Sir Edmund Pekham was appointed special treasurer to receive the money coming of the sales. In the year from Michaelmas, 1552 to Michaelmas 1553, he received £153,479 in purchase money, while £16,623 was paid into the Court of Augmentations.[45]

These ways and means proving less effective than had been expected, the council began, in December, 1552, to plan for a parliamentary grant. Northumberland approved the action, "necessarily considering that there is none other remedy to bring his majesty out of the great debts wherein for one great part he was left by his highness father . . , and augmented by the wilful government of the late Duke of Somerset, who took upon him the Protectorship and government of his own authority. His highness, by the prudence of his father, left in peace with all princes, suddenly, by that man's unskillful protectorship and less expert in government was plunged into wars whereby his majesty's charges were suddenly increased unto the

---

[43] *Journal of Edward VI*, 84. Froude, *History of England*, V, 425.

[44] *Acts of the Privy Council*, n. s., IV, 46, 133; Add. Mss., 5498, f. 29; *Journal of Edward VI*, 66.

[45] *Declared Accounts, Pipe Office*, 2080; *Augmentations Office, Treasurer's Roll of Accounts*, no. 8.

point of six or seven score thousand pounds a year over and above the charges for the keeping of Boulogne . . These things being now so onerous and weighty to the king's majesty, and having all this while been put off by the best means we have been able to devise, although but slender shifts in comparison, the same is grown to such an extremity as without it be speedily helpen by your (the council's) wise heads both dishonor and peril may likely follow. And seeing there is none other honorable means to reduce these evils grown by the occasion afore rehearsed, I think there be no man that beareth his obedient duty to his sovereign lord and country but must of consequence conform himself to think this way (of a subsidy) most honorable; for the sale of lands you have proved, the seeking of every man's doings in office you mind to try, and yet you perceive all this cannot help to salve the sore.'' In the last sentence of the letter Northumberland refers to the ''danger of murmuring or grudging that you (the council) mind to avoid.'' [46]   The difficulty of the situation which made the council fear ''murmuring and grudging'' was that it was designed to ask a tax, which was preëminently a war measure, in a time of peace. The cloak of loyalty and patriotism could not be used to quiet opposition. The interests of the crown and the people, the unity of which was the foundation of the Tudor commonwealth, were not identical here and embarrassing questions might be asked concerning the new-gotten wealth of the chief ministers. One of the council busied himself with a book of ''arguments and collections,'' apparently refuting all possible arguments against the new taxes, especially arguments based on references to the gifts of land by the council to themselves. Northumberland did not understand the new spirit of inquiry and liberalism which was in the air. He returned the book with part of his simple mind scribbled upon the margin. ''There is no need to be so ceremonious as to imagine the objects of every forward person, but rather to burden their minds and hearts with the king's extreme debts and the necessity grown and risen by such occasions and means as cannot be denied by no man, and that we need not to seem to make a count to the commons of his majesty's liberality and bountifulness in aug-

---

[46] *State Papers, Domestic, Edward VI*, XV, 73, December 28, 1552.

menting or advancing of his nobles or of his benevolence showed
to any his good servants lest you might thereby make them
wanton and give them occasion to take hold of your own arguments. But as it shall become no subject to argue the matter
so far, so if any should be so far out of reason, the matter will
always answer itself with honor and reason to their confuting
and shame.'' [47]

The grant demanded was the usual subsidy and two fifteenths
and tenths; there was nothing ''vast'' about it. Yet such was
the public temper, that even in the parliament of 1553, rather
an assembly of notables than a representative body, the measure
was debated; the commons' journal notes ''arguments'' on two
days, and a ''consultation in the Star Chamber.'' [48] Some further indication of the unpopularity of the tax may be gleaned
from the rejoicing with which Mary's remission of the subsidy
as one of her first acts was greeted. ''There was a marvellous
noise of rejoicing and giving the queen thanks in Chepeside by
the people for the same.'' [49] That the people of England in
parliament gained control of the government by virtue of parliamentary control of taxation is often stated. But it must not
be overlooked that control of the government by the people was
possible of accomplishment only as the people recognized the
government as belonging to them, and were willing to assume
the burdens of the finances of the state. This was not yet true
in the sixteenth century.

There was for Northumberland one salvation, not fifteenths
and tenths and subsidies, but the last remaining endowments of
the church, the bishops' estates. The last possible phase of
the policy begun by Cromwell had in fact already been entered.
In 1550 the newly founded bishopric of Westminster was dissolved and united to the see of London, which was forced to
neutralize any advantages of the union by the surrender of
various manors to the crown. In 1551, Ponet on his trans-
lation to Winchester alienated the whole of the patrimony of

[47] *State Papers, Domestic, Edward VI*, XVIII, 6, January 14, 1553.
[48] *Commons Journal*, I, March 6-11, 1553. The clergy also made a
grant of six shillings in the pound of the value of their livings, payable
in three years (*Statutes*, 7 Edward VI, c. 12, 13).
[49] *The Chronicle of Queen Jane and of Two Years of Queen Mary*,
(Camden Society), 48.

the see to the crown for a fixed stipend of two thousand marks. In 1552 the see of Gloucester was dissolved, its estates annexed to the crown and its diocese to that of Worcester.   True, the crown had profited little; most of the land acquired from bishops' estates had been at once regranted to courtiers.   The great attack was begun in the parliament of 1553.   A bill was passed for the division of the great diocese of Durham, with the spoliation of its lands for the benefit of the crown and Northumberland.[50]

But before the Revolution could recoup itself by further development in the way of the Henrician and Cromwellian tradition of the increase of the crown estates at the expense of the church, and rearm itself against the reaction, the boy king died.   His death came a little too soon for the success of Northumberland's plans.

50 Dixon, *History of the Church of England,* III, 197-8, 274, 471, 511.

CHAPTER XVI

RECONSTRUCTION UNDER MARY, 1553-1558

"Sterility," writes Pollard, "was the conclusive note of Mary's reign." It was a "palpable failure." Yet one exception must be taken to Mr. Pollard's sweeping condemnation. In the matter of government finance there was a real and important advance, without which the work of Elizabeth could not have begun so auspiciously. Like spendthrifts wasting their capital funds, the late Henrician and Edwardian governments had reduced and alienated crown possessions and resources to tide over financial crises. What was left was now so carefully husbanded that it was made to serve the requirements of the state for another half century. This was the constructive work of Mary's government. The religious reaction which Mary personified made it impossible to go forward to those new developments of the Tudor policy which Northumberland was planning, and had already begun, the increase of the crown lands by the annexation of the estates of the bishops. The queen's intense devotion to the old church even led to the surrender of certain resources already in hand. But the sale of lands practically ceased, and for the sources of supply which remained, conservation and intensive cultivation to effect the utmost productivity were the keynotes.

Mary enjoyed initial advantages which her brother did not have when he began to rule. The kingdom was at peace, and not threatened with war. Boulogne with its great charges had fortunately been lost. The crown was not surrounded by a group of grasping councillors, bent on enriching themselves at the expense of the state. "It must also be considered," runs a memorandum of things to be done for the good of the realm, drawn up August 4 ,1553, "that the expenses of the queen be so moderated as the crown be able to bear it and have wherewith also to resist the enemy. And for this cause all such superfluous new charges as have of late crept in are to be taken away and the size of the household, the admiralty, ordinance, mint, Ireland, Calais, Berwick and other places reduced near the same charges that they were in the latter end of King Henry VIII.''[1] The reduction of the extraordinary numbers in the armies and garrisons in Ireland, Calais and Berwick and the various forts in England was recommended and carried out. Shortly after, a special committee of the council was appointed to take general oversight of the advances for Calais, Berwick and Ireland, the North, Portsmouth, the Isle of Wight and "the Islands."[2] In Ireland alone the yearly charge which had been £42,000 in the last year of Edward VI's reign was reduced to £17,796 in the third year of Queen Mary.[3] It was recommended too, that the charges in the household be reduced, after a study of the charges of the latter part of Henry VIII's reign, with "reasonable additions thereto." But a great reduction in the household charges was not effected. During the two first years of the reign they were greater than they had been in Edward's time, though after that they were considerably reduced.[4] The expenses of the wardrobe continued very large, but were declared by a committee of the council to be satisfactory and not excessive.[5]

[1] *State Papers, Domestic, Mary,* I, 5.

[2] *State Papers, Domestic, Mary,* I, 3; III, 31.

[3] *Add. Mss.,* 4,767, f. 160. Yearly charge anno 1 Mary £37,916; anno 2 Mary £38,542; anno 3 Mary £17,769. The charges rose slightly later to £20,375 for the army and £1,735 for fees and annuities in 1559. *Ibid.,* ff. 116, 126, 129.

[4] *Declared Accounts, Pipe Office,* 1795. The charges for the year

1551-1552 were	£55,791	(Edward)
1552-1553	£51,903	(Edward and Mary)
1553-1554	£62,640	(Mary)
1554-1555	£59,353	(Mary)
1555-1556	£52,866	(Mary)
1556-1557	£54,111	(Mary)
1557-1558	£36,208	(Mary)
1558-1559	£44,824	(Mary and Elizabeth)

[5] *State Papers, Domestic, Mary,* VI, 21.

The expenses of the wardrobe for 1552-1553 were £ 5,373

1553-1554	12,307	(coronation included)
1554-1555	6,121	

P

As a retrenchment measure the union of the various revenue courts had been considered in Edward VI's reign, and authorized by parliament.[6] Mary's government at once turned its attention to the "new erected courts" and their "superfluous charges." Parliament passed a second empowering act, and on January 24, 1554, letters patent of the queen abolished the Court of Augmentations and the Court of the First Fruits and Tenths, and united them with the Exchequer. The measure might have been very reactionary in its effects, inasmuch as it aimed to restore completely the ancient course of the Exchequer, even to the use of the sheriffs as stewards of the crown lands. But there were permissive clauses in the letters patent which made it possible for the more modern system of the Augmentations Court to be continued for the administration of the crown lands in the Augmentations office of the Exchequer.

Another great economy was achieved in the matter of annuities and pensions. They were taken under consideration at the very beginning of the reign; it was found that annuities of £1,597 to Englishmen, and of £2,590 to strangers were granted during pleasure and might be stopped at once, while of the annuities paid from the monastic lands it was suspected that some had been fraudulently granted.[7] The council advised in January, 1554, that no new grants of annuities or pensions be made; and although some new grants were made, notably to those who had helped the queen at Fremlingham and to the officers of the dissolved Courts of Augmentations and First Fruits and Tenths, the total payments for pensions and annuities

1555-1556	6,029
1556-1557	missing
1557-1558	6,220
1558-1559	9,220 (coronation included)

These items are taken from *Declared Accounts, Pipe Office*, 1795, 3027 to 3032.

The household and wardrobe took all the clear revenues of the Duchies of Lancaster and Cornwall, and the Court of Wards and Liveries in Mary's reign. What was still lacking to meet their charges was paid from the Exchequer.

[6] *Statutes*, 7, Edward VI, c. 2. The General Surveyors and Augmentations had already been united, January 1, 1547.

[7] *State Papers, Domestic, Mary*, I, 22.

decreased markedly. From Easter, 1557, to Easter, 1558, they were only £5,978 as compared with £20,000 a year in Edward's day.[8]

Yet the problem which confronted Mary's government could not be solved by economies and curtailments alone. The rise in prices, the advance in the standard of living, and the higher level of salaries led necessarily to an increase in the household and wardrobe charges and in the cost of the permanent military and naval establishments. With all the economies possible, the total government disbursements in normal years of peace were considerably greater than they had been in 1540, and constantly tended to rise. It was essential that the government's revenues be increased. The time was not yet ripe to use taxation regularly to supply the new funds. Nor could the depleted estates of the crown be augmented on a grand scale as in the past. Northumberland's attainder and execution restored some of the lands which he had so unjustly gathered into his hands. As a possible means of recovering more of the fraudulently alienated estates, an investigation was proposed of all exchanges or gifts of land granted since the death of Henry VIII,[9] but nothing was done. Yet despite all the alienations of the past two decades, the crown estates were still absolutely very large, and if they could not be increased in extent, they could be made much more productive of revenue. That rise in prices which so increased the costs of running the state, increased also the potential value of the royal lands. Rents responded to the advance in prices of agricultural products, though the crown did not immediately, or automatically profit by the rise in rents. In 1555 the committee of the council appointed for lands and possessions thought it good that a survey be made of all the queen's possessions in every shire and hundred as the first step toward increasing her majesty's income; but on the next points the sub-committees entirely disagreed. One party favored the letting of all lands, possessions and manors to farm for twenty-one years, as in that way the revenue would be made more certain, and the expenses of stewards, bailiffs, auditors, surveyors and receivers much

---

[8] *Exchequer of Receipt, Misc. Books*, 259, Issues of the Exchequer.
[9] *State Papers, Domestic, Mary*, I, 5.

P *

reduced.[10] "Farming" the revenues was beginning to find the favor of experts; it was concurrently urged for the customs, where the "example of other kingdoms and dominions" showed how advantageous it was. The farming of the lands and manors was not, however, adopted. More careful attention was paid to the making of new leases, which were to be drawn up only by the officers of the courts; fines for entry seem to have been increased, and rents raised. The land revenues steadily increased throughout Mary's reign, and this increase continued without interruption in Elizabeth's time. The clear yield of the crown lands in the Court of Augmentations was £26,883 in the year 1552-1553, the last year of Edward VI and the first of Mary; in the year 1556-1557 the yield of the lands in the Augmentations office of the Exchequer was £47,723, and in the first year of Elizabeth £69,628.[11] In the Duchy of Lancaster the issues of crown lands show a similar, but smaller increase from £6,628 in the year 1552-1553, to £7,808 in the year 1558-1559.[12] The land revenues thus incremented again became the most important in the state.

But though land was the chief source of wealth in early Tudor times, investments were also taking other forms. Commercial wealth, especially the riches derived from foreign commerce had for a long time been rising to a more exalted place in the national economy. The healthy growth of trade, stimulated by Henry VII's fostering care had continued in his son's reign. In the latter years of Henry VIII however, the returns from the customs fluctuated, and in the time of Edward VI they declined.[13] The prosperity of the trading classes was shown by their ability to purchase land in great quanities when the monastic and chantry properties were offered for sale. The prestige of English merchants abroad was so great that the

[10] *State Papers, Domestic, Mary,* VI, 22; Add. Mss., 12,504, ff. 164, 166; *Cotton. Mss.; Titus B.* IV. f. 135.

[11] *Augmentations Office Treasurer's Roll of Accounts,* no. 8; *Exchequer of Receipt, Declaration Books, Pells, I; Lansd. Mss.,* 4, f. 182.

[12] *Duchy of Lancaster, Assocunts Various,* bundle VIII.

[13] The average receipts 1538-1539 to 1546-1547 were £40,120 (Schanz, *Englische Handelspolitik,* II, 12). The receipts in the year 1550-1551 were £23,386 in the ports of England, and £2,511 at Calais. The Calais customs were however, unusually small this year. In 1548-1549 they had been £6,752, and in 1549-1550 £4,164 (Add. Mss., 30,198).

credit of London merchants would secure loans in Flanders for which the credit of the king was not sufficient; their resources were again indicated by the ability of the Merchant Adventurers and the Merchants of the Staple to advance great sums to the king by way of loans. By the time of Edward VI the influence of the London merchants had become so great as to secure the revocation of the privileges of the Steelyard, and their confidence and initiative sufficient to lead them to undertake the beginning of the Muscovy Company in the voyage of Willoughby and Chancellor in 1553. These are all indications of a vigorous and increasing foreign trade in the middle of the sixteenth century. The decline in Edward's customs revenues meant not a decline in English trade, but a maladjustment of the revenue system. For this there were several causes. There was laxness and dishonesty in the custom houses and dues were not truly paid.[14] More important than this, all dues were collected on the valuations of the national books of rates of 1536 and 1545, which were themselves the valuations fixed in the London book of 1507. With the rise in prices, these valuations no longer corresponded to the actual market prices of goods in the middle of the century. In the third place, articles like wool, on which the customs revenues were formerly very great were exported in smaller quantities, while the existing duties on commodities like cloth, beer and wine, in the increased exchange of which the growth of commerce consisted, were too low. As far as the official valuations were concerned the situation was clearly recognized by a royal commission in Edward VI's reign. Pointing out the discrepancy between the market price and the rated value, the commission declared it meet to take measures for the profit of this custom, and that additional returns from new valuations were necessary. A committee of the council studied the matter in Mary's reign, and reported: "It seems necessary that goods of all sorts are imported and exported and shall

[14] *State Papers, Domestic, Mary*, XIII, 49, 50, charges of loss to the queen through fraudulent weighing of wools; *Historical Mss. Commission Reports, Hatfield Mss.*, I, 148, complaint of great funds in the custom house on the part of the customers and controllers, who are often in business for themselves. Cf. Dowell, *History of Taxes*, I, 180; Cunningham, *Growth of English Industry and Commerce*, I, 549.

be specified in a book with their true modern value, and that customs and subsidies (of tonnage and poundage) shall be paid according to the true value and quality of the same goods at these times.''[15] On May 28, 1558, the new Book of Rates with modern valuations, based on recent inquiry was issued. It raised the older rates by approximately seventy-five per cent, on the average. The privy seal prefixed to this book of rates remedied the decrease in the customs caused by the falling off in the export of wool. Because ''much less wool is shipped . . . and much more wool is made into cloth within our realm and carried out of the same in cloth by way of merchandise . . and because the custom and subsidy of wool carried out of this realm in wool doth far exceed the custom and subsidy of so much wool after the rate clothed . . we therefore minding in reasonable sort to maintain our customs as the most ancient and certain revenue of our crown . . have assessed upon cloths to be carried forth by way of merchandise (new) rates for the customs and subsidy.''[16] By this new duty upon cloth, called the Impost which replaced the former dues upon cloth, the cloth trade was made to contribute a fairer share to the necessities of the state. A few weeks before the issue of the new book of rates and the impost upon cloth the council had laid similar imposts upon the wines of France, and French dry wares imported, and upon beer exported.[17] The increase brought by the new valuations, the new duties and the greater strictness in the custom houses which the council enjoined, was immediate. From £25,900 in 1550-1551 and £29,315 in the fourth year of Mary's reign, the customs revenues rose to £82,797 in the first year of Queen Elizabeth, divided as follows, — old customs, £25,797; for the rate of wares newly appointed, £20,000; custom of the Staple, £4,000; new increase upon cloth, £26,000; new increase upon wines, £4,000; the custom of beer, £3,000.[18] The new book of rates and the new duties or imposts were the second great contribution of Mary to a

[15] Add. Mss., 30, 198; Gras, *Tudor Books of Rates*, 774; *State Papers, Domestic Mary*, VI, 22; *Cotton. Mss., Titus B.*, IV, f. 35.

[16] *Lansd. Mss.*, 3, f. 143.

[17] *Acts of the Privy Council*, n. s., VI. 305, April 17, 1558.

[18] *Lansd. Mss.*, 4, f. 182; an estimate or report on the revenues for the year 1559-1560 prepared for Cecil, and annotated in his hand.

rehabilitation of the finances of the kingdom. As in the case of the lands, Elizabeth reaped the advantages of Mary's innovations. Elizabeth's councillors extended the new imposts to all wines, and reissued the Book of Rates at various times. The customs became of almost equal importance with the land revenues as the basis for national finance, just as commercial wealth was tending to greater equality with landed wealth.

But it must not be supposed that all was smooth sailing in the financial history of Mary's reign. The constructive policies were slow in their development. Throughout the reign the government needed money, for the support of the increased establishments, and in the last year for the war with France, which fortunately was quick and decisive. But crown lands were not sold, and the coinage of debased money was not resumed. The government depended chiefly upon loans and taxes to meet its exigent demands. The debts beyond seas had been decreased in the last months of Northumberland's administration, to £61,000 by midsummer 1553. This reduction had been effected by allowing the payments in the various government departments to fall very much further into arrears.[19] Northumberland had been anxious to repay the Flanders loans, the debts of the realm abroad, possibly to strengthen his international position; Mary's council seems to have decided that it was better to pay the charges and expenditures of the state promptly, and to accept frankly, as necessary aids in doing this, further foreign loans, even at twelve and fourteen per cent, which the future could redeem. As in the latter part of Edward VI's reign, Sir Thomas Gresham was the general agent in Flanders for the loans. Between March 21, 1554, and July 31, 1557, he repaid forty-nine bonds, with the interest and brokerage charges of foreign bankers, together with certain sums due to the Staplers and Merchant Adventurers to the amount of £312,984 5s. 9d. He negotiated new loans, many of them prolongations of former loans to the value of £234,733 4s. 4d. The total interest and prolongation charges for the period were £31,224, which is possibly only a small part of the saving realized by the state by the prompt payment of its officers, servants, purveyors and

---

[19] *State Papers, Domestic, Mary*, I, 14. The foreign debt is put at £72,000 at about the same time in another paper, *ibid.*, IV, 6.

other like creditors. For certain money, 300,750 ducats, raised
by bills in Antwerp, he had to go to Spain. The money was
delivered to him by the bankers of Medina de Rioseca and Medina
del Campo at Seville; from Seville he had to carry it to the
seaside packed in great boxes, some of which broke with a loss
of 231 ducats, — which the commissioners refused to allow when
his account was made before them. In his dealings such was
"his wisdom," as his declaration of account modestly phrases
it, that he raised the value of English money in exchange to be
of more value than the money of Flanders, two shillings in the
pound in March and April 1554, one shilling in May 1557, and
six pence in August 1555.[20]

Though most of the loans were raised in Flanders, the queen
occasionally called upon the city of London for advances. On
the first Sunday of September, 1553, she demanded £20,000 of
the city of London. The sum of £10,000 was actually advanced,
and repaid within the month. In August, 1556, the city of
London advanced £6,000. In March, 1558, after the loss of
Calais the queen demanded a loan of 100,000 marks of the city,
which was reduced to £20,150 12s. 1d. when it was paid. The
queen pledged lands worth £1,007 10s. 7¼d. a year for repayment, and paid interest at twelve per cent, for the taking of
which, contrary to the usury laws, the London alderman had
to receive special licenses from the queen. The Merchant Adventurers were so "forward" and liberal at this time that the
queen wrote them a special letter of thanks, promising them
her special favor in any reasonable suits.[21]

The taxes of parliamentary grant used to eke out the crown
resources were the subsidies, very similar to those of the latter
period of Henry VIII's reign, and the fifteenths and tenths of
the laity, and the subsidies of the clergy. In her first parliament
the queen rèmitted the last subsidy granted to Edward VI,
unpaid at his death. In 1555 a subsidy payable in 1556 and
1557 was granted by the laity, and a subsidy of six shillings in
the pound by the clergy. Parliament was willing at this time

[20] *Declared Accounts, Pipe Office,* 18. The accounts of Gresham's
transactions are continued in 23, 26.

[21] Wriothesley, *Chronicle,* II, 100; *Acts of the Privy Council,* n. s., IV,
343, 353; V, 321; *State Papers, Domestic, Mary,* XIV, 83; XII, 66.

to make a further grant of two fifteenths and tenths which the queen was graciously contented to refuse with her thanks.[22] In January, 1558, as a war measure, a subsidy of one fifteenth and tenth were granted, besides a clerical subsidy of eight shillings in the pound. Of interest in connection with the subsidies of Mary's time is not the frequency with which they were asked, nor their yield, but the stiffening resistance of parliament to the taxes, and the insistence of the government on more exact and complete payment, with the punishment of those who sought to evade the taxes.[23]

Near the end of the reign too, the century-old device of the forced loan, half arbitrary tax, and half loan, was revamped. In 1556 the richest subjects of the kingdom were called upon to lend the queen £100 apiece, to be repaid within a month of All Saints Day, (November 1), 1557.[24] In September, 1557, to raise money to repay the loan of the past year, and to supply other needed sums, a more elaborate loan was "practiced." Commissioners sat in every district, as in the case of a subsidy, and rated each man's value with the assistance of the subsidy books, and the testimony of neighbors. Having made the assessments, the commissioners were to collect the money taking not under £10, nor more than 100 marks (£66 13s. 4d.). Those who firmly refused to pay without cause were to be cited before the council, as indeed many persons were. Certain counties, Derby, Chester, Lancashire, York and Nottingham were exempted from the loan, because of the service which they had "done us in the war amongst our enemies the Scots." The loan realized £109,267 0s. 4d.; of this £42,100 was used to repay the loan of 1556, and the rest was apparently used for the general purposes of the state, since the recovery of Calais was not immediately attempted. Though privy seals were given as receipts to those who had contributed, no promise of repayment was made as

22 *Commons' Journal*, I, 28, 31.

23 The *Commons' Journal* notes "arguments" on the necessity of summoning members of the house before the queen in connection with each one of the grants of the reign. For insistence upon more complete and speedier payment of taxes, see *Acts of the Privy Council*, n. s., V, VI. The yields of the Marian subsidies are listed in the Appendix, *Subsidies*.

24 *Cotton. Mss., Cleopatra F.*, VI, f. 299, a privy seal for the loan.

in the previous year, and no repayment seems ever to have been made.[25]

Note must be taken finally of the retrogressive steps in the financial history of Mary's time. These are closely connected with the political, and especially the religious situation; they proceed partly from the queen's sense of loyalty and gratitude to the church, partly from her sense of stern honor and exact justice. The confiscations and forfeits accruing to the crown by the ruin of her enemies, Mary balanced by restoration to name and lands of persons attainted by her father and brother.[26] She reërected the Hospital of St. John of Jerusalem, she restored the abbey of Westminster, and returned the monastic lands in Ireland to their original uses. She was even resolved to restore all the monastic lands in crown possession to the church, and actually ordered perfect declarations made and presented to this end. ''She preferred the salvation of her soul to the maintenance of her imperial dignity, if it could not be furnished without such assistance.'' But the councillors would not take the necessary steps; their passive resistance defeated her purpose.[27] She was however, able to accomplish the surrender of the first fruits and tenths of the clergy, and the alienations of the rectories, parsonages, glebes, benefices impropriate and other spiritual livings in the hands of the crown, though the bill for this purpose was bitterly opposed in parliament.[28] The surrender was made as a gift to the church, to be placed at the disposition of the Cardinal Pole, for the augmentation of the poor livings of the priests. The surrender of the first fruits and tenths alone would have been a dead loss to the royal revenues of something less than £25,000 a year. But the alienation was not so immediately serious as Mary's enemies in Elizabeth's reign and since have alleged. For the gift to the church carried with it the payment of pensions and corrodies of the late monks, nuns and chantry priests to a very great sum. The pensions of

[25] *State Papers, Domestic, Mary*, XI, 44, 45, 46; XVI, 49; XIII, 36. The last is the account of Richard Wilbraham receiver-general of the loan.

[26] A paper in *State Papers, Domestic, Elizabeth*, I, 64, gives the value of lands restored to such persons as £9,799 a year.

[27] Dixon, *History of the Church of England*, IV, 359.

[28] The debates and arguments are noted in the *Commons'* and *Lords' Journals*.

the chantry priests alone were £11,147 a year;[29] the entire payments of this nature which were transferred with the gift were
£44,861 in the year 1550-1551.[30] In time these pensions and
charges would cease, and then there would be at the disposal
of the church a goodly sum for the benefit of its most poorly
paid priests, but it was eighteen months after the passage of
the act of surrender before the fund sufficed to do more than
pay the charges, and remit the tenths of the smallest livings.
The net loss to the crown was not actually very great; before the
pensions became markedly smaller than the gross value of the
gift, it was resumed. The greatest and practically the only change
which Elizabeth made in the financial policy of her sister and
her sister's government was the revocation of the various restor-
ations which Mary had made to the church; especially the repeal
of the Act of 1555, and the resumption by the crown of the first
fruits and tenths, and the spiritual livings.

Revenue, to paraphrase Burke a little, is the chief problem
of the state, nay more, it is the State. This is certainly valid
for fifteenth and sixteenth century England. A sufficient revenue was the insistent difficulty of Tudor statesmen. Their
solution was circumstanced by two conditions, the determination
of the crown after the humiliation of the fifteenth century to
be independent, and the self interest of the middle classes,
in whose alliance a large part of the king's power consisted,
which made them reluctant to accept taxation as a method of
governmental finance. The conquest of the feudal nobility was
Henry VII's greatest opportunity to increase the resources of
his crown by stripping them of their wealth and estates, thus
providing a revenue for the state on the basis of landed estates,
independent of control, and satisfactory to the middle classes.
Cromwell furthered his work by the seizure of a large part of
the property and wealth of the church. At a time when their
system was on the point of disintegration, Mary and her advisers were strong and capable enough to gather together the
remaining resources, and so conserve, husband, and increase their
productivity by raising the rents of the crown lands, and by
issuing a new book of rates for customs, and levying new im-

[29] *Historical Mss. Commission Reports, Hatfield Mss.*, I, 75.
[30] *Add. Mss.*, 30,198.

posts, that with the careful parsimony of Elizabeth, reorganization was put off until the seventeenth century. When the necessity for a new financial system forced itself upon the Stuarts, they were too weak, and too incompetent to deal with it. The example of Holland, and the Long Parliament were necessary before it could be set up, and with it, the promise of the Confirmatio Cartarum realized.

All must acknowledge the titanic achievements of the early Tudors. It is axiomatic that their strong governments were needed in the England of their day to discipline the national life, and that their governments were strong largely because of their solid financial basis. Great recognition is due to the masterly way in which there were turned to the service of the state the greater economic unification of England and the chief forms of wealth of the time. It may even be granted that in some of their work the Tudors stood for real progress, especially in their destruction of the outworn vested control of the Exchequer over national finance. But care should be taken not to sanctify their success. For fundamentally they faced away from Liberty. The permanent success of their plans for securing income for the crown apart from the will of the people would have meant the end of freedom.

Fortunately, Henry VIII by his active foreign policy defeated these plans, and by his wastes and drains for war unwittingly made possible the revival of the representative control in England, after his father and himself had so nearly destroyed it. The miseries and wretched sufferings of the people of his own day may be the Vicarious Atonement by virtue of which in part, we in our day have salvation.

INDEX